As Christians we are called to be *change agents*. We are to be used of God to point people to Christ and let Him do the changing. If people are being changed, society and culture will be changed as well. Os Hillman does a great job of showing how we can be change agents of the Lord Most High in the realms of our lives.

—David Green
Founder and CEO, Hobby Lobby

The Holy Spirit is very serious about calling forth an aggressive army of God to transform our society. One of the tangible indications of this fact can be seen in the remarkable mushrooming of superb literature on the subject. Os Hillman's *Change Agent* is the latest and arguably the best transformation textbook now available. Let's regard this as our operations manual for pushing back the enemy and inviting God's kingdom to penetrate our society! Let's all get it, read it, digest it, and act on it! We can truly be change agents!

—C. Peter Wagner
Chancellor Emeritus, Wagner Leadership Institute

More than any other, the concept of "seven mountains" has captured the imagination of Christian leaders internationally. It would be important for us to hear what Os Hillman has to say.

—Landa Cope
Founding International Dean of the
College of Communication with Youth With A Mission
University of the Nations

Master storyteller Os Hillman has written a book here that should be read by every layman in the country. It presents a good overview of the issues facing our culture today and what we as Christians can do about it. It's also a great small group study for people who are willing to rethink many of the culture concepts they have been living with.

—Ralph Palmen
President, Pinnacle Forum America

This book is very timely written as the world groans for the "sons and daughters to arise" as change agents to bring solutions to lives, society, and nations. There is a prophecy that shall be fulfilled by a passionate group of kingdom-minded leaders: "The kingdoms of this world have become the kingdoms of our Lord and of His Christ, and He shall reign forever and ever!" (Rev. 11:15). I believe this book casts a vision for believers to impact our world as change agents in the seven mountains or kingdoms of influence. It will challenge and motivate the readers as it provides a track for understanding God's processes in the making of great leaders who as catalysts shall become change agents.

—Pat Francis, PhD
Senior Pastor, Kingdom Covenant Center

God has called you to impact the culture in your sphere of influence, and Os Hillman shows you exactly which steps to take. This will be an invaluable tool for you of biblical models, current examples, and spiritual insights as you seek to be God's *agent of change*!

—KENT HUMPHREYS
AMBASSADOR, FCCI / CHRIST@WORK

I loved the book because it showed a balanced and personal view on being a change agent. This has absolutely, truly blessed my socks off! I am excited for the readers who will glance into their destiny through this book. Outstanding!

—CHERYL A. HILL, DDIV
PRESIDENT, GOD'S GREEN AFRICA

The Bible says to pray, "Your kingdom come; Your will be done, on earth as it is in heaven." But what does that look like, and what are Christians to do in the face of the dramatic moral decay of society today? Os Hillman answers those questions with a comprehensive blueprint for change agents. First, he grounds the reader in a biblical worldview framework for society. But before he says, "Charge into the battle," he takes the reader through the refining process of character preparation. Finally he paints the picture of how change agents can extend the kingdom on earth through the seven mountains of society. In this book Os has given Christians an essential tool to equip them for God's call on their lives in one of the most tumultuous periods in history.

—JOHN MULFORD, PHD
DIRECTOR, REGENT UNIVERSITY CENTER FOR ENTREPRENEURSHIP
PROFESSOR, SCHOOL OF GLOBAL LEADERSHIP AND ENTREPRENEURSHIP
FORMER DEAN, SCHOOL OF BUSINESS

Os Hillman's book offers a great explanation of where God's kingdom has come from, where it is at, and where God is leading. Hillman does a masterful job of depicting heroes of the marketplace and other mountains while explaining how we all can become change agents. I recommend this book for all those who have prayed, "Thy kingdom come; Thy will be done."

—AL CAPERNA
DIRECTOR, CALL2ALL BUSINESS NETWORK
CEO, CMC GROUP

Not only does Os Hillman provide an honest and comprehensive view of today's culture, but he also shows us how we can significantly impact it by becoming God's change agent. Think you can't make a difference? Think again. This book will both challenge and encourage you to live a life greater than what you thought possible.

—LARRY JULIAN
AUTHOR OF GOD IS MY CEO, GOD IS MY SUCCESS, AND
GOD IS MY COACH

Many marketplace leaders and others are tired of going to conferences and reading books that load them down with information. This book not only provides great biblical teaching in a relative and easily understood manner, but it also provides great tools that can be immediately applied to bring *change agents* into their destinies and actually see transformation in their cities.

—FORD TAYLOR
COFOUNDER, TRANSFORMATION CINCINNATI/N. KENTUCKY

I am convinced that God is calling Christians to engage both people and social structures with His transforming gospel. Over the years Os Hillman's books have inspired, challenged, and equipped me for this task in my own business life. I would highly recommend *Change Agent* to every Christian who is serious about engaging strategically in God's call to a ministry of transformation and influence in all of the various spheres of society.

—GRAHAM POWER
CHAIRMAN, THE POWER GROUP OF COMPANIES
FOUNDER OF GLOBAL DAY OF PRAYER AND UNASHAMEDLY ETHICAL

In his book *Change Agent,* Os Hillman combines extensive research, anecdotal referencing, and his personal experiences to deliver another profitable book to the body of Christ. Those who desire to be a part of reforming our society will find this to be compelling reading.

—JOHNNY ENLOW
PASTOR, DAYSTAR CHURCH, ATLANTA, GA
AUTHOR OF *THE SEVEN MOUNTAIN PROPHECY*

I believe Os Hillman's book is part of a "trumpet call" the Lord is making to His church, especially in the West. *Change Agent* is a call to action for Christians to put God's will and His kingdom ahead of selfish agendas. Transformation starts from within, and this book inspires total surrender to God's will for our lives at the foot of the cross, especially in areas of influence. Through the power of the Holy Spirit, God wants us to "blossom" for Him wherever He has planted us. Os's latest book is a wonderful encouragement for us to live radical lives for Jesus Christ.

—GERARD LONG
PRESIDENT, ALPHA USA

Change Agent empowers everyone who desires to cause change. Written with a wealth of experience, this book should be required reading for everyone who calls themselves a ministry and marketplace leader. I wish I had this book as a young man. Thank you, Os, for leading the way!

—ROBERT WATKINS
PRESIDENT, KINGS & PRIESTS INTERNATIONAL

Os Hillman is one of the most recognized and respected marketplace leaders in the Christian church today. He is a successful entrepreneur himself, so he is especially qualified to teach us some of the practical and important principles of Christian entrepreneurship. I strongly recommend this helpful and encouraging book to you.

—Paul Cedar
Chairman, Mission America Coalition

Os Hillman has produced a profound and practical book that both informed and inspired me. This work will be a tremendous resource for those with a passion for cultural transformation. Well done!

—Wes Lane
Former District Attorney, Oklahoma City
Author of *Amazingly Graced*

"If the foundations are destroyed, what can the righteous do?" (Ps. 11:3). This is the cry of many in our modern-day society, as we have seen the critical foundations of the seven cultural mountains destroyed right before our eyes. In his book *Change Agent*, Os Hillman gives us reasons as to why and how these foundations have been destroyed, as well as very practical solutions regarding what we can do now to rebuild our society on solid biblical principles.

—Craig Hill
Founder, Family Foundations International

In recent years, we have heard about God's last days' mandate for real, societal transformation. We have seen the glorious evidence of this societal work in pockets here and there. We have heard this mandate preached about at conferences and in churches. Os Hillman's important book *Change Agent* will not only bring clarity and definition to this mandate, but it will also blow the clarion call for what is the message of our generation! Os's book is filled with deep, biblical insight that will challenge and inspire you to move from the ordinary to the extraordinary. I believe it will soon become a leadership manual for change.

—Paul L. Cuny
President, MarketPlace Leadership International
Author of *Secrets of the Kingdom Economy*

CHANGE AGENT

ENGAGING YOUR PASSION TO BE
THE ONE WHO MAKES A DIFFERENCE

OS HILLMAN

CHARISMA
HOUSE

Most CHARISMA HOUSE BOOK GROUP products are available at special quantity discounts for bulk purchase for sales promotions, premiums, fund-raising, and educational needs. For details, write Charisma House Book Group, 600 Rinehart Road, Lake Mary, Florida 32746, or telephone (407) 333-0600.

CHANGE AGENT by Os Hillman
Published by Charisma House
Charisma Media/Charisma House Book Group
600 Rinehart Road, Lake Mary, Florida 32746
www.charismahouse.com

Unless otherwise noted, all Scripture quotations are from the New King James Version of the Bible. Copyright © 1979, 1980, 1982 by Thomas Nelson, Inc., publishers. Used by permission.

Scripture quotations marked AMP are from the Amplified Bible. Old Testament copyright © 1965, 1987 by the Zondervan Corporation. The Amplified New Testament copyright © 1954, 1958, 1987 by the Lockman Foundation. Used by permission.

Scripture quotations marked NIV are from the Holy Bible, New International Version. Copyright © 1973, 1978, 1984, International Bible Society. Used by permission.

Cover design by Gearbox Studio
Design Director: Bill Johnson

Please visit the author's website at www.marketplaceleaders.org.

Library of Congress Cataloging-in-Publication Data:
Hillman, Os.
  Change agent / Os Hillman. -- 1st ed.
     p. cm.
  Includes bibliographical references (p.   ).
  ISBN 978-1-61638-182-0 (trade paper) -- ISBN 978-1-61638-567-5 (e-book) 1.
Christianity and culture. 2. Change--Religious aspects--Christianity. I. Title.
  BR115.C8H545 2011
  261--dc23
                                        2011017415

First Edition

11 12 13 14 15 — 9 8 7 6 5 4 3 2 1
Printed in the United States of America

To the Father, Son, and Holy Spirit,
our only true source for change.

Now it shall come to pass in the latter days that the mountain of the LORD's house shall be established on the top of the mountains, and shall be exalted above the hills; and all the nations shall flow to it. Many people shall come and say, "Come, and let us go up to the mountain of the LORD, to the house of the God of Jacob; He will teach us His ways, and we shall walk in His paths."

—Isaiah 2:2–3

"In that day," says the LORD, "I will assemble the lame, I will gather the outcast and those whom I have afflicted; I will make the lame a remnant, and the outcast a strong nation; so the LORD will reign over them in Mount Zion from now on, even forever."

—Micah 4:6–7

Contents

Foreword

IN WORLD WAR II the Allies needed a breakthrough in dealing with Nazi-occupied strongholds in Europe, and so the legendary 482nd Bombardment Group was formed. This group was equipped with the first generation of radar technology, and with that they were able to penetrate targets formerly obscured by cloud cover and subject only to "blind bombing." This elite group was called *Pathfinders*, and that is what best describes Os Hillman. He is a Pathfinder.

I first met Os while speaking in Connecticut about the seven mountains in the year 2000. I knew other people were hearing something similar but did not know any but a few national ministries. It was C. Peter Wagner who extended to me his platform and circle of friends and introduced me to Os. He described him as a pioneer who possessed a unique grasp of what God was doing in the marketplace globally. He was right! Os and I have had a growing friendship ever since. He has been stalking this subject for more than twenty-five years, ever sharpening his focus, combining resources, and providing insight and commentary that penetrate with clarity what the enemy obscures with cloud cover. This book, *Change Agent*, provides both a map and the indispensable radar upgrade needed so that our days of "blind bombing" in prayer, evangelism, and social activism can get recalibrated in expectation of hitting the target and having the impact we all intuitively know our message should carry. This latest book lays a foundation for personal and institutional impact that is both practical and paradigm jarring!

While there is only one gospel, Os points out that the gospel we have primarily preached throughout the earth focuses on individual salvation. The gospel of salvation redeems souls but only indirectly redeems economic, educational, political, or artistic institutions. The gospel of the kingdom, on the other hand, includes the gospel of salvation but encompasses the larger and more ambitious project of teaching to save nations while preaching to save souls. Making disciples of entire people groups and nations is the end game. It is thrilling to consider that the cry "Thy kingdom come. Thy will be done in earth, as it is in heaven" makes heaven available through you right now to potentially fix whatever is broken in any earthly system you are assigned to. This is God's desire. In the end the leaves of the tree of life are "for the healing of the nations."[1]

Our eschatology has put us at a disadvantage, causing us to be more pre-occupied with His coming than strategic in how we occupy till He comes. This confusion is problematic because the last days are a time of great shaking. The key is not to assume that every shaking is evidence of the collapse of civilization or the expansion of anti-Christ forces. Shaking can also remove what is militating against the advance of God's kingdom so "that the things which cannot be shaken may remain."[2]

What we have lacked up until now is a template to work with. Transformation is a complex subject, but Os clarifies the terrain and helps us get handles on our task.

Change Agent provides an updated map surveying the seven mountains that shape culture. Here also Os adds an important distinction; those at the top, the elites and their networks, are but a remnant—wielding power totally disproportionate to their numbers. He makes clear that it is a mistake to think that the majority shapes culture—it's quite the opposite; it is always a remnant at the top. In the past we have engaged a wrong strategy. More prayer for more conversions or trying to get more Christians thinking more biblically will not produce more results. We are praying for a move of God, but what is needed is a move of people from the periphery in the bleachers to the very center of the coliseum floor where decisions are made and culture is produced. In matters spiritual and natural, proximity is power. The strongman's goods are at peace in spite of all our noise because they are only spoiled when the stronger one goes up into his house. A new breed of gatekeepers needs to arise. The church needs to be in proximity to the gates of hell, and those gates are in "them thar hills." This company of change agents, recruited in sufficient force, will catalyze the awakening we have been praying for.

Indeed, it is amazing how this message is suddenly taking hold on a global scale. As this fresh perspective is preached, faith is quickened and people are coming alive. Clarity is power! Believers who embrace this paradigm are instinctively energized as they begin to envision what God wants to do through them in every sphere of society. As this army advances—by means covert and overt—a genuine move among nations becomes possible. We need healers and deliverers of economies and prophets and poets with pens who war against corruption. We need filmmakers and comedians who will marginalize the mouths that mock what is righteous. We need artists and architects who are authorized to save the soul of cities, and we need a new breed of Great Awakeners called to stir the slumbering giant in the religion mountain. George Whitefield, the fiery evangelist, formed William Wilberforce, the statesman who in turn abolished slavery and restored a nation's conscience. Both Whitefield, the overt, and Wilberforce, the often covert, were successful agents of change.

Of particular importance in this journey is the emphasis Os puts on prayer and networking. Lasting change does not come through the ingenuity of man-made carts, but rather God advances His government upon the soft shoulders of Levites, just as the ark of old was carried. Heaven's ark touches down on earth to the degree it finds earthly carriers. Change agents and intercessors are a combined force, a heavenly nitro and glycerin that, when combined, explode strongholds. Change agents, like the Levites who carried the ark, bear the weight of their assignment as a team, staying connected because they know the dangers of going alone.

This book provides both a big-picture perspective and a very personal application. The Joseph journey is the pathway of transformation that change agents experience, as their dreams of the future seem dashed by the contradictory circumstances of the present. Multitudes will find comfort when they realize that they, like Joseph, are not prisoners of circumstance but rather a prisoner of a process preparing them to come out of confinement into a large place. At first Joseph's own brothers did not want to hear him, but in the end he stood in Pharaoh's court, "[teaching] his elders wisdom."[3]

Someone once told me, "Three years from now you will be the same person you are today except for the books you read and the people you meet." Read this book, pass it on, and meet with like-minded change agents. It will make you a sharper instrument and will prosper your journey. In fact, lately as I think of this book and the mountains we are called to harvest, I am reminded of a word Isaiah prophesied to Israel when the people described their condition as that of "a worm and not a man."[4] God promised new clarity, decisiveness, and success to those who drew near to serve His purposes. He assured them, saying, "I am with you....Behold, I will make you into a new threshing sledge with sharp teeth; you shall thresh the mountains and beat them small, and make the hills like chaff."[5] I believe God is extending that promise to you and me as we join Him in what He is doing in the earth.

—LANCE WALLNAU

Introduction

CALLED TO A BIGGER STORY

Then I will raise up for Myself a faithful priest who shall do
according to what is in My heart and in My mind. I will build him
a sure house, and he shall walk before My anointed forever.
—1 SAMUEL 2:35

D EEP IN THE heart of every human is a desire to make a difference in their world—they want to be change agents. Simply stated, a change agent is a person chosen to bring about change. Sometimes that desire is buried under insecurities, hardships, and wounds we have never recognized or faced. You will meet some of these change agents in this book, including the biblical examples of Abraham, Moses, Esther, Joseph, and others from our world today. Each of these people made a difference in his or her world. God's calling to each included hardship, testing, a crisis of belief, failure, and grace—all mixed into a life that made an impact. This is a part of every change agent's journey.

Each of us was created to solve a problem. Abraham solved a problem—he birthed a people and nation that would represent God. Joseph solved a problem for his employer Pharaoh by providing a solution to a famine in the land, and in the process he became a world leader. Moses solved a problem for God and the Israelites by freeing his people from slavery. Paul solved a problem by bringing the gospel to the Gentiles. Solving problems—whether for God, your government, your employer, or your city—raises the value of your *influence capital*.

For years we thought that the best way to influence culture was to have an evangelism campaign in our cities. These activities alone, though important, do not change society. They must include the dynamic of believers positioned at the top of each sphere of influence that defines culture who become problem solvers in that culture, thereby giving godly influence over it.

Humans are born into a world at war. Each human being is born to discover and live out his or her personal story and thereby impact the larger story of the world that person lives in. Our story is usually always about us in the beginning—our desires, our needs, our crisis. This often leads us to a bigger story as a result of trying to reconcile our smaller story.

Braveheart is one of my favorite movies of all time. It is a movie about one man's story, which became other people's story. William Wallace wanted to live a peaceable life in the countryside of Scotland. However, there was war going on in the land, brought on by a wicked king in England. In the movie his wife is killed by the English army. Wallace responds by revenging her death, killing those who killed his beloved bride. His warrior reputation spread to the common people throughout the land, who held the same hatred of the English as he did, but did not have the heart or courage to fight the English. Wallace inspired something in them. They joined him in the fight and ultimately defeated the English in many battles. Wallace was not able to finish the fight. He was betrayed by one of his own and executed by the English. It would take Robert the Bruce to finish the work of freeing the Scottish people from the control of the English. But William Wallace was a change agent who became part of a larger story.

Similar stories could be told of people like Martin Luther King Jr., Nelson Mandela, the apostle Paul, and Rosa Parks. Each of these people was drawn into a personal crisis that led to a larger story that pushed them into living for a cause greater than themselves. Others became part of the cause they were fighting for. *Personal crisis is often the front door to our larger story in life.* For Joseph it began with the pit, for Paul it began with blindness on the Damascus road, for Martin Luther it began with ninety-five theses, and for Martin Luther King Jr. it began when a woman refused to give up her seat on a bus.

Rarely do change agents grow up wanting to change the world. Most of us settle for our smaller story. We don't think we have what it takes, so we resign ourselves to making the best of our circumstances merely to get by. "Change the world? I am just trying to make it to the next paycheck" is often the sentiment for many of us. But God says there is more than our personal plight. There is a bigger story we are each called into. And God allows a crisis to take place in our smaller story to ignite the larger one that resides in each of us.

God calls every human being to be a change agent for His kingdom. He does not see us living only in our smaller story. When God came to Gideon in the winepress, Gideon was trying to avoid being seen by his enemies and, at the same time, make a living. The angel of the Lord came to Gideon and said, "Oh, mighty warrior!" Gideon found the words strange. "Who, me? Warrior? You must have the wrong address. I am just a farmer."[1] God saw Gideon's future. God needed a change agent for such a time as that, and Gideon was His man.

CALLED INTO BATTLE

When God created the earth and Satan was thrust from his heavenly domain, a war began for control of the earth. Adam and Eve sinned against the perfect world that God created for them, thereby opening the door to Satan, whose mandate was to *devour your destiny*. He has been seeking to fulfill that mandate ever since. "Be sober, be vigilant; because your adversary the devil walks about like a roaring lion, seeking whom he may devour."[2]

Satan attempts to kill God's change agents and their destinies before we are ever born. He tried to kill Moses at birth and then tried to shut his mouth up through a stuttering spirit that caused him great insecurity. Moses's woundedness caused him to become so stubborn that even God could not convince him to use his voice to deliver the people. He insisted that his brother Aaron be his mouthpiece. You see, Satan always tries to turn our glory into shame.[3] He wants your past to become your future. He wants to convince you that you have no purpose or destiny.

Satan tried to kill Jesus at birth, forcing Him to flee to Egypt to escape the knife of Herod. Heaven watched this battle play out for the Son of God coming to Planet Earth.

> And war broke out in heaven: Michael and his angels fought with the dragon; and the dragon and his angels fought, but they did not prevail, nor was a place found for them in heaven any longer....And the dragon was enraged with the woman, and he went to make war with the rest of her offspring, who keep the commandments of God and have the testimony of Jesus Christ.
>
> —REVELATION 12:7–8, 17

Satan is killing the destinies of God's sons and daughters every day through legalized abortion and through the killing of our spirits through dysfunctional family systems. Jesus came to the earth to redeem what had been lost in the garden.[4] What was lost in the garden was the intimate relationship with God the Father, dominion over the earth, and a meaningful purpose for our lives— all losses designed to encourage us to live for our smaller story rather than God's bigger story of His kingdom here on earth.

How many of us settle for the smaller story of our lives? God calls us to something great, but because of the wounds we receive as children, we cannot get past the pain and the insecurity it causes in our lives. For some of us it comes as a simple fear of standing in front of people to speak. Or it may come as fear to lead a small group Bible study. For others it may come through poor self-confidence because of a father or mother who shamed us growing up. Still others build walls of protection through performance designed to keep us safe and secure. Life's wounds affect how we view life as an adult. This is Satan's strategy to keep change agents from fulfilling their larger calling, their larger story. As I stated earlier, many times the pain caused by these situations become the catalyst to start us toward the journey of God's larger story for our lives.

Jesus came to give us life abundantly, not simply to make our life meaningful. It is part of our preparation for becoming a warrior for the battle. Today men and women in the marketplace are being called into battle. We have sat on the sidelines too long. We have been told that we are second-class spiritual citizens. This is changing. God is calling forth His remnant to awaken us to our destinies, which are larger than the nine-to-five calling we often settle for. We are first called into a personal and intimate relationship with God through Jesus Christ. If we are married, husbands are to reflect that love to their wives by sacrificially loving and caring for their brides just as Jesus sacrificially gave Himself for His bride, the church. The family mountain is one of our weakest mountains, unfortunately, and it must be reclaimed.

Next, the nine-to-five calling is the place where God will allow you to intersect your personal, home, and vocational callings to affect the world. The very thing you were made for is the very place where your story is to be lived for 60–70 percent of your time. The prophet Joel tells us that in the last days we will exchange that which the world views as simply tools to make a living into tools to wage a war of love for the Creator of the universe.

> Proclaim this among the nations:
> "Prepare for war!
> Wake up the mighty men,
> Let all the men of war draw near,
> Let them come up.
> Beat your plowshares into swords
> And your pruning hooks into spears;
> Let the weak say, 'I am strong.'"
> Assemble and come, all you nations,
> And gather together all around.
> Cause Your mighty ones to go down there, O Lord.
>
> —Joel 3:9–11

You were created for the battle. In the following chapters you will learn where the battle is being waged and how you can become part of the larger story as God's change agent.

THE CALL TO CHANGE CULTURE

Chapter 1

CULTURE GONE AWRY

Now it shall come to pass in the latter days
That the mountain of the LORD's house
Shall be established on the top of the mountains,
And shall be exalted above the hills;
And all nations shall flow to it.

—ISAIAH 2:2

IN 1975 BILL Bright, founder of Campus Crusade, and Loren Cunningham, founder of Youth With A Mission, had lunch together in Colorado. God simultaneously gave each of these change agents a message to give to the other. During that same time frame Francis Schaeffer, founder of L'Abri, and Pat Robertson of Regent University and the Christian Broadcasting Network were given a similar message. That message was that if we are to impact any nation for Jesus Christ, then we will have to affect the seven spheres, or mountains of society, that are the pillars of any society. *These seven mountains are business, government, media, arts and entertainment, education, the family, and religion.* There are many subgroups under these main categories. In essence, God was telling these four change agents where the battlefield was. It was here where culture would be won or lost. Their assignment was to raise up change agents to scale the mountains and to help a new generation of change agents understand the larger story.

During the last fifteen years God has been igniting men and women to see their work lives as holy callings from God. They have begun to realize the spiritual calling upon their lives. In the last few years the message of the seven mountains has begun to reemerge through many leaders simultaneously, many not knowing one another. I recall when God began speaking to me about this through my friend Lance Wallnau. I began to teach and prepare to share this message at an international conference. I had been traveling internationally and had not been in my church for more than three months. When I returned, my pastor, Johnny Enlow, was in his third message on the "Seven-Mountain Strategy." This series of messages became a book titled *The Seven Mountain Prophecy.* When God speaks simultaneously to leaders, we understand that

God is initiating something through His church. However, this message is largely being released through men and women in the marketplace.

Landa Cope, dean of the Youth With a Mission (YWAM) International Schools and author of the *The Old Testament Template*, has spoken in more than 110 nations. She explained to me that this was not just a message for America but that it was being implemented around the globe in various forms. Her book discusses eight cultural spheres of influence. She adds science and technology as her eighth mountain. "Some nations are years ahead of the United States in the implementation of a strategy focus on the core cultural spheres as a means to influence culture," she said.

Henry Blackaby once said, "You never find God asking persons to dream up what they want to do for Him. When God starts to do something in the world, He takes the initiative to come and talk to somebody. For some divine reason, He has chosen to involve His people in accomplishing His purposes."[1]

How Culture Is Defined

Culture is defined by a relatively small number of change agents who operate at the tops of these mountains. It takes less than 3–5 percent of those operating at the tops of a cultural mountain to actually shift the values represented on that mountain. This is exactly what the gay rights movement has done through the mountains of media and arts and entertainment. They are gradually legitimizing their cause through these two mountains. We will discuss this more in the chapter on the family mountain.

Mountains are controlled by a small percentage of leaders and networks. James Hunter, in a 2002 Trinity Forum briefing, highlights what sociologist Randall Collins says about civilizations in his book *The Sociology of Philosophies*. According to Collins, civilizations have been defined by a very small percentage of cultural philosophers who influence seven gates and supporting networks since our birth as a civilization. Hunter summarizes, "Even if we add the minor figures in all of the networks, in all of the civilizations, the total is only 2,700. In sum, between 150 and 3,000 people (a tiny fraction of the roughly 23 billion people living between 600 B.C. and A.D. 1900) framed the major contours of all world civilizations. Clearly, the transformations here were top-down."[2]

What an amazing piece of information. Imagine that. *Culture has been defined since the beginning of time by no more than three thousand change agents, a tiny fraction of the population.* That is why we must realize that making more conversions will not necessarily change culture. It is important to have conversions, but it is more important to have those who are converted operate at the tops of the cultural mountains from a biblical worldview.

Those at the tops of these mountains are expressing a worldview about each influence. The more liberal and ungodly the change agents at the top, the more liberal and ungodly the culture. The more godly the change agent at the top, the more righteous the culture will be. *It doesn't matter if the majority of the culture is made up of Christians. It only matters who has the greatest influence over that cultural mountain.* And the mountain of family must undergird all other cultural mountains.

In November of 2007 I had the privilege of interviewing Loren Cunningham. Following is an excerpt of that interview as he describes the meeting with Bill Bright that day in 1975.

> As we came in and greeted each other [we were friends for quite a while], and I was reaching for my yellow paper that I had written on the day before, he said, "Loren, I want to show you what God has shown me!" And it was virtually the same list that God had given me the day before. Three weeks later my wife, Darlene, had seen Dr. Francis Schaeffer on TV, and he had the same list! And so I realized that this was for the body of Christ.
>
> I gave this message for the first time in Hamburg, Germany, at the big cathedral there to a group of hundreds of young people who had gathered at that time. I said, "These are the areas that you can go into as missionaries. Here they are: First, it's the institution set up by God first, the family. After the family is church, or the people of God. The third is the area of school, or education. The fourth is media, public communication, in all forms, printed and electronic. The fifth is what I call celebration, the arts, entertainment, and sports, where you celebrate within a culture. The sixth would be the whole area of the economy, which starts with innovations in science and technology, productivity, sales, and service. We often call this area business, but we sometimes leave out the scientific part, which actually raises the wealth of the world. Anything new, like making sand into chips for a microchip, increases wealth in the world. And then, of course, predicting sales and service helps to spread the wealth. The last is the area of government. Now government, as the Bible shows in Isaiah 33:22, includes three branches of government: judicial, legislative, and executive.
>
> "So we make whatever we do, if we do it as unto the Lord, a sanctified or a holy work. It is holy unto the Lord. It's not just standing in the pulpit on Sunday—that's one of the spheres. It's also all the other spheres together, and that's how we achieve advancing the kingdom of God."[3]

Loren proceeded to explain how they began to equip young people with these seven spheres in mind through the schools they have established all over the world.

WHAT HAPPENED?

As I listened to his story, I could not help but ask myself, "With so many wonderful Christian leaders like Loren Cunningham impacting the world with the good news of the kingdom of God, why is our own nation in the condition we are in today?" We seem to be making some strides in other parts of the world, but in our own nation we seem to be losing the cultural battle.

One plausible explanation for the lack of progress in our nation may be the fact that it has not been until the last fifteen years that an awakening among men and women in the workplace has begun. This silent majority—that had been satisfied simply to sit on the sidelines and write a check each week to their local church—was awakened by a very real move of God to the spiritual nature and value of their calling in and through their vocations. Martin Luther brought the Word of God back to the people, but the Faith at Work movement is bringing the work of God back to the people.

Francis Schaeffer seemed to understand this dichotomy when he established L'Abri Fellowship in 1955, which has study centers in Europe, North America, and Asia. These study centers are designed to stimulate students in an intellectually and deeply spiritual foundation to give representation to faith within the seven spheres of society.

We are each called to become change agents in the sphere of influence God has called us to impact. As each of us does this, we reclaim the culture one person at a time, one industry at a time, one mountain at a time. This becomes our larger story. In the end, we know God will establish His kingdom on the top of every cultural mountain.

James Hunter, in his book *To Change the World*, states, "Imagine…a genuine 'third great awakening' occurring in America, where half of the population is converted to a deep Christian faith. Unless this awakening extended to envelop the cultural gatekeepers, it would have little effect on the character of the symbols that are produced and prevail in public and private culture. And, without a fundamental restructuring of the institutions of culture formation and transmission in our society—the market, government-sponsored cultured institutions, education at all levels, advertising, entertainment, publishing, and the news media, not to mention church—revival would have a negligible long-term effect on the reconstitution of the culture."[4]

OUR CURRENT STATUS IN CULTURE

When the righteous are in authority, the people rejoice;
But when a wicked man rules, the people groan.
—PROVERBS 29:2

For the last several decades culture has become increasingly secular and liberal in the United States. But God has always raised up His change agents to represent His interests and agenda on Planet Earth. God is raising up His change agents for such a time as this. We know that Jesus will return for a bride that "He might present her to Himself a glorious church, not having spot or wrinkle or any such thing, but that she should be holy and without blemish."[5] So, despite the trends we may see, I believe we need to operate from a victorious eschatology viewpoint. God's current activity in the marketplace is part of this. He is calling His church to "love the LORD your God with all your heart, with all your soul, and with all your mind."[6] This means applying God's mind to the natural order expressed through the cultural mountains of society.

THE FROG IN THE KETTLE

There is an analogy that best describes American culture today. It goes like this: A frog jumped into cool water in a kettle, not realizing the heat had been turned on. Gradually the heat began to build, and the frog adjusted to the warmer temperature. However, the heat became very hot, and the frog did not notice the extreme heat until he was burned to death in the kettle. America has been sitting in the kettle of a cultural slide into liberalism that is just now beginning to alarm Christians to the point they are ready to do something about it. How did we get here? *UnChristian* coauthor Gabe Lyons says, "America was practically Christian just a handful of years ago, but in the past several decades, our country's predominant self-perceptions have been challenged and replaced. . . . So although many of us still *feel* like we reside in Christian America, that reality is dead."[7]

We have been losing the seven mountains of culture to liberal influences for three distinct reasons. The first reason is very simple: We have separated ourselves and our nation from God. As we became more prosperous as a nation, we became less dependent on God. Unfortunately, humility and prosperity often do not coexist. We gave up dominion when Adam and Eve fell, and we have failed to reclaim it because of our own sins of self-satisfaction and complacency toward God.

You see, our enemies didn't have to kill us; we simply disobeyed God, which entitled our enemies to take our mountains. Over the centuries there have been major tipping points in our culture that led to a continual falling away from the foundations God gave us to live by in our nation. God laid out His requirements to the nation of Israel, which can be applied to every nation on earth.

> However, if you do not obey the LORD your God and do not carefully
> follow all his commands and decrees I am giving you today, all these

curses will come upon you and overtake you: You will be cursed in the city and cursed in the country. Your basket and your kneading trough will be cursed. The fruit of your womb will be cursed, and the crops of your land, and the calves of your herds and the lambs of your flocks. You will be cursed when you come in and cursed when you go out.

—DEUTERONOMY 28:15–19, NIV

BIBLICAL WORLDVIEW

And Joshua said, "By this you shall know that the living God is among you, and that He will without fail drive out from before you the Canaanites and the Hittites and the Hivites and the Perizzites and the Girgashites and the Amorites and the Jebusites."

—JOSHUA 3:10

Johnny Enlow, author of *The Seven Mountain Prophecy*, cites seven enemies found in the Book of Joshua, which can be correlated to the seven cultural mountains. The meaning of the names behind each of these enemies can be tied to a specific cultural mountain. We will discuss this in a later chapter. However, these enemies seek to distort our views of God and culture through an unbiblical worldview.

What percentage of Christians in the United States hold a biblical worldview? Glad you asked. George Barna has been asking this question in his surveys for many years. Here is how he defines a biblical worldview: "For the purposes of the survey, a 'biblical worldview' was defined as believing that absolute moral truth exists; the Bible is totally accurate in all of the principles it teaches; Satan is considered to be a real being or force, not merely symbolic; a person cannot earn their way into Heaven by trying to be good or do good works; Jesus Christ lived a sinless life on earth; and God is the all-knowing, all-powerful creator of the world who still rules the universe today. In the research, anyone who held all of those beliefs was said to have a biblical worldview." Barna's 2008 Barna survey found that only 9 percent of the general audience surveyed had a biblical worldview, and those who claimed to be born-again Christians were 19 percent.[8]

Unfortunately, the trend is not looking very promising among the next generation, a group George Barna and David Kinnaman refer to as the *Mosaics* (born between 1984 and 2002) and the *Busters* (born between 1965 and 1983). David Kinnaman, coauthor of *UnChristian*, states that among two-thirds of young adults who have made a commitment to Jesus at one time in their life, only 3 percent of both groups embrace the criteria listed earlier that defines a biblical worldview.[9]

Dr. Henry Blackaby gives his observation of what has happened to America. "If I were to attempt to find the beginning of what I believe is a national neglect of God, I would return to the early 1960s. It seems as though God removed the hedge of protection from around America in that decade. We began to see unrestrained things take place from the '60s to this present day. There seems to have been nothing to hold back the tide of injustice in society. A deep departure from God in the churches has continued since that decade. It is as if the hedge of His protection has been broken down, and God is letting us experience the consequences of our own sin."[10]

Michael Lindsay, in his book *Faith in the Halls of Power*, chronicles the systematic decline of Christian influence in our nation. "In the nineteenth century, American evangelism was so influential that, in the words of one historian, 'it was virtually a religious establishment.' Conservative Protestants populated the faculties of Harvard, Yale, and Princeton. Evangelicals were also active in politics, helping drive the temperance and women's suffrage movements as they had done decades earlier with abolitionism."[11]

TIPPING POINTS IN CULTURE

There have been several tipping points in American society that are landmarks where our *frog* felt the heat go up several degrees.

In 1963, prayer in schools was ruled unconstitutional. This became a major tipping point in our nation. God made sure we knew it was this activity that began a decline in the moral fiber of our nation, as there is a very distinct declining curve that can be graphed off major societal ills that began to be evidenced since 1963.

Since 1963:

- Premarital sex increased 500 percent.

- Unwed pregnancy was up 400 percent.

- Sexually transmitted disease was up 200 percent.

- Suicides were up 400 percent.

- SAT scores dropped 90 points from 1963–1980 (lowest in the industrialized world).

- Single-parent families were up 140 percent.

- Violent crime was up 500 percent.[12]

The Baby Boomer generation has not done a very good job during our spiritual watch over the nation. Ten years after prayer was banned in school, conservative Christians lost one of the most important battles when abortion was legalized in 1973, as the result of the famous *Roe v. Wade* Supreme Court case.

It's Now Hard to Tell the Difference

Influence in culture is only possible when those who want to exert influence have a message and a life that others see and desire. This is the nature of a truly transformed life. Unfortunately, there is evidence that Christianity in America has lost its power and its influence at the foundation level. *UnChristian* authors Kinnaman and Lyons also conducted extensive research to determine our influence on culture. Their findings are disturbing.

> In virtually every study we conduct, representing thousands of interviews every year, born-again Christians fail to display much attitudinal or behavioral evidence of transformed lives. For instance, based on a study released in 2007, we found that most of the lifestyle activities of born-again Christians were statistically equivalent to those of non-born-again. When asked to identify their activities over the last thirty days, born-again believers were just as likely to bet or gamble, to visit a pornographic website, to take something that did not belong to them, to consult a medium or psychic, to physically fight or abuse someone, to have consumed enough alcohol to be considered legally drunk, to have used an illegal, nonprescription drug, to have said something to someone that was not true, to have gotten back at someone for something he or she did, and to have said mean things behind another person's back. No difference.[13]

These findings are a contrast to what took place during the Roman Empire. We know that during that time, Christians took care of the terminally ill at the risk of their own lives and were such a testimony to the love and power of Christ in a life that they drew people into faith by their very different lifestyle. Constantine proclaimed Rome the *Holy Roman Empire*, not for political reasons, but merely stating the obvious that was being demonstrated by the people. *Christians transformed culture by the way they lived.*

God and Government

Our worldview has a direct impact on our ability to influence the world around us. Loren Cunningham, in his book *The Book That Transforms Nations*, told a story that illustrates this point.

> Nabis, an Egyptian friend of mine, overheard three Arabs talking as they watched airplanes taking off in Kuwait. One of them said, "Why is it we can fly those jets but we can never create one?" A good question. Why? Isn't wonderful technology flowing from Middle Eastern nations? Those nations have as many intelligent gifted people per capita as any others in the world. But their worldview has hobbled their

people with concrete thinking, legalism, and rigid hierarchy—qualities that prevent a rise to world leadership. Their worldview hinders the progress of Middle Eastern culture and keeps people from developing innovative ideas.[14]

The further we move away from a biblical worldview, the less influence I believe we will have in the world.

Today there is a move in society to remove God from government altogether. One lawsuit in 2006 sought to remove God from the Pledge of Allegiance. Another sought to remove prayer from public school commencements. The move to remove God from all government is growing in our nation, and unless there is a remnant with the backbone to stand against it, we will fall to the way of Europe, which is becoming increasingly pagan. How sad, when we think that some of our greatest spiritual leaders came from places like Germany and England. In spite of the fact our national motto is "In God We Trust," which appears on every currency in America, we are seeing an eroding of this belief. This is evidenced by President Barack Obama's statement in a speech in Turkey in April 2009, when he said, "We do not consider ourselves a Christian nation."[15] It is becoming increasingly difficult to bring up the name of God in a public forum.

American church attendance is steadily declining. According to an *Outreach* magazine article in May/June 2006, in 1990 20.4 percent of the population attended an Orthodox Christian church on any given weekend. In 2000, that percentage dropped to 18.7 percent and to 17.7 percent by 2004.[16] However, George Barna's figures are not quite as bleak but still show a declining trend. One pastor reflects on Barna's results from a 2009 study:

> My research shows that church attendance in the U.S. is as low as 15–20% of the entire population on any given Sunday, and in some areas of the country is likely even lower. The problem is not that Christians are transferring to another (non-Christian) religion as much as it is that traditional versions of Christianity are being rejected. A better headline than that which appears above (and on the report) may be that the "traditional version of Christianity is no longer the default religion in the U.S." The population is increasingly unchurched as traditional versions of Christianity fall out of favor.[17]

RELATIVISM

Another major trend we have seen develop in our generation is the move toward relativism. Relativism means there are no absolutes. Today's mantra goes like this: "Whatever feels good to you and does not impose your views on others is good." No one wants to offend anyone else. Consequently we have a whole new generation being raised who don't want to offend anyone by implying there really is a right and wrong way to do something and who are unwilling to stand upon convictions that might be rooted in a moral faith. This is why we have a leadership vacuum in our nation.

Here is the rub. Change agents want to be influencers of culture, but when we make choices that alienate the culture in our attempt to remain true to absolute truth, we run amuck. George Barna, in his research on the most culture-changing megathemes of 2010, cited the difficult balance that Christians have in maintaining an absolute Christian worldview while still loving those in the culture. "The challenge today is for Christian leaders to achieve the delicate balance between representing truth and acting in love. The challenge for every Christian in the U.S. is to know his/her faith well enough to understand which fights are worth fighting, and which stands are nonnegotiable. There is a place for tolerance in Christianity; knowing when and where to draw the line appears to perplex a growing proportion of Christians in this age of tolerance."[18]

Stanley Grenz is a well-respected author and theology professor who died in 1900 but extensively studied postmodernism (the emerging worldview). In his book *A Primer on Postmodernism*, he describes the major tenets and sociocultural implications of the changes occurring in our society in the early stages of the twenty-first century. He defined postmodernism as a "questioning, and even rejection, of the Enlightenment project and the foundational assumptions upon which it was built, namely, that knowledge is certain, objective and inherently good. Consequently it marks the end of a single worldview. Postmodernism resists unified, all-encompassing and universally valid explanations."[19]

This leads society to the conclusion that there is no absolute truth, which contradicts the Bible, which is based upon absolute truth.

In the midnineties the Spirituality at Work movement ushered in a new sensitivity and acceptance in corporate America to allow the worker to embrace spirituality in his or her working life. However, Patricia Aburdene, in her book *Megatrends 2010*, cites that instead of this being a move toward bringing Christianity into the workplace, it has ushered in all forms of New Age, transcendental meditation, and other forms of spirituality, because the new societal rule is to "connect with God any way you can."[20] In other words, there is no right and wrong way to God. The Bible becomes irrelevant as *the* way to God because it represents just *another way* to God in a postmodern society. Those who would have the audacity to say that Jesus is *the* way are now considered rigid and backward for a modern and progressive society because of the obvious diversity of faiths and ethnicity held by so many in our postmodern society. Yet the Bible warns us, "There is a way that seems right to a man, but its end is the way of death."[21]

In summary, the first reason we have lost culture is due to our own disobedience. We have entitled our enemies to take our mountains because of our own disobedience.

In the chapters that follow, we will seek to better understand how far we have fallen away from the ideals that were the foundations of our nation and what we must do to reclaim them through an existing and new generation of change agents. We have fallen for our own smaller stories while giving up the larger one God has called us to live.

QUESTIONS FOR REFLECTION

1. Cite some of the reasons we have lost culture listed in this chapter.

2. Explain how relativism has influenced culture and the church today. How are we to maintain absolutes and still impact the culture?

3. Read 2 Chronicles 7:14. Based on this verse, what is the first step we must do? Contrast the difference between the smaller story and the larger story as it relates to culture.

Chapter 2

KING KONG AND THE GARDEN OF EDEN

Then God blessed them, and God said to them, "Be fruitful and multiply; fill the earth and subdue it; have dominion over the fish of the sea, over the birds of the air, and over every living thing that moves on the earth."
—Genesis 1:28

I N 1933 A movie was released titled *King Kong*, set in America's Great Depression, and a remake of the movie was produced in America in 2005. It was the story of a movie producer who traveled to a place called *Skull Island* on the ship *Venture*. A giant ape lived on the island, and he captured a beautiful woman and fell in love with her. The ape was larger than life and had great strength and power to protect *and* harm the young woman. Initially the woman had great fear. But that fear gradually moved to love and compassion for her captor. He would pick her up in his palm and gaze into her eyes. He provided for her every need and protected her. The longer she remained in captivity, the more the young woman began to have feelings for this dangerous, giant gorilla. He was dangerous, but he was good.

When the men from the ship captured the gorilla, she opposed their actions. She defended her captor. She became his advocate when the men tried to turn this grand creature into a spectacle. They commercialized their catch. They failed to recognize the sensitive personality of the gorilla, wanting only to capitalize on the marquee value of the ape.

There are some similarities between this fictitious movie and the Garden of Eden described in the Book of Genesis. Dream with me for a moment. Imagine living in a world without sin—a world where God is your intimate friend. You can speak to Him at any time. You know He loves you and keeps you safe. He invites you to get to know Him. You know He is dangerous, but you also know He is good. Your initial perception is fear; however, you discover you are totally safe in the protected environment of the garden. All your needs are met—for companionship, love, food—everything is provided, without sweat and toil. The Bible says that the Garden of Eden where Adam and Eve lived was a perfect kind of life before the fall.

Although Adam and Eve lived in the Garden of Eden where everything was provided for them, they still had to work. Work was considered another means of worship of their Creator. Work was very different. Adam and Eve were given dominion over every living thing. They named all the animals; they could tell the animals what to do, and they would do it. Their vegetables were not susceptible to insects. If they needed anything, they simply asked God. There was no competition. There was no sickness. There was no need for manipulative sales ploys. No one had impure motives. There were no jails because there was no crime, and no hospitals because there was no sickness. There was no sexual perversion—all was pure and innocent. There would be no scams coming from Nigeria through your e-mail, no evil dictators like Saddam Hussein to wreak pain and suffering. And there was nothing more beautiful than the Garden of Eden.

ADAM AND EVE WERE GIVEN DOMINION OVER THEIR WORLD

God's original intent was for man to rule and reign over the earth, together with Him, by the authority entrusted to them. "The heaven, even the heavens, are the LORD's; but the earth He has given to the children of men."[1] God blessed them and said, "Be fruitful and multiply; fill the earth and subdue it; have dominion over the fish of the sea, over the birds of the air, and over every living thing that moves on the earth."[2]

God extended His ownership over everything He created *and* over the people who lived on the earth. "The earth is the LORD's, and all its fullness, the world and those who dwell therein."[3] This is why Jesus prayed that whatever was in heaven would be manifested on the earth. He was wanting to restore all that had been lost. His desire for His people has always been for them to be at the top of every sphere of society, not because we are better than others, but because He wants to reveal His love in every human being in every aspect of society. He told the people of Israel this in Deuteronomy 28:13–14:

> And the LORD will make you the head and not the tail; you shall be above only, and not be beneath, if you heed the commandments of the LORD your God, which I command you today, and are careful to observe them. So you shall not turn aside from any of the words which I command you this day, to the right hand or to the left, to go after other gods to serve them.

The context of this verse was in Israel's relationship to other nations. Israel had a problem with adopting the idols of other nations. God said, "Be faithful to Me, and you will be above the other nations." An important understanding must be stated at this point. *Dominion, or perhaps a better word to use is influence, is a result of our love and obedience to God, not a goal to be achieved.* It is the fruit of our obedience. Otherwise we begin to use fleshly strategies to exploit and subjugate others to our way of thinking. Jesus never sought to have dominion; rather, He encouraged others to love and obey God. It is better that we avoid the word *dominion* in our culture today due to the connotation that comes with this word of control and manipulation of others. It also reminds people of a flawed movement in the body of Christ called dominion theology that caused great harm to many.

When we operate from love and service, we will be attractive to the world. They will desire to follow. We become solution providers to the issues of mankind. Jesus solved people's problems, which resulted in greater influence in people's lives. Influence without humility and relationship (with Jesus and others) means we operate from our individual personal agendas, which is what the evangelical church has done in many instances.

God describes His nature by His position as King over all domains. In her book *An Introduction to the Old Testament Template,* Landa Cope lists His positions:

- King of kings—the Lord of justice
- Jehovah Jireh—Lord of economics
- Father—Lord of the family
- Creator God—Lord of science and technology
- Living Word—Lord of communication
- Potter—Lord of the arts and beauty
- Great Teacher—Lord of education[4]

He is also the Great Physician, the healer of our bodies.

So, you can see that God's original mandate was to rule and reign on the earth through His creation. His mission wasn't simply for man to receive salvation. Salvation was only the entry point. His ultimate goal was for man to rule by His grace, love, and power in order to be a testimony of His love to the world He created.

Gabe Lyons explains: "Christ's death and Resurrection were not only meant to save people *from* something. He wanted to save Christians *to* something. God longs to restore his image in them, and let them loose, freeing them to pursue his original dreams for the entire world. Here, now, today, tomorrow. They no longer feel bound to wait for heaven or spend all of their time telling people what they should believe. Instead, they are participating with God in his restoration project for the whole world. They recognize that Christ's redemptive work is not the end or even the goal of our stories; redemption is the beginning of our participation in God's work of restoration in our lives and in the world. Understanding that one idea literally changes everything."⁵

MAN HAD FREEDOM AND BOUNDARIES

When God created man, He created them to manage the earth within certain freedoms and boundaries. There was a tree of life in the garden that was off limits to Adam and Eve. "Out of the ground the LORD God made every tree grow that is pleasant to the sight and good for food. The tree of life was also in the midst of the garden, and the tree of the knowledge of good and evil."⁶ Knowledge can be dangerous when it replaces our trust and obedience to our heavenly Father. This is what has happened to education today. Education and knowledge have become idols.

"Then the LORD God took the man and put him in the garden of Eden to tend and keep it. And the LORD God commanded the man, saying, 'Of every tree of the garden you may freely eat; but of the tree of the knowledge of good and evil you shall not eat, for in the day that you eat of it you shall surely die.'"⁷ God had a boundary line that Adam and Eve had to respect in order for God to protect them. However, man decided that being a steward was not good enough. He wanted to be like God and have all knowledge. Satan convinced man that God was holding out on them.

What did God mean when He said, "You shall surely die," if they ate from the tree? It didn't mean physical death. It meant that their relationship with their Creator would die. It meant that sin would enter the world. Sin means separation from God. All that was good in the garden would be tarnished, and the entire planet would be impacted by Adam and Eve's sin. Everything, yes, *everything* would change. Satan would be allowed to have dominion instead of man. Their intimate relationship with God would now be broken.

A "sublease" to the earth was permitted to Satan when Adam and Eve sinned. They no longer controlled Planet Earth. We see evidence of this in several New Testament passages. When Jesus was tempted by the devil, Satan offered to Jesus "all the kingdoms of the world and their glory."⁸ His influence was limited by God's sovereignty, but he was still able to exercise great power over the world's activities. Jesus did not dispute Satan's claims. Jesus acknowledged that Satan was "the ruler of this world."⁹

In another account Satan is referred to as the "god of this age."¹⁰ In his first epistle, John states that "the whole world lies under the sway of the wicked one."¹¹ Jesus came to the earth to reclaim all that had been lost in the garden¹² and give the keys back to man. However, it was man's responsibility to be His representative in this reclamation process. Prayer and exercising our authority would be the primary tools to do this.¹³ Some of God's desired activity does not happen because there is no intercessor vessel for Him to use to execute His will, which He has limited Himself to using.

Evidence of these consequences came in many ways. Adam and Eve realized their nakedness and covered themselves. No longer was everything pure and holy; sin had come into their world. Their work now required sweat and toil, because the ground had been cursed and had thorns and thistles. Their dreams for a great future died.

Until this time they had known no evil. The tree of the knowledge of good and evil became the basis for the battle for mankind's future relationship with God and His creation. Shame, evil, murder, doubt, unbelief, and worry all came into the world with that one act of disobedience. Man began to use all sorts of deceptive and manipulative means to gain provision. Greed and mammon were the results. The marketplace was tainted by the sin of man.

God's boundaries were meant to protect. However, man's nature wants no boundaries. So, man rebelled against God by refusing to live inside boundaries that were designed to benefit him. It happens every day in our fallen world. God's original intent was for individuals and nations to obey God, and if they did, they would:

- Prosper in every way

- Fulfill their unique purpose

- Fulfill God's overall plan

- Receive their God-ordained inheritance individually and as a nation

In essence, all creation would have reflected His glory as a result of their obedience to Him.

God knows that man will be most fulfilled when they are led by godly people and godly principles. He tells us in Proverbs, "'When the righteous are in authority, the people rejoice; but when a wicked man rules, the people groan."[14] We each need to answer some important questions to determine where we are individually—and in our community—in regard to God's original intent. Would your community notice if your local church shut its doors tomorrow? Would your workplace notice if you were no longer there? Is your industry different because of you? Are you living the larger story God had in mind for you to be His representative change agent? What would our nation look like if each of us modeled Christlike leadership and servanthood? Would the blessings of Deuteronomy 28:1–14 rest upon our nation?

WHY JESUS WAS NECESSARY

For it pleased the Father that in Him all the fullness should dwell, and by Him to reconcile all things to Himself, by Him, whether things on earth or things in heaven, having made peace through the blood of His cross.

—COLOSSIANS 1:19–20

Jesus returned to reclaim His Lordship over all domains of influence through His representatives—not just as Lord over salvation. After Jesus returned to heaven, it was up to His followers to appropriate what He did on the cross by reclaiming out of obedience all that had been lost. We are His representatives on the earth. Many Christians believe the earth is not God's but is now in control of Satan, and so they have abdicated rulership to him. Many are simply awaiting the *rapture from this evil world*. This is not biblical theology.

One of Jesus's last instructions to the disciples related to His authority and His passing of that authority to those of us on earth. Matthew 28:18–20 states, "And Jesus came and spoke to them, saying, 'All authority has been given to Me in heaven and on earth. Go therefore and make disciples of all the nations, baptizing them in the name of the Father and of the Son and of the Holy Spirit, teaching them to observe all things that I have commanded you; and lo, I am with you always, even to the end of the age.'" Jesus was officially passing His authority to us. Jesus was giving His representatives *power of attorney* to represent and enforce His interests on the earth. That is our role.

We are to enforce and teach what Jesus has instructed us to do and what He has said. *Our role is to enforce His will through intercessory prayer by claiming His promises and defeating the works of the enemy.* Jesus came to defeat the works of the enemy. "For this purpose the Son of God was manifested, that He might destroy the works of the devil."[15] We too are called to defeat the works of the enemy on earth because we are to live as Jesus did on earth. Jesus said we would do even greater works than Him.

The *escape theology* assumes the influence of the church will decrease on earth until Jesus returns. This view sees the influence of the church waning in the last days. Genesis 1:28 and Matthew 28:19–20 provide the basis for a theology that believes that the return of Christ has more to do with the maturity of the bride versus a timetable. This theology does not intend to imply absolute dominion, as in a sinless earth, but a preparatory dominion, as in the earth being prepared for the return of the King. When Jesus prayed the Lord's Prayer, He prayed that what was in heaven would be manifested on the earth through His representatives.[16]

The Bible teaches that through modeling the love and servant leadership that Jesus modeled, we will have influence upon our worlds. This is so Jesus can come back for a mature bride. In order to reclaim the earth, God needs His change agents. God chooses to work through man. Are you ready to start this reclamation process by being one of His change agents?

QUESTIONS FOR REFLECTION:

1. Consider the role Adam and Even had before the sin in the garden. What do you think work was like?

2. Jesus paid a price to reclaim what was lost. What are we to do in response to what He did?

3. How would you define being a change agent?

Chapter 3

DEVELOP A BIBLICAL WORLDVIEW

Your kingdom come.
Your will be done
On earth as it is in heaven.

—Matthew 6:10

I WANT YOU TO imagine a conversation between Joshua and God. "Now Joshua, I have called you to take the leadership from Moses, and I want you to take My people across the Jordan River into the Promised Land. However, once you cross the Jordan River, I want you and all your people to sit down. Your mission is done."

"Ridiculous!" you might say. I would agree with you. But in many ways, this is exactly what the American church has done in the last fifty years. We have preached the gospel of salvation, but we have not taught the people to apply the message of the gospel to their everyday life. This is the difference between the gospel of salvation and the gospel of the kingdom. This is the second reason I believe we have been losing the culture.

Jesus did not come merely to give us a ticket to heaven. He came to bring us much more—the kingdom of God on earth. Nowhere in the Bible will you find the phrase *gospel of salvation*. The church does not exist for heaven but for earth. If it existed only for heaven, then upon conversion, each of us would immediately be taken to heaven. Oswald Chambers said, "It is not a question of being saved from hell, but in being saved in order to manifest the Son of God in our mortal flesh."[1] There would be no reason for us to remain on earth if there was not a work to be done. So why has God allowed us to receive this new birth and remain on earth? It is so that we might bring the kingdom of God into our world—to our families, our workplace, and our communities.

Jesus talked about the kingdom of God more than seventy times in the New Testament—much more often than He mentioned salvation. While salvation is part of bringing the kingdom of God on earth, it includes much more. When Jesus came to earth, He came in order to penetrate the very kingdom of darkness with light. He came to bring healing to sickness, replace sadness with joy, and fill meaninglessness people with purpose. He came to change things for the better in a world that had no hope outside of God. Chuck Colson says, "Genuine Christianity is more than a relationship with Jesus, as expressed in personal piety, church attendance, Bible study, and works of charity. It is more than discipleship, more than believing a system of doctrines about God. Genuine Christianity is a way of seeing and comprehending all reality. It is a worldview."[2]

God wants you to bring the kingdom of God into the territory He has given you so that His will can be done on earth as it is in heaven. Your domain is your workplace, family, and community. *When the gospel of the kingdom comes into a life and a community, everything in its wake is impacted.*

We need to understand how the church arrived at this place of being stuck on the gospel of salvation.

In 1999 we hosted a marketplace conference in Atlanta. One of my speakers was Landa Cope, Dean of the College of Communication for Youth With A Mission University of the Nations. Landa teaches all over the world. At that time she was writing a book, and she taught us from her notes. Today her book *An Introduction to the Old Testament Template* addresses the issue of the failure of the church to operate from Jesus's paradigm of the gospel of the kingdom versus the gospel of salvation. She believes this is why we have had such little impact in the Western church.

Her opening chapter tells a story about her sitting in her living room one day watching a television program where a British journalist was saying that Christians believe that the more Christians there are in a community, the more that community will be affected for good—the greater the Christian presence, then the greater the benefit to the society at large.

The TV journalist went on to describe a research project that was designed to discover if this was true. He evaluated the most Christianized city in America to see how this influence worked out practically. He defined "most Christianized" as the community with the largest percentage of church attendance regularly—Dallas, Texas. He looked at various statistics and studies, including crime, safety on the streets, police enforcement, and the justice and penal system. He looked at health care, hospitals, emergency care, contagious diseases, infant mortality rate, and the distribution of caregivers. He reviewed education, equality of schools, safety, test scores, and graduation statistics. Jobs, housing, and general economics were also evaluated. Each of these categories was evaluated using racial and economic factors. Was there equity regardless of color, creed, or income? And so on.

By the time the journalist was finished with the conclusions of the Dallas study, Landa was devastated. No one would want to live in a city in that condition. The crime, the decrepit social systems, the disease, the economic discrepancies, the racial injustice all disqualified this community from having an adequate quality of life. And this was the *most Christianized* city in America! Landa wanted to weep.

The television host took this devastating picture of a broken community to Christian leaders and asked for their observations. One by one each pastor viewed the same facts about the condition of his city. With simplicity the narrator asked each minister, "As a Christian leader what is your response to the condition of your community?" Without exception, in various ways, they all said the same thing, "This is not our concern...we are *spiritual* leaders."[3] Martin Luther said, "A gospel that does not deal with the issues of the day is not the gospel at all."

God is doing a unique work in the earth today. There are seasons in which the Holy Spirit speaks things to the church. During one decade it might be a focus on evangelism. During another it might be a greater awareness of the Holy Spirit. During another it might be a focus on social problems in cities.

BIRTH OF THE WORKPLACE MOVEMENT

For the last several decades we have seen the church focus on proclamation evangelism. This has been true in the workplace movement as well. In 1930 Christian Businessmen's Connection (CBMC) began with a focus on evangelizing men in the workplace. Twenty years later Full Gospel Business Men's Fellowship International (FGBMFI) was birthed through Demos Shakarian. This too was a focus on winning men to Christ. Billy Graham rose in prominence during the fifties and sixties. His crusades won many to Christ. However, in the workplace movement we began to see some discrepancies, similar to Landa's story. We would often hear comments from Christians and non-Christians alike, who said, "I will never work with a Christian. The last time I did I got burned." The reason this was happening was that people were getting saved in the marketplace, but their lives had not been transformed. Their souls had been redeemed, but their working lives had not. In other words, the gospel of the kingdom had not been realized in their lives.

It wasn't until the 1980s that this began to change in the workplace movement. Groups like the International Christian Chamber of Commerce (ICCC) emerged in 1985 and began helping men and women apply the Word of God to *how* they worked. Work was no longer a platform for sharing the gospel; it was now a place to bring the presence and power of God into the very ways we operate our businesses. Many other marketplace groups were birthed during the same time frame, also with a focus on applying the Word of God to how individuals worked.

In the nineties we began to see a new focus emerge. This focus was on social entrepreneurship and social transformation. Groups like the Pinnacle Forum and Halftime with Bob Buford began to promote social agendas using entrepreneurship from a Christian viewpoint to impact the culture. Our organization, Marketplace Leaders, was birthed in 1996. Our mission is to help men and women fulfill their purpose in and through their work life.

It was also this time frame when the Billy Graham organization, Henry Blackaby, Peter Wagner, and Ed Silvoso entered the marketplace movement. They had not been focused on this area until then. They recognized something was going on in the workplace, and they wanted to support it. Ed Silvoso, who resides in California but originates from Argentina, became one of the most active practitioners who modeled city and community transformation by combining marketplace initiatives with intercession, local church leadership, and working initiatives to solve community problems in cooperation with city government officials. In essence he was combining the gospel of salvation with the gospel of the kingdom, which resulted in a changed community and even nations.

Gospel of Salvation vs. Gospel of the Kingdom

The simplest way to understand the distinction between the two kingdoms is to recognize that the gospel of salvation deals only with salvation for your soul. The gospel of the kingdom deals with all things that the cross affected, including not only salvation but also reconciliation of all things—including the material world that was lost in the Fall.

It is helpful at this stage for us to define what we mean by a *kingdom*. Myles Munroe, author of *Kingdom Principles*, describes a kingdom in these terms: "A kingdom is the governing influence of a king over his territory, impacting it with his personal will, purpose, and intent, producing a culture, values, morals, and lifestyle that reflect the king's desires and nature for his citizens."[4] Jesus's desire was for God's kingdom to be manifested on earth. When He taught the disciples to pray, He petitioned His heavenly Father by asking, "Your kingdom come. Your will be done on earth as it is in heaven."[5] While we may never see God's kingdom completely manifested on earth as it is in heaven, Jesus *is* telling us that we should ask for it and expect it. Moses was led by God, not to establish a religion, but to establish a nation of people who would love, serve, and honor God. In other words, God wanted His kingdom expressed completely through their lives.

An Incomplete Gospel

The following comparison between attributes of the gospel of the kingdom and the gospel of salvation provides a better understanding of the two. When Jesus prayed the Lord's Prayer, He prayed for the manifestation of what was happening in heaven to happen on earth. "Our Father in Heaven, hallowed be Your name. Your kingdom come. Your will be done on earth as it is in heaven."[6] His emphasis was more than salvation.

Gospel of Salvation	Gospel of the Kingdom
Focus: Evangelism/salvation	Focus: Taking dominion
Eternal, heavenly focus	Material, social, earthly, secular
Addresses only the soul	Address soul *and* body
"Rapture escape" mentality	"Possess the land" mentality
Sacred vs. secular—dualism	Impacts all aspects of society
Goal: Transaction, "Win the next soul"	Goal: Influence through servanthood, godly leadership, active faith
Example: Nigeria	Example: Almolonga, Guatemala

This diagram shows the contrast between the gospel of salvation and the gospel of the kingdom. One is passive; the other is active, with a goal of taking possession as Joshua was instructed. One of the problems in the church today is that we often talk about "escaping this evil world" through the Rapture instead of influencing the world. Some research tells us that as much as 60 percent of the population of the country of Nigeria may be born again. Yet the culture has some of the greatest problems with crime and corruption of any nation in the world. That is because the gospel of salvation has been the primary message.

Contrast Nigeria to Almolonga, Guatemala, where 90 percent of the population is Christian, and there are no jails—because they are not needed.[7]

Books like the Left Behind series may be good fictional reading that has some level of truth, but they can instill in our minds a mind-set that Christians are to wait for the *great escape* instead of focusing our time and energy on occupying the land and changing the culture. Jesus said He wants to return to a mature bride; that means a vibrant church that is actively impacting our world.

A FLAWED ESCHATOLOGY

Our early spiritual leaders had a different view of eschatology than many contemporary teachers. They believed God was not coming back until His church/bride was mature. A few quotes give us an indication of their views:

> I myself believe that King Jesus will reign, and the idols be utterly abolished; but I expect the same power which turned the world upside down once, will still continue to do it. The Holy Ghost would never suffer the imputation to rest upon His holy name that He was not able to convert the world.
>
> —CHARLES H. SPURGEON[8]

> Satan's kingdom shall be overthrown, throughout the whole habitable globe, on every side, and on all its continents. When these times come, then doubtless the gospel shall have glorious success, and all the inhabitants of this new-discovered world shall become the subjects of the kingdom of Christ, as well as all the other ends of the earth.
>
> —Jonathan Edwards[9]

> All unprejudiced persons may see with their eyes, that he [God] is already renewing the face of the earth: And we have strong reason to hope that the work he hath begun, he will carry on unto the day of the Lord Jesus; that he will never intermit this blessed work of his Spirit, until he has fulfilled all his promises, until he hath put a period to sin, and misery, and infirmity, and death, and reestablished universal holiness and happiness, and caused all the inhabitants of the earth to sing together, "Hallelujah, the Lord God Omnipotent reigneth!"
>
> —John Wesley[10]

Scripture helps us understand what must happen before these last days are concluded. "And this gospel of the kingdom will be preached in all the world as a witness to all the nations, and then the end will come."[11] In a conference presentation, Harold Eberle, author of *Victorious Eschatology,* said, "In other words, the church is not sitting around *waiting* for the return of Jesus. It is *working* for the return of Jesus. It is the job of the redeemed sons and daughters of God to make disciples of every nation and prepare the earth for His return."[12] God's Word gives a similar instruction: "Let us be glad and rejoice and give Him glory, for the marriage of the Lamb has come, and His wife has made herself ready."[13]

There are many other factors, such as what must take place among the people of Israel, before the End Times come that could be discussed here, but that would take us down an eschatology path. I trust you get my point here. It is clear we have some time left on this earth, and we need to be about His business.

The World Is Looking for a Solution, Not Necessarily a Christian Solution

The people in the world are not looking for a Christian solution to problems in the world; they are just looking for solutions. They do not care who provides the solution. Christians should be like Joseph, who provided a solution to Pharaoh's problem of interpreting his dream, which led to dealing with a famine in the land. He became a change agent with a solution. He also became the man to manage the solution. He went from prisoner to second in command in one day.

Not all solutions have a fish on its sleeve or a gospel tract provided with the solution. Kingdom solutions sometimes need stealth solutions so that the secular world can accept them. Such was the case in Uganda. HIV prevalence in Uganda peaked at around 15 percent in 1991 and then fell to 5 percent by 2001. An increase in sexual abstinence has recently been highlighted as a primary cause of the declines; however, large increases also occurred in two other aspects of sexual behavior—monogamy and condom use—and these changes made important contributions to the reduced risk for HIV infection.[14] One of the factors motivating these necessary behavior changes was input from the pastors of the nation, who came together and impressed upon government leaders the need to do three things: promote sexual abstinence among unmarried people, stress the importance of monogamy among marriage partners, and place a high priority on instructions in preventative hygiene to the people. Because of the willingness of these Ugandan pastors to be change agents in their own country, the entire nation reaped the benefits and stopped the alarming rise of AIDS. Since the late 1980s, the Ugandan government, a wide array of nongovernmental organizations (NGOs), and activists have promoted programs and policies designed to influence these three behaviors through a comprehensive approach to prevention, termed "ABC" (Abstinence, Be Faithful [monogamy], and Use Condoms).[15]

ALMOLONGA, GUATEMALA

Today God is speaking very clearly to the church about societal transformation. He is raising up His change agents throughout the world to impact all aspects of society. Fifteen years ago the idea of a community being totally transformed through the gospel of Jesus Christ was a foreign concept. However, according to George Otis Jr., director of the Sentinel Group, there are more than five hundred communities that are in some form of quantifiable transformation process throughout the world today.[16]

The defining characteristic of a community that is being transformed is that the socioeconomic traits are being positively affected. The crime rate goes down, the economy is improved, and the number of Christians in the city increases. Prayer increases and the city leaders become Christians. In order to go beyond the gospel of salvation to the gospel of the kingdom we must exercise a different level of faith for our communities.

Almolonga, Guatemala, is a city that models the gospel of the kingdom. George Otis Jr. featured a transformations documentary story on this amazing city and community. Mariano Riscajche was one of the first in a wave of supernatural conversions in 1974 that swept through Almolonga. He later became a leading pastor in the city and spearheaded the revival that was to come. A call to repentance and holiness was followed by a period of intense spiritual warfare against the rampant alcoholism and idol worship in the city.

Today it's been estimated that more than 90 percent of Almolonga's people are now born-again Christians. A generation ago there were only four churches. Today there are twenty-three! The last jail closed down in 1988, because there's virtually no crime in this town. Once there was rampant alcoholism; now bars have been closed or torn down and rebuilt into church halls.[17] All of this is due to a gospel of the kingdom focus versus just salvations.

If we are going to become change agents, we must make the gospel an integral part of our life, our worldview, and our passion. That is what it means to apply the kingdom of God to our lives and our culture. Almolonga is one example of what it means to bring *heaven to earth* as Jesus prayed in the Lord's Prayer. The apostle Paul said, "For if we live, we live to the Lord; and if we die, we die to the Lord. Therefore, whether we live or die, we are the Lord's."[18]

Charles Spurgeon understood this theology of the requirement to influence the culture when he wrote these words: "If God had willed it we might each of us have entered heaven at the moment of our conversion. It was not absolutely necessary for our preparation for immortality that we should tarry here."[19]

God left you and me here after conversion to influence our world for Him.

Questions for Reflection

1. What has been your Christian experience to date? Would you classify it more as a gospel of salvation or a gospel of the kingdom?

2. What can we learn from the two cities mentioned in this chapter—Dallas, Texas, and Almolonga, Guatemala?

3. What steps do you need to take to live the gospel of the kingdom in every area of your life?

Chapter 4

ELIMINATE THE GREAT DIVIDE

*Then the L*ORD *God took the man and put him in
the garden of Eden to tend and keep it.*
—GENESIS 2:15

I MAGINE FOR A moment that Jesus has just completed His three years of training with the disciples. He has been crucified and is now commissioning the Twelve to go into the world and disciple the nations. Now imagine Him also making this statement to them: "Dear brothers, it is now time for you to share what you have learned from Me. However, as you share with others, be sure that you keep what I taught you separate from your work life. The principles I have shared with you only apply in the synagogue. The miracles you saw in Me can only be done in the synagogue. Keep this in mind when thinking about praying for the sick or the lost. These truths will not work in the marketplace."

Sound preposterous? It may, but this is the mind-set of many in our world today—the spiritual does not mix with the everyday workplace. God created us to reflect His glory in what we do. "Now the Lord is the Spirit, and where the Spirit of the Lord is, there is freedom. And we, who with unveiled faces all reflect the Lord's glory, are being transformed into his likeness with ever-increasing glory, which comes from the Lord, who is the Spirit."[1] Like Christ, we are a creative people designed to work and take care of the earth. Each of us is endowed with ability and creativity. Satan wants us to view our labor as something that should be placed around our neck, forcing us to live under slavery, something very unspiritual, instead of a way to reveal God's glory. The church has played into Satan's hand by reinforcing this message, because we have not understood or applied Paul's exhortation: "Whatever you do, do it all for the glory of God."[2] In another letter he said, "It is the Lord Christ you are serving."[3]

The first two reasons we lost culture, in my opinion, were due to our own sins as a nation and an overemphasis on the gospel of salvation versus the gospel of the kingdom. A third reason I believe we have lost the culture is the result of the church not having a biblical view of work and calling. When Jesus came to earth, He came as a carpenter, a man given to work with His hands and to provide an honest service to His fellow man. He did not come as a priest, although He was both a king and a priest.[4] When it came time to recruit those for whom the church would be founded, He chose twelve men from the marketplace—fishermen, a tax collector, a farmer, and so on. They all came from the marketplace. Interestingly enough, none of His disciples were priests in the Jewish church, a natural place to recruit from if you were going to start a religious movement. Jesus called them all from the marketplace of life. Was it an accident that He called men from the marketplace to play such vital roles in His mission? I think not. During a conversation with Henry Blackaby, I asked him where he believed that spiritual leadership was most evident in our nation. He said, "It is not coming from our churches or from Washington; it is coming from men and women in the marketplace."

When God created the earth, He demonstrated something right up front to human beings. He believed in work. He was, above all else, the Master Creator. He was an artist, designer, strategic planner, organizer, project developer, assessor, zoologist, biologist, chemist, linguist, programmer, materials specialist, engineer, and waste management technician. This work did not end when He created man but was only the beginning in His continued care for mankind. Whether we call our work *sacred* or *secular*, all legitimate work reflects the activity of God. God is honored when we work with the goal of reflecting His life through our life and work. So why and how did society begin to draw a separation between faith and work?

The Great Divide: Elevating the Spiritual at the Expense of the Secular

If you were to conduct a survey on an average city street to determine if people thought religion belonged in the workplace, chances are high that they would say no.

Most people today see no relevance between God and work in today's fast-paced marketplace. Why is this? Why do many Christians even believe this also? Well, it goes back to our early years. Os Guinness, in his book *The Call*, provides us the necessary history of how we got to this segmented view of work and life.

> The truth of calling means that for followers of Christ, "everyone, everywhere, and in everything" lives the whole of life as a response to God's call. Yet this holistic character of calling has often been distorted to become a form of dualism that elevates the spiritual at the expense of the secular. This distortion may be called the "Catholic distortion"

because it rose in the Catholic era and is the majority position in the Catholic tradition.

Protestants, however, cannot afford to be smug. For one thing, countless Protestants have succumbed to the Catholic distortion as Wilberforce nearly did. Ponder, for example, the fallacy of the contemporary Protestant term *full-time Christian service*—as if those not working for churches or Christian organizations are only part-time in the service of Christ. For another thing, Protestant confusion about calling...has led to a "Protestant distortion" that is even worse. This is a form of dualism in a secular direction that not only elevates the secular at the expense of the spiritual, but also cuts it off from the spiritual altogether.[5]

Therefore it is understandable why we are where we are today. Over many centuries we have been trained to believe that the two worlds of spiritual and secular are to be separated. This misunderstanding has led to the highly debated issue today of separation of church and state. As change agents, we will need to fully acquaint ourselves with the current issues being debated in our nation and world and become prepared to hold ourselves and others to a sound, biblical, godly worldview.

FULL-TIME VS. PART-TIME

Although it isn't evident in God's Word, a class distinction exists today, particularly in the church, between those in *full-time Christian work* and those who *work secular jobs*. People testify of leaving *regular* jobs to go to the mission field or some other *full-time Christian work*. Yet, from the beginning of time, work was the primary means of creativity for human beings to reflect God's glory through man. God was a worker. God worked six days in Genesis, and on the seventh He rested.

When we think about a theology of work, we need to consider some of the reasons why God designed work:

1. *We work to meet human needs.* He gave everyone a unique DNA to pursue a vocation that would meet a human need.

2. *He wanted us to view our work as ministry.* Work often involves serving others. The Greek word for *service* is the same word as *ministry* (*diakonia*).[6] When we serve others, we are actually performing ministry to the Lord, even when it is a secular form of work.

3. *We are to view our work as worship to God.* All of life should be conducted as a form of worship. When the Olympic runner

Eric Liddell described his gift of running to his sister in the classic film *Chariots of Fire*, he said, "When I run, I feel His pleasure." We too should feel His pleasure when we work unto Him. The words *work* and *worship* are both derived from the Hebrew word *avodah*.

4. *We are to use our work as a platform to share the love of God.* Our work allows us to build relationships with others to demonstrate the love of God to them in a tangible way. A popular saying states, "People don't care how much you know until they know how much you care." Building relationship with others is the first step to demonstrating the love of God.

5. *We work to earn money to fund God's work on the earth.* For most of us, work will be the primary means of supplying our needs for food and clothing. Deuteronomy 8:18 tells us that God gives us the ability to create wealth in order to establish His covenant upon the earth.

6. *We work to care for the poor.* When Boaz allowed the gleanings to be left behind from his harvest, he was establishing a kingdom principle for those of us in business. He allowed the poor to come and collect what was left. They still had to work, but the owner of the field intentionally left the gleanings for the poor.[7] Businesses should think of how this principle applies to care for the poor.

7. *We work to transform culture.* From the beginning God intended that man would reflect His glory through man's work, that it might affect all of culture. God cares about our cities and nations and wants to see every person influenced for Jesus Christ.

8. *We work to bring glory to God.* God takes us through the process of life and allows us to develop specific skills and talents for His purposes. The marketplace is where many of us have the greatest opportunity to display these gifts.

David began his working career in the fields as a shepherd. Scripture tells us that David had encounters with a lion and a bear. This was part of his preparation for the day he would meet Goliath. He was chosen by God through a divine appointment with Samuel, the prophet who made a house call to anoint David as the next king of Israel. Then God orchestrated a divine circumstance that transformed David from a caterer of food to a deliverer of a nation in one afternoon. During David's training period, he was assigned to serve King Saul, who tried to slay him repeatedly. David's training period appears to have been about thirteen years, until he finally became king at age thirty, the age of maturity in the Jewish culture.

When young David went up against Goliath, he was only a small shepherd boy. King Saul offered David his armor to protect him from the big Philistine, but David knew the weight of the armor would be a hindrance to him. Instead, David used the skills he had developed as a shepherd to protect his sheep. A slingshot and stones were his weapons. When the time came for David to exercise his faith in God to slay the giant, he used the talents God had trained him to use and the authority he had in God.

The shepherd fields were David's training grounds. There he learned to fight lions and protect his sheep. As king of Israel he would protect God's sheep. God gives us the same talents to achieve the things He wants us to achieve. However, not all of us will be heroes. Some of us have been called to use our talents to serve others to benefit the kingdom of God. David's faith was the reason God gave him victory. David declared to Goliath that he came in the name and authority of the living God and that the whole world would know the God of Israel because of the defeat of the giant by a small shepherd boy.[8]

This is why God gave him victory over Goliath—so the world may know the living God. The workplace is a training ground for most of us. It is the place where we deal with the everyday challenges of life, but it is also here where God wants to reveal His glory so that the world might know that He is God.

For most of us, we will have many *jobs* before we will fulfill God's ultimate work for our lives. In our lives the place of convergence is often at the point where all of our gifts and talents align to perform our greatest work. God uses the early training, as He did with David, to prepare us for future battles and experiences that He will use for His purposes in our lives. Winston Churchill led the British through the dark hours of World War II. He said, "I felt as if I were walking with destiny, and that all my past life had been but a preparation for this hour and for this trial."[9]

God wants to use you and me to reflect His glory wherever we are. He also wants us to use the talents and abilities He has allowed us to be trained with for His greater glory in this world. We can find comfort in the knowledge that there is no higher calling than to be where God calls us, regardless of whether it is in *full-time* Christian mission work or working at the local hardware store.

QUESTIONS FOR REFLECTION

1. What has been your personal experience of the concept of *sacred* versus *secular*?

2. Have you ever considered your job a ministry? Explain.

3. Based on the information in this chapter, explain why God views secular work as important.

PREPARATION
TO BECOME A
CHANGE AGENT

Chapter 5

GOD'S RECRUITMENT PROCESS

*Now the man Moses was very humble, more than all
men who were on the face of the earth.*
—NUMBERS 12:3

I CAN ONLY IMAGINE the life of Moses at age eighty before God paid him a personal visit. I can see him sitting in the desert wasteland, herding sheep. He had been doing it for forty years—think about it, forty years in the hot sun, tending sheep. Imagine his thoughts—during his earlier years in Egypt he had the best of everything. He had the best education a man could have. He was trained in hieroglyphics, a very difficult language system, and was a bright and educated man. He was being groomed to be an international change agent for the nation of Egypt. He ate the very best food, and he was trained to be an army general.

He probably recalled his Egyptian counterparts making coarse jokes about the Hebrew shepherds, a profession that was considered the lowest of all professions. It was detestable in the eyes of an Egyptian. This is why years later Joseph told his brothers not to tell his counterparts what they did for a living. He did not want his associates to think more disparagingly of his Hebrew brothers than they already did.

But the good years in Egypt were just a distant memory. At age forty he killed an Egyptian who was persecuting a Hebrew slave. He had a very great conflict in his soul. Deep down he knew there was a calling from God upon his life. But he did not really know this God; it was only an abstract idea in his mind at this point. He tried to help his people the only way he knew how— through the Egyptian way of retaliation and force.

Why forty years in the desert? The answer is simple. God was giving Moses on-the-job training to live and adapt in a harsh environment—one he would have to weather for the next forty years. *When God gives a saint an assignment, the training ground fits the assignment.* Do you ever wonder why it seems like God leaves us in a holding pattern or actually brings an assault against us? God is performing the deeper work in us. It is the work of the soul that only hardship, isolation, and waiting can accomplish. When we are out of control, it means God is in control.

The future was about to change for Moses. God was about to engage His change agent. He was to deliver an entire nation from slavery and teach a nation what it meant to be under God's rulership. His preparation for this assignment was complete. There was enough humility in Moses for God to be able to work with him. D. L. Moody once said, "Moses spent his first forty years thinking he was somebody. He spent his next forty years learning he was nobody. He spent his third forty years discovering what God can do with a nobody."

Life is often seen backward. Many times we do not understand the ways of God until we have passed through the valleys and can stand upon the mountaintop and see the path behind us. Only then can we appreciate why this or that lesson was required in our process. For Moses, it was absolutely necessary for him to be raised in the court of Pharaoh, to understand their customs, their ways, and how they thought. Who better to bring a people out of Egyptian slavery than one who has been on the other side of the fence as a slave lord? He was raised near the very top of a governmental mountain, and he was called to deliver a people from that same governmental mountain. He knew what he would be up against. Perhaps that is why he argued with God so much about the assignment. Humanly speaking, he knew he couldn't accomplish such a feat.

This is a good lesson for us all. *God's training ground usually is made up of life experiences that will contribute to the ultimate assignment God has for us.* There is often a lifetime of preparation toward an assignment that God designs just for us. Moses was now at a place of convergence in his life. I mentioned earlier that convergence means that all aspects of life align to a point where God gets the greatest benefit through the skills, maturity, and resources He has entrusted to you. Moses would now make decisions based on the situation, not based on his own abilities, resources, or need. He became part of the flow of God.

LESSONS FROM A BURNING BUSH

God decided to come to Moses through a very unusual way. He allowed a bush to catch fire, but instead of burning up, it simply kept burning. Moses had probably seen brush fires in the desert because of lightning storms. But this was different. The bush was not burning up. He decided to check it out. However, when he came closer, a voice came out from the bush: "Moses, take off your shoes for you are on holy ground!" What an introduction! The God of the universe, the God of galaxies, the maker of stars, planets, human beings, the ocean, animals, deserts, and every living thing, including Adam and Eve—the one and only God—speaks through a simple burning bush. God takes something ordinary and makes it extraordinary, just as He does with you and me. He is setting a precedent for things to come. Let's examine the lessons Moses learned through his burning bush experience.

Bringing the presence of God to work

> Take your sandals off your feet, for the place where you stand is holy ground.
>
> —EXODUS 3:5

Notice that God came to Moses's place of work during his workday—his work as a shepherd in the fields. Why is this ground holy? Because God's presence was there. That is the first lesson for all of us. Our work becomes holy when the presence of God resides there. How often do you think of the presence of God in your job as a secretary, construction worker, dentist, teacher, or businessman or woman? You will never be a change agent if you do not have the presence of God in your work.

Years later Moses would come back to this region after coming down from the mountain upon receiving the Ten Commandments. The people would be left to their own devices and would get into idol worship, making the famous golden calf. Moses would almost throw in the towel. Losing one important focus almost destroyed his mission—he failed to represent the presence of God to the people. This opened them up to idol worship. Their loyalty was no longer directed to God but to any idol that came their way. Moses spoke to God in very direct terms and said, "If Your Presence does not go with us, do not bring us up from here. For how then will it be known that Your people and I have found grace in Your sight, except You go with us?"[1]

That really is the issue, isn't it? We can do good things. We can help others. We can be successful in business. But we will not really be successful in God without His presence.

A changed paradigm about your work

God asked Moses a question. This was not because God wanted information, but He was entering a process of discovery with Moses.[2] "What is that in your hand?" said God.

Moses replied, "It is my staff, Lord."

"I am going to perform miracles through your staff." What did that staff represent in Moses's life? It represented his calling as a shepherd. God was about to change his view of his work in a very dynamic way.

"Lay it down on the ground," said God.

Moses laid his staff on the ground, and God turned it into a snake. God told Moses to pick it up by the tail. God changed Moses's paradigm about something that was familiar and representative in his life. Picking up a snake by the tail contradicted all he knew about snakes. God was challenging his ideas about what he knew and what he needed to know. God turns the ordinary into the extraordinary. He turned a routine day's work into an encounter with the living God. In order to experience this, Moses had to lay his staff down on the ground. In essence, God was saying, "I want you to lay down all you have, giving it to Me, so that I can use it."

You and I must lay our vocations down and watch what God will do as we yield control to Him. God will bring His power into our vocations, and we can become stewards of His glory through that staff. Are you ready to lay down your vocation so that He can live His life through it? Are you ready to let God manifest His power through it?

Scripture says that when he picked up his staff, it was no longer the staff of Moses; it was now the staff of God. Moses became a steward of that staff. This lesson from God was a prophetic act that was rooted all the way back to Genesis and the encounter that Adam and Eve had with the snake. Moses was taking authority over the serpent that deceived Adam and Eve. No longer would the serpent be used to deceive; it would be ruled over by God.

God is picky about obedience.

Moses was ready to leave for the long journey to Egypt. His wife and sons would be making the trip as well. However, something dramatic happened on his way out of town. God threatened to kill Moses. "And it came to pass on the way, at the encampment, that the LORD met him and sought to kill him. Then Zipporah took a sharp stone and cut off the foreskin of her son and cast it at Moses's feet, and said, 'Surely you are a husband of blood to me!' So He let him go. Then she said, 'You are a husband of blood!'—because of the circumcision."[3]

Wow! When I first read those words I was incredulous! Did God invest eighty years into this man's life just to kill him over a failure to circumcise his kid? That just wasn't reasonable.

However, Christianity is not a democracy; it is a theocracy, and the King is ruler over all. We do the bidding of the King, no matter what we may think about it. His ways are higher than our ways. That is what gets us into trouble—when we think we can question His ways. Circumcision was an expression of a covenantal relationship between Israel and God. When Moses failed to uphold this covenant, which had been made hundreds of years earlier with Abraham, it was grievous in God's eyes—so grievous that God was willing to abort the mission of Moses.

I have noticed a truth now that I have lived a good bit of life. I am fifty-eight as I write this book. *The greater the calling, the greater the scrutiny with God.* The things you could get away with ten years ago are no longer allowable for God's change agent. Why is this? It is because God wants to use only holy vessels for His work. He wants only the best representatives for His work. He is an employer who has high standards of integrity, humility, and character. If you expect to be used mightily by God, expect to shore up those sins you used to be able to get away with.

The sin of Moses was that he overlooked something that was very important to God. As a result he had to separate from his wife and son. They were not able to make the journey to Egypt with Moses. There was now a rift between him and his wife. He took it like a man, but there was now a division with the second most important person in his life. *So often issues that are important to God get brought to our attention through our spouses.* They are such important issues to God that He is prepared to kill our mission and assignment if we don't take care of it. Your spouse is often where the first warning signs appear. Wives are in our lives for our protection. They are more sensitive and aware of things we men often cannot see. However, we often reject their input because we feel they are irrational and are not looking at the facts. We also push back counsel from our wives because we simply want to do things our own way. Our pride prevents us from hearing their input because we men believe it might make us appear weak if we did.

Pastor Tim Keller of Redeemer Church in New York City once said in a conference, "Life can be totally out of order, but if your marriage relationship is good, you can handle it. However, if everything is going great and your marriage is not good, no success will satisfy. You'll operate from a place of emotional despair and inner turmoil." I've experienced a lot of warfare in this area of my life and can attest that it is the first place Satan attacks a change agent.

You can achieve the greatest things in the world, but if it is at the cost of your marriage or family, it is worth nothing. Hear this, men! If your value is in your accomplishments and your work, your relationship with your spouse and family will suffer. Paul tells us that even if we can remove mountains, it does not compare to living a life exemplified by love: "And though I have the gift of prophecy, and understand all mysteries and all knowledge, and though I have all faith, *so that I could remove mountains*, but have not love, I am nothing. And though I bestow all my goods to feed the poor, and though I give my body to be burned, but have not love, it profits me nothing."[4]

God changes the rules.

The first time the Israelites needed water, God told Moses to strike the rock. When he did, water came gushing from the rock. But then there was another occasion. It was the same problem, but this time God changed His instruction. This time God told Moses to speak to the rock. However, Moses was irritated with the people and struck the rock instead of speaking to the rock.

Then the LORD spoke to Moses, saying, "Take the rod; you and your brother Aaron gather the congregation together. Speak to the rock before their eyes, and it will yield its water; thus you shall bring water for them out of the rock, and give drink to the congregation and their animals." So Moses took the rod from before the LORD as He commanded him. And Moses and Aaron gathered the assembly together before the rock; and he said to them, "Hear now, you rebels! Must we bring water for you out of this rock?" Then Moses lifted his hand and struck the rock twice with his rod; and water came out abundantly, and the congregation and their animals drank.

—NUMBERS 20:7–11

God was trying to move Moses into another dimension of his relationship with God. He wanted him to operate at God's level. God spoke things into existence. He used His authority and power through what He spoke. He wanted Moses to move to another level. However, I want you to notice that Moses still got water from the rock. This is an indication of the importance of the need of the people. God still gave water to the people because He cared more about their immediate need.

Have you ever seen a man or woman of God preach great sermons and see fruit from their ministry, only to discover they had been living in sin during those times? Sometimes our anointing still operates because the gifts and callings are irrevocable.[5] However, God was not pleased at Moses's disobedience, and it would cost Moses his ability to fulfill God's complete purposes for his life. He would not be able to touch the ground of the Promised Land. Ultimately God judges sin.

The spoken word is powerful. There are times we must use the spoken word to proclaim God's purposes over a situation or a person. The audible voice has power. The thalamus in our brain responds to audible words. It makes an imprint upon our minds. That is why words can harm or build up. When we speak words to our children, they have the power of life and death. When we speak words to our spouses, they have the power of life and death in them. Be careful what you speak.

Jesus said that we can speak to the mountain and thrust it into the sea if we have the faith of a mustard seed.[6] He was giving us a lesson on the value of the spoken word. In previous books I've shared a story where God led me to speak over a pile of books in my basement to "leave the basement to be a blessing to others." It was a Saturday when businesses were closed. A call came in that afternoon for an order of three hundred books. God was teaching me to use the authority He had given when the Holy Spirit leads me to use that authority. God calls you, as a change agent, to move at a greater dimension in your calling to experience His power.

Moses provides us with some good lessons. Take these lessons to heart, and become the change agent God wants you to become.

QUESTIONS FOR REFLECTION

Why not take time right now to pray a prayer of dedication of your work life to God? Entrust Him to work through it for His purposes.

1. Does your life represent the presence of God? Do you spend time alone with God developing that relationship?

2. Are there any things you have failed to be aware of that might prevent God from allowing you to move forward until you take care of them?

3. Do you have your priorities right at home? If not, what needs to change?

Chapter 6

SIX STAGES AND PROCESSES OF THE
CALL OF A CHANGE AGENT

As he journeyed he came near Damascus, and suddenly a light shone around him from heaven. Then he fell to the ground, and heard a voice saying to him, "Saul, Saul, why are you persecuting Me?"...And the Lord said to him, "Arise and go into the city, and you will be told what you must do."
—ACTS 9:3–6

I HAVE STUDIED THE lives of change agents and have observed, both in my life and in the lives of other change agents, six unique stages God often takes His change agents through in their spiritual pilgrimage toward becoming a change agent. I have personally gone through each of these changes in my own life.

1. *Divine circumstances:* God initiates a personal encounter with the change agent, often through a personal crisis.

2. *Character development:* God takes the change agent through a series of character tests designed to develop humility and trust.

3. *Isolation period:* A time of separation from past dependencies realigns values to a biblical economy.

4. *Personal cross:* God brings the change agent to experience his or her personal cross.

5. *Problem solvers:* Change agents become problem solvers through invention and entrepreneurship.

6. *Networks:* Change happens as a small number of change agents band together.

Lisette Malmberg grew up in Aruba, a small island of only 150,000 people in the Caribbean until she was seventeen years old. She went to the United States to study and graduated in 1982 with a bachelor's degree in science, with a major in marketing from St. Thomas University in Miami. In 1984, after several years of working in the States, she returned home to Aruba to work for her family's tourism business. Her family owns a number of tourism-related companies. Over a period of twenty years she was consistently promoted until 1994, when her father made her brother and her shareholders of the company. During those years she played a key role in many local organizations and served on boards of directors, such as the Aruba Hotel and Tourism Association, the Aruba Quality Foundation, and the Aruba Hospitality and Security Foundation. Today the company employs more than 275 persons in nine subsidiary companies, serving well over 300,000 guests per year.

Lisette came to faith in Christ in the spring of 1995. After a devastating divorce in 1985 and a series of heart-breaking relationships, Lisette said she "came to the end of herself." She said had never heard the gospel preached, did not have any religious background, and only remembered an "Our Father" she used to pray in Catholic school. After going on her knees every night for about three months, during which she was going through her heart-wrenching crisis, all she knew to pray was, "Our Father, who art in heaven..." One day at about midnight, at the end of her rope, she knelt down in the shower, lifted her fists to heaven, and prayed, "If there is a God, come and change my life, and if You prove to me that you are real, I will serve You the rest of my life."

The next day a dear friend came to her house and invited her to church; her friend had accepted the Lord the week before. Lisette went to an Assemblies of God church that Sunday, gave her life to the Lord, and experienced a radical conversion. God had heard her prayer.

Lisette began to grow in her relationship with Christ, and after seven years of serving God in that church, in March of 2002, the Lord called her to plant a church with a small group of friends of "like precious faith," and the miracles began. The church has grown to a vibrant local community of believers with more than four hundred people in attendance every Sunday. It plays a key role in serving the nation of Aruba. A weekly TV show, *The Word of Life*, is broadcast on national TV stations in Aruba, Curacao, and Bonaire and is widely viewed by all segments of the community. Lisette was becoming a change agent on her tiny island. She would later meet Pastor Sunday Adelaja, a Nigerian-born pastor of the largest church in Europe (with twenty-five thousand members, located in Ukraine) and author of the book *ChurchShift*. That relationship led to the Lisette hosting a Kingdom Impact for National Transformation conference in Aruba, which was attended by more than two thousand people and broadcast on national TV. Lisette was getting a national vision for her nation, which led to yet another initiative on her small island.

She felt there was a need to train workplace leaders on her island, and that is when the idea of a Kingdom Leadership Institute was birthed. She held meetings with local pastors in preparation for launching the institute during Pastor Adelaja's visit, and more than seventy-five pastors, representing their local congregations, attended an orientation breakfast and a subsequent breakfast with Pastor Adelaja and his team. Many acknowledged this sovereign move of God, and the strategic process for transformation began. The mission of the institute is: "To be a training center to help people grow in an intimate relationship with God and understand His kingdom in light of His Word so that they can discover their divine call and unique expression in God's purpose for their lives—as reformers and influencers of culture."

Lisette attended the Reclaim 7 Mountains conference our ministry hosted in Atlanta in 2008, and later hosted our workshop, The 9 to 5 Window, as part of her curriculum. Then, in November of 2010, I taught my Change Agent Intensive Workshop to their Kingdom Leadership Institute students and spoke in her church that Sunday morning.

The institute is unique in that it actually prepares leaders to understand the theology of social transformation, the kingdom of God, the seven mountains that need to be reformed, and to identify their places of assignment and be equipped to operate in their unique gift mix to bring the kingdom of God to bear on their mountain. The institute program ends with a three-session "Deployment Strategy," during which students of each mountain are brought together for brainstorming and intercessory prayer seeking the Lord for strategies and actual initiatives to transform their segment. Lisette is impacting her nation at every level of the seven mountains of cultural influence and has been instrumental at the highest level of her government.

Lisette is a change agent who had become lost in her career and life, with no spiritual compass. God reached out to her, and she responded. As with many change agents God calls, His deepest work in our lives often comes after a series of crises that led to conversion and to an intimate relationship with Christ and a vision larger than ourselves.

The Calling of Change Agents

As is often the case, God recruits His change agents in the midst of personal crisis situations. Every follower of Christ yearns to experience His presence and His power and to be used in His kingdom. We are all part of a larger story that God desires us to flow into. Frederick Buechner describes calling and receiving our personal vision this way: "Personal vision is the place where your deep gladness and the world's deep hunger meet."[1]

Henry Blackaby, in his very popular Bible study *Experiencing God*, states that fulfilling our purpose has more to do with what God is doing with us than with what we are doing without Him. We are joining God in His agenda, not simply going out and doing a work for God. We are responders of His invitation to join Him. God always works through human beings to accomplish His work on Planet Earth.

Like Lisette, change agents impact the status quo. It can be a good person or a bad person who makes change. Change agents cause tipping points in culture. A tipping point is a measurable shift in culture or a product because of some external force that causes the change to take place. When network television allowed two women to kiss on prime time, it led to a tipping point on what is socially acceptable to show on television. Gay rights tipped the scale toward their agenda of promoting a homosexual lifestyle as acceptable to the mainstream public.

Adolf Hitler and Saddam Hussein were two of the world's most hideous change agents. They were responsible for the deaths of thousands of innocent people. Charles Darwin was a change agent who had a very negative impact on our culture by convincing the scientific community and the general population that evolution is how mankind came into being. This theory has impacted many areas of culture, including changing our entire educational system and how we interpret law today.

Rosa Parks, who decided in 1955 not to give up her seat in the back of the bus in Montgomery, Alabama, became a change agent who inspired Martin Luther King Jr. and others to help blacks become liberated from racial discrimination in America. A change agent is not limited to age, race, position, or economic status.

THE ROLE OF CRISIS AND DIVINE CIRCUMSTANCES

God initiates a personal encounter with the change agent, often through a personal crisis. Lisette did not grow up thinking, "I want to be a change agent." It is often more a result of a *circumstantial calling*. The person responds to a situation into which he or she was thrust. David was thrust into a situation where Israel was unwilling to fight Goliath. This was not acceptable in David's mind, despite his youthful age. He responded, and now you and I know the rest of the story. God described David's life this way: "Now then, tell my servant David, 'This is what the LORD Almighty says: I took you from the pasture and from following the flock to be ruler over my people Israel.'"[2]

Martin Luther was struggling with his own personal spiritual condition when he discovered the idea of *saved by grace*. This led to greater revelation, which compelled him to speak out about what he saw in the Scriptures. Before long he became an affront to long-held religious traditions that impacted spiritual power bases in the Roman Catholic Church. He was thrust into a movement before he knew it.

Earlier I discussed William Wallace, the Scottish crusader who rebelled against the tyrannical rule of England over Scotland and became Scotland's most prominent change agent. It began as a personal response, but it drew the Scottish common people into the fight as they were inspired by his courage and leadership.

A seven-year crisis in my life put me in circumstances that allowed me to see the hand of God personally in my adversity. One time I was on the island of Cypress, and a man came up to me and said, "God had to remove your finances to reserve the reward He has for you in heaven." I had never met the man, and he could not have known that I had just lost $500,000 in the previous year. Divine circumstances can change the course of our lives.

Others have had a direct and personal encounter with God. Moses had a personal encounter with God at the burning bush. King Saul was handpicked by Samuel the prophet to be the first king of Israel after the loss of the family donkeys, which led him to the prophet Samuel. Saul discovered that his crisis was about his calling to be the first king of Israel—it was not about lost donkeys. Paul was blinded by Jesus and personally recruited to be an apostle. God still speaks to His change agents and creates circumstances by which they are recruited for His purposes.

God may recruit you through a divine circumstance that disrupts your life—but connects you to a purpose and destiny. Sometimes the crisis is a direct result of our sin, and we cry out in our pain, which leads us to seek God in our lives. However, in other cases it can be a direct consequence of a call upon our lives, as was the case with Joseph. God may be orchestrating events to enlist us into His plan. In either case, these divine disruptions get our attention in a dramatic way. You may react to the situation by trying to solve your problem. However, be aware this may be God's stage of enlisting you into relationship first; then the fruit of that relationship will lead to your assignment.

God Develops Character Through Testing

> And you shall remember that the LORD your God led you all the way these forty years in the wilderness, to humble you and test you, to know what was in your heart, whether you would keep His commandments or not.
>
> —Deuteronomy 8:2

Preparation for a change agent involves character development. God takes the change agent through a series of character-building tests designed to develop humility, trust, and intimacy with God.

God does not test us to find out what we will do; He tests us to let us know what we will do. This is one way we get to see how faithless, unloving, or uncommitted we are to Him or another person. We get to see how we respond to those who treat us badly. We get to see if we are going to pout like little children or embrace the experience as one who needs to grow up. What comes out of you when you are squeezed?

David knew that God tests His people. "I know also, my God, that You test the heart and have pleasure in uprightness."[3] David didn't pass several tests. He flunked the test with Bathsheba—his child died, and he had a lifelong generational bout with lust and sexual problems in his family. He flunked the test on numbering the troops—seventy thousand people lost their lives because he did that. David was one of the few leaders in the Bible whose sins did not disqualify him from achieving his ultimate purpose. This was due to his repentant heart and his extravagant love of God, which came from his heart.

Joseph also had some tests. He was tested to see if he would retaliate against his brothers for betraying him and throwing him into a pit. He forgave them. He was tested sexually when Potiphar's wife decided she had to have him. He fled, but he still got prison time for being righteous. He passed that one. He was tested with an extended time of isolation in prison to see if he would persevere and experience God's presence in his circumstance. He passed that one too. He was a model prisoner. God's Word says, "But God was with him."[4] Finally Joseph was tested to see if he would be a good steward with the position, power, and influence God gave him. He passed with flying colors.

Testing is designed to prepare us for greater things.[5] God brings tests into our lives to develop character and to prepare us for greater use in the kingdom. There is no other way to find out how we will do without real world experiences to test our mettle. David understood this when he said, "Blessed be the LORD my Rock, who trains my hands for war, and my fingers for battle."[6] There's no place like the battlefield itself to find out how we are going to do.

James tells us that testing is designed to develop patience and perseverance, which mature our faith. "My brethren, count it all joy when you fall into various trials, knowing that the testing of your faith produces patience. But let patience have its perfect work, that you may be perfect and complete, lacking nothing."[7]

CRISIS AND PAIN LEAD TO COMMITMENT, OBEDIENCE, AND INTIMACY

Emotional pain can be excruciating. It can devastate you like nothing else. Divorce, loss of a child in an accident or illness, death of a spouse, abandonment by a wife or loved one—these experiences test our faith in God and in human beings. I have had more than my share of very close relationships that ended in betrayals. Many of them reconciled, but some did not reconcile until years later. Those were difficult times. There were times I literally felt my heart was bleeding from the inside out. David must have been feeling this when he wrote this psalm:

For it is not an enemy who reproaches me;
Then I could bear it.
Nor is it one who hates me who has exalted himself against me;
Then I could hide from him.
But it was you, a man my equal,
My companion and my acquaintance.
We took sweet counsel together,
And walked to the house of God in the throng.

—Psalm 55:12–14

Emotional pain drives us deep into the arms of our heavenly Father like nothing else. It helps us to identify with the cross. Ultimately, it should motivate us to greater levels of intimacy and obedience. The psalmist wrote, "Before I was afflicted I went astray, but now I keep Your word."[8] The pain our Savior endured was designed to create greater obedience in His life: "Though He was a Son, yet He learned obedience by the things which He suffered."[9]

We will all experience betrayal at some point in our journey. You may be experiencing emotional pain as God is preparing you to be a change agent. God wants you to follow the example of His Son, who washed the feet of Judas. Oh, how difficult this test is to pass. We don't want to forgive those who hurt us deeply. But Jesus said that if we don't forgive others, He doesn't forgive us.[10] Not a very good option! Jesus chose to tear up the "You hurt me deeply—you deserve to pay" ticket. So must we. You hold yourself and others in a prison if you do not forgive.

Change Agents Operate From a Place of Weakness

God calls His change agents to operate from a place of weakness, not strength. On the surface it may appear that God's change agents are operating from a place of great strength. However, many struggle to balance their influence and role with faith and humility. Paul had great influence, but he also operated from a place of physical weakness. He was not a great speaker or impressive in stature. But God assured Paul, "My grace is sufficient for you, for my power is made perfect in weakness." With God's assurance of grace, Paul was able to say, "Therefore I will boast all the more gladly about my weaknesses, so that Christ's power may rest on me."[11]

If you are a change agent in the making, expect God to take you through a season of character refinement designed to develop humility and trust. Expect also that God's grace will be all you need.

QUESTIONS FOR REFLECTION

1. Describe a situation that caused you the greatest emotional pain in your life. What did you learn from it?

2. Describe a period of testing God took you through. Did you pass or fail?

3. Have you experienced betrayal from someone close? How did it end?

4. Is there anyone you still need to forgive?

Chapter 7

EMBRACING THE CROSS
THROUGH BROKENNESS

*And being found in appearance as a man, He humbled Himself and
became obedient to the point of death, even the death of the cross.*
—PHILIPPIANS 2:8

IN DECEMBER 2008 a movie hit the theaters titled, *The Day the Earth Stood
Still*. It was a remake of a movie produced in the 1950s by the same name.
I remember the movie, because it scared me to death as a kid. In the new
version, actor Keanu Reeves was an alien who came to earth on a spaceship.
He developed a relationship with a woman in the film who wanted to know
why he came to earth. The alien said that the reason was because humans had
not taken care of the planet, and so they were here to save the planet from
humans. In other words, they were planning to wipe out humanity because of
what humans were doing to the planet and to each other.

As the story developed, the woman pleaded for another chance on behalf
of her human race. "But we can change," said the desperate woman.

"I am not sure you can," said the alien.

During the movie the alien watched the woman's relationship with her
young son and saw her model a more caring side of humanity. When the
destruction began, she pleaded, "We can change; we can change!"

The alien turned to the woman and said, "Many times change does not
really occur until one is brought to the point of desperation. Change occurs
when there is a threat of losing something very dear to us, or there is enough
pain in our lives that it motivates us to make a change." The alien was sharing
a profound spiritual truth.

THE JOURNEY TOWARD INTIMACY WITH GOD

Our fourth stage of the journey to become a change agent is the cross stage.
Several years ago I discovered there are three phases to our journey toward a
deeper relationship with God. Most of us begin our journey in the *convenience
phase*. In this phase life is OK, and we make choices based on our perception of

the outcome. If we think a decision benefits us, we make that choice. If we don't see a benefit, then we pass. Another way of describing this is it is an outcome-based method of living.

Then God allows a *crisis* into our life designed to increase our obedience and desire to seek Him. God desires intimacy with His creation. He does not want His creation to relate to Him based on convenience or outcome. Often He will allow things to happen in our lives that create a crisis. This crisis forces us to our knees, and we cry out to Him for a solution. Our emotional pain motivates us to a greater level of obedience, because we are motivated to seek God for deliverance from the pain of our situation. This is an example of the way God allows us to experience our personal cross. It is a sign of adoption for every believer. "In this you greatly rejoice, though now for a little while, if need be, you have been grieved by various trials, that the genuineness of your faith, being much more precious than gold that perishes, though it is tested by fire, may be found to praise, honor, and glory at the revelation of Jesus Christ, whom having not seen you love."[1]

These times of *cross bearing* are designed to lead us to a personal revelation of Jesus Christ in our lives. We tend to be such strong leaders that often it takes a great deal of personal pain to stop us in our current course—one that God knows is not His best for us. Through this process we experience Galatians 2:20 in our lives: "I have been crucified with Christ; it is no longer I who live, but Christ lives in me."

The third phase is the *conviction phase*. This phase is designed to move us into a life of deep intimacy with God. We live our life based upon Him and desiring to please our heavenly Father just as Jesus did. For many of us, this process is the first time we experience an intimate encounter with the living God. For Moses, it was the burning bush. For Joseph, it was the day he became prime minister of Egypt and saw his dream supernaturally fulfilled by God. For Paul, it was the blinding light that led to his salvation.

Every believer is called to experience the cross: "Let this mind be in you which was also in Christ Jesus, who, being in the form of God, did not consider it robbery to be equal with God, but made Himself of no reputation, taking the form of a bondservant, and coming in the likeness of men. And being found in appearance as a man, He humbled Himself and became obedient to the point of death, even the death of the cross."[2]

It took three nails to crucify our Savior to the cross. God says that if we are to allow Christ to live through us, then the old man must be crucified. We can voluntarily crucify our flesh, but we cannot complete the process by ourselves. *It usually requires another person who pounds that third nail of betrayal into our old man of flesh, which allows the work to be completed in us.*

- For Jesus, it was Judas.

- For David, it was Absalom.

- For Joseph, it was his brothers.

Betrayal is a nail that will either complete the death process or cause us to linger in unforgiveness and bitterness, which will result in an even worse state—partial death. Either we become bitter or we become better as a result of the process.

Betrayal is one of the instruments God uses in the lives of His change agents to make them like Jesus. It is the severest of all the tests God brings to those who would be His change agents. I like to think of betrayal as God's graduate level course for leaders. Jeanne Guyon, a sixteenth-century writer, explains: "You will not find any comfort from man when you have been put on the cross. The believer who loves the cross finds that even the bitterest things that come his way are sweet. To the hungry soul every bitter thing is sweet."[3]

Jesus told His disciples that forgiving those who wrong us is not optional. He minces no words: "But if you do not forgive men their sins, your Father will not forgive your sins."[4] He goes further by saying that not only are we to forgive, but also we are actually to love our enemies: "But I tell you: Love your enemies and pray for those who persecute you, that you may be sons of your Father in heaven."[5] When there is death, there is new life and freedom for the believer.

Spiritual Deposits Through the Cross

The cross is designed to make spiritual deposits into our lives.[6] During a seven-year period of adversity, God made deposits into my life that resulted in a whole new direction and led to my current ministry to men and women in the marketplace. In hindsight, I can see that some of my suffering was due to generational sins I could not recognize until I began to reap the fruit of those sins. Some adversity was a consequence of a new calling, which required preparation through tests of adversity. It led to the writing of *TGIF: Today God Is First,* which is being used around the world to encourage men and women in the workplace. All of this would not have happened if I had not responded to the pain that led me into a place of seeking Him with all my heart. At the end of the seven-year period, God restored all I had lost.

Through a battle we did not choose, God invites us to live for a cause greater than ourselves. It is in this battle that we learn the reality of our faith. It is there we discover that the God in whom we intellectually believed can be trusted with the outcome of our lives. For many, this becomes the launching pad for a deeper faith experience, but for others, it becomes a crossroads for a shipwrecked faith. They become victims to their crisis instead of victors.

Oswald Chambers describes the death process this way: "'They that are Christ's have crucified the flesh'—it is going to cost the natural in you everything, not something. Jesus said—'If any man will be My disciple, let him deny himself,' i.e., his right to himself, and a man has to realize who Jesus Christ is before he will do it. Beware of refusing to go to the funeral of your own independence. The natural life is not spiritual, and it can only be made spiritual by sacrifice. If we do not resolutely sacrifice the natural, the supernatural can never become natural in us."[7]

Walking successfully through your season of cross bearing gives you the authority to minister the message God deposits into your life during that season and to fulfill the purpose for which God created you. *The level of adversity corresponds to the level of call and to the depth and width of the ministry and purpose He plans through your life.* If your foundation is not solid, then Satan will pick you off as you scale any mountain of influence.

THE CROSS IS A SIGN OF ADOPTION

Many people think that suffering is a sign of God's displeasure. Certainly we can suffer because of our own sin. There are three reasons you and I may suffer adversity in our lives:

1. *Sin.* Sometimes we experience a crisis because we have sown the seeds of sin, and we reap what we sow. This becomes motivation to come to the cross, often for salvation.

2. *Generational sin* (subconscious strongholds). Sometimes we have generational issues that are not recognized until problems surface that are rooted in these issues.

3. *Calling.* Sometimes we experience adversity simply because of the call upon our lives, like Joseph.

You can quickly discern that you are entering a season of the cross when you have feelings like these:

- "Why am I going through this?"
- "This makes no sense, God. I'm not in sin! Why is this happening to me?"
- "My world is falling apart."

- "I feel like I'm in a freefall and have nothing to hang on to. I can't control anything."

- "It's not true! How could they think such lies?"

- "How could he/she betray me like this?"

The cross often makes no logical sense to us. We feel we are being wrongfully treated, and there is emotional and sometimes even physical pain associated with the cross. However, God's ultimate purpose in the cross is this: *The cross is a custom-designed assault to remove pride and self-assurance.* Its primary goal is humility, greater dependence upon God, and increased intimacy with the Father.

Ultimately, we want to see a resurrection to our situations. Death without resurrection is no victory. Paul spoke of this resurrection when he said, "We were therefore buried with him through baptism into death in order that, just as Christ was raised from the dead through the glory of the Father, we too may live a new life."[8]

Death of a Dream Can Birth True Vision

We see this principle in Joseph, who had a dream to rule over his brothers one day. That dream died but was later fulfilled in ways he could never have imagined. Abraham had a vision for a great nation and tried to help God fulfill that dream by conspiring with Sarah to lay with her maidservant and give birth to Ishmael instead of waiting for Isaac, the promised son. The disciples had a vision for an earthly kingdom, only to see that dream die when Jesus died on the cross.

We must wait for God to birth His vision. I thought I was called to the faith and work area and published a magazine with that focus, but it failed. Through the death of my dream, God birthed a new vision later and gave me the tools to use.

The birthing process may come in a time of darkness. In Genesis 15:12 we read that "horror and great darkness fell up" Abram. In the depths of that strange and terrible darkness, God told Abram that his descendents would one day be slaves in a strange country, but they would come out of that nation with great possessions and return to the land God had promised to Abram, which we now call the Holy Land. The ways of God may be painful, and may require a depth of soul experience to fulfill the purposes of God in our lives. A. W. Tozer once wrote: "It is doubtful whether God can bless a man greatly until he has hurt him deeply."[9]

Leadership is often birthed through pain. Tozer said, "A true and safe leader is likely one who has no desire to lead, but is forced into a position of leadership by the inward pressure of the Holy Spirit and by the pressure of an external situation."[10] Such was the case with Martin Luther. He was surprised to be used by God to reform the church. Luther was simply struggling for salvation before God and was the most surprised person of all to set off the cataclysmic sixteenth-century movement we know as the *Reformation*.

The same can be said of me. My seven-year pit experience of 1994–2001 took me through an incredible time of adversity. It was during that period that God birthed TGIF and my leadership in the faith and work movement. I was the most surprised person the first time I heard someone identify me as *the leader of the faith and work movement*. There were many before me who could claim that, but God had placed me into leadership in this area during this season.

God will use failure in your life to break down that strong desire in your heart to see your name in lights. He will destroy the false-self, performance-driven personality we have lived with to gain acceptance. When He finally breaks you of that lust for recognition, He may place you before the lights in ways you never imagined.

What Is the Goal of the Christian Life?

The goal is DEATH—so that Christ may live through us! *Both God and Satan want you dead, but for different reasons.* God wants your old nature dead. Satan wants to kill your destiny.

The cross is for every believer. Jesus told His disciples, "If anyone would come after me, he must deny himself and take up his cross and follow me. For whoever wants to save his life will lose it, but whoever loses his life for me will find it."[11] One day a mentor said to me, "I would kill you myself if I could." I was struggling to get past my own stuff. I was trying to birth something only God could birth by embracing the cross.

In 1 Samuel 2:35 we find these words: "I will raise up for Myself a faithful priest who shall do according to what is in My heart and in My mind. I will build him a sure house, and he shall walk before My anointed forever." Are you ready to be that faithful change agent through whom God can reveal His life? The only way to do this is by embracing the cross and allowing His life to be fully realized through you.

Consider these words from the apostle Paul: "For I am persuaded that neither death nor life, nor angels nor principalities nor powers, nor things present nor things to come, nor height nor depth, nor any other created thing, shall be able to separate us from the love of God which is in Christ Jesus our Lord."[12]

Michael Molinos summarizes spiritual death for the believer: "Dying—dying to the self—belongs to those who are being completed in Christ."[13]

Friend, if you've never asked God to crucify all that is in you that is not of Him, let me encourage you to pray that prayer right now.

Questions for Reflection

1. Are you experiencing a difficult time right now? If so, ask God to reveal the reason. If there is no overt or hidden sin in your life, it may simply be a result of your calling.

2. What are the benefits of the cross?

3. Why does it require a third person to complete the work of the cross in you?

Chapter 8

THE ROLE OF ISOLATION

David therefore departed from there and escaped to the cave of Adullam.
—1 SAMUEL 22:1

OW DID IT all come to this? Haven't I honored Saul? Haven't I honored God? Didn't You anoint me to be king, God?" David must have been thinking these thoughts as he looked out from his cave over the rocky cliffs below. Rejected. A fugitive. A man without a country. No army. No resources. He had just faked madness to stay alive. He must have had a sick stomach. Hope deferred makes the heart sick.[1] How did life get to this dead end? Such can be the fate of a leader in whom God is doing the deeper work. David must have identified with the same feelings as Job when he too could not make sense of his calamities.

> Look, I go forward, but He is not there,
> And backward, but I cannot perceive Him;
> When He works on the left hand, I cannot behold Him;
> When He turns to the right hand, I cannot see Him.
> But He knows the way that I take;
> When He has tested me, I shall come forth as gold.
> My foot has held fast to His steps;
> I have kept His way and not turned aside.
> I have not departed from the commandment of His lips;
> I have treasured the words of His mouth
> More than my necessary food.
> —JOB 23:8–12

God handpicked David to be the heir to King Saul's throne over Israel. He removed Saul due to his disobedience. God instructed the prophet Samuel to make a house call to Jesse's family. Jesse had eight sons, and one of them was to be the next king of Israel. In one day God took David from delivering lunch to delivering a nation.

David is a man whose character was tested much as Joseph's was. After David was anointed by Samuel to be the next king, he did not immediately go into *king-to-be* training school. The Bible tells us he went back to shepherding sheep. It is noteworthy that David did this. When we get a dramatic word from God, how many of us want to go out and try to fulfill that word rather than wait for God to fulfill it in His timing?

When there is an anointing on your life, you will bring a blessing on those you serve. Soon after this commissioning by Samuel, God orchestrated the events that would bring David into the first phase of his calling as change agent for the nation of Israel as its greatest king. Although merely a teenager, he was invited to serve Saul through his musical abilities. David became a source of comfort for Saul when he played for him. You never know when God is going to choose to elevate you to a place of influence.

Once the access door was opened, God orchestrated another opportunity for David. David volunteered to fight Goliath when no other soldier, including Saul, would fight him. David was given a platform to demonstrate God's favor on his skills as a warrior, even at this young age. David solved a problem for Saul and Israel. The greatest miracle I find in this story is not his defeat of Goliath but that King Saul risked the entire Israeli army on the merits of a teenager. This should have been Saul's battle. However, David defeated Goliath and won the hearts of all Israel. This favor from God increased as David won more battles.

This caused jealousy and insecurity to grow in Saul, which led to Saul's later decision to attempt to kill David. David had to flee as a fugitive for doing his job too well. *Sometimes obedience does not yield less adversity; it actually increases it.*

Have you ever done your job so well that others become jealous? David became a fugitive for being great at what God called him to. The training ground for a leader in the kingdom can often mean years of difficult, unfair treatment. David was forced to flee from Saul, and he was tested to see if he would take things into his own hands. Although Saul was wrong in what he was doing, David understood that it was not his right to remove Saul from power. David recognized the office more than the individual in the office. He knew it was God who placed men in their places of power. David passed this test with flying colors, in spite of his followers advising him to kill Saul and affirming to him that he would be justified in doing it.

DAVID'S LOW POINT

David's low point came when he had to escape the fury of Saul by running to the Cave of Adullam. Alone in his cave, David may have felt abandoned by God. Every change agent that would wield spiritual and physical influence with men must first win it in some hidden place. I am sure David asked the question, "Is this how you train the next king of Israel?"

Such are the ways of God. *The ways of God are fraught with unfairness, crisis, isolation, and doubts on the road to leadership.* During this low point in his life, David penned these words:

> I cry out to the LORD with my voice;
> With my voice to the LORD I make my supplication.
> I pour out my complaint before Him;
> I declare before Him my trouble.
>
> When my spirit was overwhelmed within me,
> Then You knew my path.
> In the way in which I walk
> They have secretly set a snare for me.
>
> —PSALM 142:1–3

Elijah spent time in a cave after fleeing for his life from Jezebel. This became a time when God had to bring Elijah out of a great time of despair and deception to correct a belief he held about the number of God's prophets who were in the land. He thought he was the only one left. He wanted to die. He had lost hope in his life. That is what Jezebels do in their attempts to destroy God's work among His prophets through intimidation and threats. "The word of the LORD came to him, and He said to him, 'What are you doing here, Elijah?'"[2] God went on to tell him there were actually seven thousand of His prophets in the land. Life gets distorted when we are thrust into despair. God helped Elijah. He will help you and me too.

We will all enter the Cave of Adullam at some time in our lives if we are called to be change agents. Doubt may be such a cave. Persecution may be such a cave. Sickness may be such a cave. Bereavement may be such a cave. Conflict and betrayal in relationships can be such a cave. However, there is no cave dark enough to shut out God, although it may certainly feel like it. This is the dark night of the soul. Adullam was a place of safety for David, but it was more—it was a place to do business with God. If God calls us into darkness in order to enter His presence, then that darkness will become an entry door to new levels of relationship with a God who longs for fellowship with you and me.

God was testing David's mettle and preparing him for a new chapter in his life. Charles Swindoll describes the role that isolation and the cave may play in a leader's journey:

> David has been brought to the place where God can truly begin to shape him and use him. *When the sovereign God brings us to nothing, it is to reroute our lives, not to end them.* Human perspective says, "Aha, you've lost this, you've lost that. You've caused this, you've caused that. You've ruined this, you've ruined that. End your life!" But God

says, "No. No. You're in the cave. But that doesn't mean it's curtains. That means it's time to reroute your life. Now's the time to start anew!" That's exactly what he does with David.[3]

What happens next is truly remarkable. David's family and the down-and-outers of society all come to his hideout. They join him in the fight. They become his army of misfits, but after he trains them for battle they become known as "David's mighty men." Such are the ways of God.

David was first used to solve a problem for Israel and to replace Saul's ungodly leadership with godly leadership. Now David begins the phase of training his men as a network or, in this case, his army. Networks are always necessary to create change in culture. No one man can do it by himself, as we will discuss later in this book.

Isolation May Come as a Result of Our Own Sin

Some of us do not enter our cave of isolation as a result of the call of God upon our lives; rather, we enter because of our pride, arrogance, and presumption. However, God uses the cave of isolation to deliver us from generational iniquity, which causes us to behave un-Christlike and leads us to make decisions that send us into the cave of isolation. Even so, God uses this time to sanctify our lives for the purpose and calling He has for us, if we are willing to repent and gain the freedom this process is designed to achieve in our lives. At other times, this cave time can come as the result of the call on our lives, as we see in the case of Joseph.

Joseph was the eleventh son to be born to Jacob in his old age. However, he would not be the last; that notoriety would belong to Benjamin. Joseph was a favored son because he was born to Rachel, Jacob's beloved wife, who birthed Joseph and Benjamin, his younger brother. Jacob showed much favoritism to Joseph, which enraged the other ten brothers. When Joseph received his dream from God that someday he would rule over them and had the boldness and arrogance to flaunt that dream before his brothers and his father, bitterness began to grow in his brothers. It almost resulted in murder, but Reuben interceded on his behalf.

This was the first evidence we have of Joseph's youthful pride. This pride launched Joseph into his first *isolation experience* when he was sold as a slave. However, Joseph's indiscretion did not fit the punishment. Apparently something greater was at work.

His second isolation experience was when he was serving as a slave and servant of Potiphar's house. He was a faithful servant, and his character was unquestionable. Potiphar's wife made several attempts to seduce Joseph. However, we find that Joseph made a strategic error on one occasion: "But it happened about this time, when Joseph went into the house to do his work, and none of the men of the house was inside, that she caught him by his garment, saying, 'Lie with me.' But he left his garment in her hand, and fled and ran outside."[4]

Joseph was the overseer for all of Potiphar's household. Could he have prevented this ultimate setup by Potiphar's wife by having others in the house? We can never know for sure. What we do know is this led to Potiphar's judgment against him. Joseph could not defend the accusation, because he did not have a witness. This led to his isolation in prison and personal cave experience for many years. I can only imagine the many dark nights in that dingy, dirty, and smelly Egyptian prison cell.

Many of us men can relate to the error of Joseph. As Christian men, we should not do certain things that open the door to the enemy's schemes against us. In this day of openness and anything goes, it is easy to get caught in the web of inappropriate actions that can lead to our downfall. For instance, making it a policy to keep doors open when there are meetings with someone of the opposite sex in the office is wisdom. Never traveling with the opposite sex without your wife or another male is another wise policy. Recognize the value of a witness.

Joseph's adversity was not commensurate with his lack of discernment or his pride. In God's economy, what we experience may have little connection to the level of crisis or the fairness of what we face. God's ways are always higher than our ways. God can use our indiscretion as a catalyst to usher us into a process designed to accomplish His greater purposes for our lives and for the benefit of others in the future.

Those God uses to significantly impact the kingdom are often required to experience the deepest level of adversity, which will light the torch to illuminate the often dark passageways for those yet to follow. They are our teachers. And the teacher must always know the lesson better than the student. God's desire is to bring us into maturity and joy and to help us to discover our true selves and purpose in Him.

MESSES INTO MESSAGES INTO MESSENGERS

God knows the stubborn human heart. He knows that if He is to accomplish His deepest work, He must take us into isolation in order to give us the privilege of being used in His kingdom. Isolation changes us and removes things that hinder us. God uses isolation to force us to draw deep upon His grace. Isolation is only a season in our lives. When He has accomplished what He wants in our lives in the isolation, He will bring us out. The desert may mean being put on the shelf for a season, but from your perch of the shelf you will experience the reality of a living God like never before.

For some, God gives us a mission that can only be fulfilled after we have spent adequate time in preparation in the desert, which is another form of isolation God uses. Fear not the desert, for it is here you will hear God's voice. It is here you become His bride. It is here you will have the idols of your life removed. It is here you learn to adapt to a new environment that often has less resources to draw upon.

When David left his cave of isolation, he said, "'He brought me out into a spacious place; he rescued me because he delighted in me."[5] Jesus chose times of isolation with His disciples to explain parables to them. The times when we are alone and away from the distractions of life can be the most productive times for us to hear the voice of God in our lives. We must initiate these times ourselves by meeting with God in the early morning. There are other times when God initiates these times in order to get our undivided attention for a work He may be preparing for us to do. This may come in the form of an unpleasant circumstance like a job loss, illness, or marriage separation. C. S. Lewis said, "God whispers to us in our pleasures, speaks in our conscience, but shouts in our pains: it is his megaphone to rouse a deaf world."[6]

The cave is also a place to process our pain and receive a message from God for our own lives and for the benefit of others. As the result of being placed in a cave, many servants of God have received divine revelations that benefited the entire body of Christ. Daniel coined these words about the cave experience: "He reveals deep and secret things; He knows what is in the darkness, and light dwells with Him."[7] When we are placed in a season of isolation, we must view it as a time orchestrated by God to seek Him more in our lives. "It is the glory of God to conceal a matter, but the glory of kings is to search out a matter."[8]

Isolation Because of Our Obedience

Ezekiel was in a place of isolation and captivity as the Book of Ezekiel opens. "Now it came to pass in the thirtieth year, in the fourth month, on the fifth day of the month, as I was among the captives by the River Chebar, that the heavens were opened and I saw visions of God. On the fifth day of the month, which was in the fifth year of King Jehoiachin's captivity, the word of the LORD came expressly to Ezekiel the priest, the son of Buzi, in the land of the Chaldeans by the River Chebar; and the hand of the LORD was upon him there."[9]

During this season, God will reveal deep spiritual insights. They are like spiritual jewels. It is the depth and width of your cross experience that will determine the degree of fruit that will come from your life.

It was during an extended time of isolation that I wrote *TGIF: Today God Is First*, a daily devotional read daily by hundreds of thousands of people worldwide. The prophet Isaiah helped me understand what God was doing in me at that time: "I will give you the treasures of darkness and hidden riches of secret places, that you may know that I, the LORD, who call you by name, am the God of Israel."[10] Hosea tells us He "[brings] us into the wilderness" to speak to us.[11] He reveals Himself and His messages in us during the isolation times.

The apostle Paul wrote many of his epistles from a prison cell. His perspective on his isolation was revealed in the way he signed his letters—"prisoner of the Lord." The apostle John wrote his vision of Revelation from the isle of Patmos. The prophet Jeremiah understood isolation: "While Jeremiah was still confined in the courtyard of the guards, *the word of the Lord came to him a second time....* 'Call to me and I will answer you and tell you great and unsearchable things you do not know.'"[12] Notice that while Jeremiah was confined, the word of the Lord came to him.

Yes, this is often the way of God. Sometimes God intentionally hides His people for a season to accomplish a deeper work in order to craft a message through their life. "You shall hide them in the secret place of Your presence."[13]

John Bunyan, who wrote *Pilgrim's Progress*, grew up in poverty and taught himself to read. He struggled with feelings of not being forgiven by God. His wife died of a sudden illness, and he turned totally to God in his pain. He began to preach throughout England, but because he did not have a license, the authorities arrested him and eventually imprisoned him for twelve years for preaching without a license. While in prison he experienced God's presence in a special way and wrote the classic best seller *The Pilgrim's Progress*—a book that could only have been written by someone being refined by the fires of adversity. Yes, God turns our messes into His messages and His messengers.

Well-known Chinese leader and deep-thinking writer Watchman Nee was led into extended isolation periods after contracting tuberculosis. He was forced to get away to rest in a more favorable climate. He was completely alone and isolated, but he concluded that God used isolation in the lives of Christian leaders to develop character and wrote about it during this time. There were also other times when Nee was forced into isolation periods resulting from persecution, conflicts, and further illness.

Nelson Mandela was hidden for twenty-seven years before he became the "Joseph" of his nation. The apostle Paul wrote many letters from his prison cell. John the apostle wrote his vision of Revelation from the isle of Patmos. Elijah was sent to the brook of Cherith to be alone and fed by ravens. Life isn't about waiting for the storms to pass; it's about learning to dance in the rain.

David wrote three psalms while he was in his cave—Psalms 34, 57, and 142. Each of them reveal the condition of his heart—the absolute low point of his life.

David was a man looking for purpose in all of his troubles. I am sure he wondered how he went from being a king's favored son to being an outlaw who had to fake madness just to stay alive. He probably thought of the day as a teen when Samuel anointed him as the next king of Israel. Like many of us, he thought, "So where are You now, God? I thought I was Your man." But David also exhibited an amazing faith and hope in God at the conclusion of Psalm 142: "You shall deal bountifully with me."[14] It takes courage to make such a statement in the face of total defeat.

When God takes us into our own cave of Adullam, we must remember this is a time of intentional hiddenness and preparation. If handled correctly, others will be drawn to your anointing, and they will find themselves transformed as you allow your anointing to destroy the yoke of bondage—it will fall off of you and onto others you will serve.

Dr. Robert Clinton, author of *The Making of a Leader*, cites the reason many change agents will experience an isolation period in their journey:

> One way that God forces a leader into reflective evaluation and into "being" (versus doing) stage of the upward development pattern involves isolation. It is one of the most effective means for maturing a leader. Several times in a leader's lifetime, the leader may be set aside from his or her normal ministry. Causes may include crisis, disciplinary action, providential circumstances (such as war, oppressive government action, illness) or self choice. The thrust of the processing is on the recognition that the isolation is God's work and that it is a call to a deeper relationship and experience of God. Isolation is often used by God to teach important leadership lessons that could not be learned while experiencing the pressures of their normal work.[15]

God is working while His agents wait and wait and wait. Each is being selected for a handpicked assignment. This waiting is preparation for a greater depth of use and greater anointing that cannot be accomplished otherwise. *Because of the waiting and testing you endure, you will be given even greater authority. The waiting period actually creates a level of authority for you to carry out your assignment from God.*

My friend and intercessor Bradley once said to me, "God doesn't prune dead trees, only fruitful ones." But the process can be extremely painful. I have written my best works during times of isolation and adversity that forced me into the soil of God's grace as a result of desperation and pain. This book that I am writing now is being written during an isolation period.

COME OUT OF THE STRONGHOLD

God doesn't allow us to remain in our own cave of isolation. If we remain there too long, we become defeated by our circumstance. It is interesting that the prophet told David, "Do not stay in the stronghold; depart, and go to the land of Judah."[16] *Judah* means praise. If we are to overcome our circumstances, we must do something that seems unnatural—we must praise God in the midst of our circumstances. We don't praise Him *for* the circumstance; we praise Him for *who He is* and that He is our deliverer.

What did the cave do in the life of David? Well, God turned the mess of the cave into one of our greatest messengers, who wrote many of the psalms that have comforted millions of people over the centuries. We learn the lessons from tears he shed in those times, and they are a spring from which we drink:

> As they pass through the Valley of Baca,
> They make it a spring;
> The rain also covers it with pools.
> They go from strength to strength;
> Each one appears before God in Zion.
>
> —PSALM 84:6–7

There is a spiritual law in the kingdom of God. Every great leader in the kingdom will pass through the Valley of Baca. *Baca* means "to weep." It comes from the Hebrew word *bakah*, meaning "to weep; generally to bemoan."

However, Baca is also a place of springs. There is nothing better on a hot day when you're thirsty and weary than to drink water from a mountain spring. It refreshes. It renews. It gives you a second wind to continue your journey. Those who commit themselves to a pilgrimage with God will experience the Valley of Baca. But in the midst of Baca they will discover that in this valley they will also drink from a very special spring that refreshes with a different kind of living water.

Baca becomes the source of "secret things in hidden places" reserved only for those willing to journey on the great pilgrimage with God. Once you drink from this spring, you will be energized in your spiritual man from strength to strength. Each Valley of Baca will result in a new spiritual spring from which you will drink. It is handmade just for you by God. But know this; it will be used to provide a refreshing drink for others you will encounter who are also on their pilgrimage.

Ultimately Baca leads to the presence of God. There is something about being in a place with God that results in our weeping and crying out to Him. Do you find yourself in this place with God today? If so, know that His springs are also available to you. Ask Him today to give you a drink from His spring only available in the Valley of Baca.

Do you find yourself in an isolation chamber? Perhaps you are a change agent in the making. Perhaps there is a deposit God is seeking to make into your life that will be used for many others. If so, let God do the deeper work through this isolation period. Let Him temper those things in you that have needed to be tempered.

Do you find yourself in an isolation chamber? If so, let me encourage you with these words: "Let him who walks in the dark, who has no light, trust in the name of the Lord and rely on his God."[17] May the Lord be your stronghold in this stage of your journey. Learn to listen during this time, and let God develop intimacy with you by spending focused time of praise, study, prayer, and quiet listening.

QUESTIONS FOR REFLECTION

1. Are you in a time of isolation? Are you able to identify some spiritual benefits to your time? Name a few of them.

2. Name two or three of the most important reasons listed in this chapter for an isolation time from God's perspective.

3. Name some people and the length of their isolation times. What came from their lives as a result?

Chapter 9

AVOID THE TRAPS OF PERFORMANCE, PASSION, POSITION, AND POSSESSIONS

Behold, You desire truth in the inward parts,
And in the hidden part You will make me to know wisdom.

—PSALM 51:6

T HE APOSTLE PAUL understood that *the higher you go up a mountain of influence, the greater the level of spiritual warfare.* "For a great and effective door has opened to me, and there are many adversaries."[1] He understood that his calling penetrated spiritual forces in high places. It was not just a matter of his communication and professional skill that would make him effective in impacting his culture; it was overcoming the principalities that ruled the mountains he was seeking to claim.

Oswald Chambers also understood this truth: "When you get higher up, you face other temptations and characteristics. Satan uses the strategy of elevation in temptation, and God does the same, but the effect is different. When the devil puts you into an elevated place, he makes you screw your idea of holiness beyond what flesh and blood could ever bear, it is a spiritual acrobatic performance, you are poised and dare not move; but when God elevates you by His grace into the heavenly places, instead of finding a pinnacle to cling to, you find a great tableland where it is easy to move."[2]

If you have not gained a victory over Satan's traps of performance, passion, position, and possessions before you are elevated as a change agent into a leadership role, you will be an easy prey for Satan and his demons. Many leaders' integrity is not strong enough to keep them at the top of a mountain once the prosperity, fame, and prestige hit them. Heinz Ketchup founder H. J. Heinz once said, "Quality is for a product what character is to a man."

Chuck Swindoll once heard a seasoned pastor warn a group of ministers about the primary temptations that come to leaders who achieve a level of success. He said, "Along with the kind of temperament, winsomeness, and charisma it takes to be a dynamic spiritual leader, there also comes a series of easy faults to fall into. To make them easy to remember, he used four words that began with the same letter, S: *silver, sloth, sex,* and *self.* Stop and think of the dynamic leaders who have fallen. Almost without exception, one or more of these four has the avenue of failure."[3]

In 1 John 2:16 we find Satan's primary strategy to unseat change agents from their calling: "For all that is in the world—the lust of the flesh, the lust of the eyes, and the pride of life—is not of the Father but is of the world." Satan has no new strategies. They've worked very effectively since the Garden of Eden. You will find at least one of these strategies at the root of every leader who fell to sin. They deal with sins of passion, possessions, and position. I believe that there is another trap Satan uses also, and that is the trap of performance. In this chapter we will look at all four of these traps and learn to avoid them.

When Jesus was led into wilderness to be tempted, He was tempted in three specific areas. "Then Jesus was led up by the Spirit into the wilderness to be tempted by the devil."[4]

1. *His identity.* "If you are the Son of God…"[5] Jesus was tempted to believe a lie about who He was. Satan wanted to make Him doubt whom and what He came for. We are also tempted to believe a lie about who we are. We are tempted to live through our own wounds and insecurities and believe we are not worthy of being a son of our heavenly Father, so we try to perform to gain acceptance. Jesus knew He was the Son of God and knew His mission was to honor His Father and fulfill His purpose.

2. *His authority.* Satan's second temptation was to make Jesus believe He had to tangibly demonstrate His spiritual authority by using His power inappropriately and at the wrong times. Jesus knew He only did what the Father told Him to do. Satan does this with us by tempting us to prove our spirituality through our own performance. We end up living as slaves versus sons when we fall for this.

3. *His strategy.* The third temptation was to use the wrong strategy to accomplish His assigned mission. Satan said, "All these things I will give You if You will fall down and worship me."[6] We employ manipulative and controlling strategies rooted in our flesh to justify our ends.

These same three temptations show up in our approach to changing culture and generally in living out our Christian life.

Avoid the Performance Trap

No king is saved by the multitude of an army;
A mighty man is not delivered by great strength.
A horse is a vain hope for safety;
Neither shall it deliver any by its great strength.

—Psalm 33:16–17

One of the core traps the enemy sets for change agents is the performance trap. As a young boy, it was my weekly job to mow the grass. One day I missed a few sections of grass. Mom promptly took me to the front yard and showed me where I had missed. Mom loved working in the yard and took pride in it. It became clear to me that if I was going to mow her yard, it had to be right. I never missed a spot ever again. Even today I cannot mow my own yard and not have it perfect. Early in my childhood, the trap of performance was laid for me with the purest of sugar coating through my experience in mowing the lawn. I was ensnared to perform by wanting to gain my mother's approval on a job well done. Shame will produce a person driven to perform in order to gain love. If you never had words of affirmation or emotionally caring parents who validated your worth as an individual, more than likely you sought to gain love through your performance. This is especially true for men. It can sabotage your destiny as a change agent.

I was shy growing up. Mom and Dad thought I should get involved in sports to bring me out. I loved playing pickup football in the neighborhood, and we always had the best yard for football. I was a cut above others my age. I was always picked first in the pickup games. After all, I played in the Gravy Bowl as quarterback and defensive halfback. I made a game-winning interception in the Gravy Bowl. Then came Little League baseball. I started in right field and graduated to first base. My coach taught me how to throw, and I began pitching. I became an all-star pitcher with a mean curveball for a twelve-year-old. I made the all-star team as a pitcher and pitched in the big game. My curveball was really working. I would aim for the batter and watch it cross right over the plate. At first the umpire called my pitches as balls instead of strikes because he thought they were going to hit the batter. He came up to me after the game and said he had never seen the amount of movement on a curveball like I was able to put on it.

Then came basketball. I played junior-high ball and was moderately good. But it was not until I got to high school that I had developed into a good basketball player. I was in between sizes for a guard or forward at six feet two inches. I often played both positions. I developed a deadly jump shot. My coach would put me out on a wing and get the ball to me. One game I scored twenty-six points and led scoring. When I was hot, I could drop them from anywhere.

However, I was slow and not a great ball handler, so my jump shot was about it. We won the 4A state championship during my junior year.

Then came golf. When I was eleven, I began to play golf. Soon I began caddying for my dad on Saturdays. Five bucks for two heavy bags equaled ten dollars! I was rich! Dad introduced me to the game, and I was a natural. I loved the game, and it became my sport. I lived on the golf course during summers, arriving at the course at 8:00 a.m. and often playing forty-five holes while carrying my golf bag. By age fourteen I had broken seventy several times and had three hole-in-ones. I won all the junior tournaments in my area, and at age fifteen I qualified for the US Junior Amateur that was held in Boston, Massachusetts, at Brookline Country Club, where the US Open has been played. During the first two rounds I played with Gary Koch, who later played on the PGA Tour and is now a golf analyst for NBC. Ben Crenshaw also played in that tournament.

I say all of this only to clearly establish the early childhood pattern of performance. Performance equaled value, validation, and love. Because validation was very limited in words or emotional intimacy while I was growing up, I sought to compensate for my unmet needs through my performance.

As an adult, this translated into performance in business and in relationships. I performed subconsciously in the way I thought others wanted me to perform to gain their love and validation. This is called operating from a false self, or *poser* personality. I struggled to experience the unconditional love of God. Intimacy in relationships was difficult. The bottom line was always performance, but this was subconscious, and I could not recognize it on the surface. We often derive our identity from the input our lives have on those who make up our audiences or circle of influence. This leads us to gain our validation from others instead of God.

God will always force us into our wound to destroy the lie that was spoken to us through it. It would be many years before I would discover that lie. That lie would allow me to sabotage many good things in my life. It would place me on a treadmill of performance that would create a false self that posed as *the* successful Christian businessman. Underneath I would struggle to have intimacy with God and others. This was directly related to the wounds of childhood, where I failed to learn or receive emotional intimacy, which was not modeled by my parents toward me. These wounds remained until God helped me recognize and heal these wounds as an adult.

I was in my forties and fifties before I discovered how deep-seated performance had impacted every area of my life. I thought I had dealt with performance issues many years earlier. However, there were more layers waiting to be uncovered. I discovered that performance made me view others through my performance glasses. I placed a subconscious requirement on others to live under my performance standards. If you did not operate at a level of performance or excellence I expected, I would make it known, sometimes in direct ways and other times in subtle ways.

Do you ever get angry with others when they don't perform the way you think they should? We should expect excellence in the marketplace, but we must be aware of how dysfunction can play a role in our lives and surface as we live out our calling.

For me, it showed up in so many ways, from honking my horn at imperfect drivers, to having a bad attitude with a ticket agent who was taking too much time, to having a critical spirit when people performed poorly. It was subtle, but it tainted my view of the world. The internal, subconscious message was: "If I must live under this performance mandate, you must also." I projected my life wound on everyone else. Now, it was not always visible because I was a strong Christian leader who had discipline. Some might never see visibly the turmoil that was going inside of me. This too was another form of performance.

John Eldredge, coauthor of *The Sacred Romance,* says that we "choose anesthesia of the heart through some form of competence."[7] This was certainly my drug of choice. Once God began to shatter the performance trap in my life, I invested myself into understanding and accepting the love of God in my life. I renounced the lie of performance Satan had been speaking to me. I discovered the Father's love. This was not an easy process, and it took months to appropriate. I'm still a work in progress, but God led me to write a book on this topic entitled, *Experiencing the Father's Love.*

EXPERIENCING THE FATHER'S LOVE

One encounter of personally connecting with the love of the Father came through a mentor. I was fourteen when I lost my earthly father in a plane crash, so abandonment and rejection issues played into my performance issues. This man, in some ways, became a father figure to me. He lives in another country. We were talking about my crisis at the time, and he stopped midstream in our phone conversation and said, "Os, you must know something. I love you. I really love you. I believe God has given us a special kind of relationship. I just want you to know that."

I was taken by surprise at his comment and felt unprepared to respond. I said a respectful, "I love you too. You have meant a lot to me." But there was no emotion behind the words because I did not know how to respond. The following day, as I walked around a lake where I walk every day, my mind went back to his phone call, and I began to weep. I wept for thirty minutes. The Lord was saying that He loved me through the love of my mentor. He reminded me that I had not heard those words from my father, even though I knew he did love me. He simply did not verbalize it.

I was discovering how truly difficult it was to love myself unconditionally and to be vulnerable enough to let God love me unconditionally. I began to let go of performance activities that were subtle traps designed to entice me to *earn* God's love.

If you are going to be a godly change agent, you must live from the heart, not performance. God wants us to relate to each of us through a heart connection, not through our performance. Our motivation to obey should be rooted in our heart connection to our heavenly Father. "I will give you a new heart and put a new spirit within you; I will take the heart of stone out of your flesh and give you a heart of flesh. I will put My Spirit within you and cause you to walk in My statutes, and you will keep My judgments and do them."[8]

Don't Get Trapped by Passion

> Do not love the world or the things in the world. If anyone loves the world, the love of the Father is not in him. For all that *is* in the world— the lust of the flesh, the lust of the eyes, and the pride of life—is not of the Father but is of the world. And the world is passing away, and the lust of it; but he who does the will of God abides forever.
>
> —1 John 2:15–17

Bill Clinton's sexual indiscretions with Monica Lewinsky in the White House brought shame to him, his family, and the nation. To make matters worse, he tried to cover it up by lying to the American people on national television and later explained it away as "not being sex." It led to impeachment proceedings but amounted to only a slap on the hand from Congress. Nevertheless, Clinton will forever be remembered in the history books for his indiscretions.

Tiger Woods, the most recognized sports figure in the world today, took pride in crafting a well-protected self-image. He sought to present a family image and prided himself in his ability to keep his private life out of the media. This was so important to him that he even named his yacht *Privacy*. However, all that changed in December of 2009 when Tiger attempted to hide information surrounding his car accident, which took place in his private residential neighborhood. Several affairs were revealed through the national tabloid media a few days later. Despite his attempts to conceal this, a voice mail message between him and a woman led to his exposure. This is yet another example of how the age of the digital media has become a tenacious posse designed to reveal things done in darkness.

Passion is the lust of the flesh. It is what makes us feel good. These are the temptations that arouse the physical impulses of our lives. When David looked at Bathsheba from his balcony and decided he had to have her, the lust of the flesh (passion) took over his life and started a downward spiraling cycle that led to even greater sins—the sin of murder and cover-up. God judged David for his sin. His judgment resulted in God taking his child, but David's life was spared after he repented.

Many a great man has fallen because of their secret lives of passion. King Solomon controlled the mountain of government. He was known as the wisest man on the earth during his lifetime. However, something changed that. King Solomon had a generational stronghold of lust and unredeemed passion that had been passed down to him from his father, David. This lust dulled his heart toward God and took him off the path God had for his life and his nation.[9]

Solomon fulfilled his own words: "Whoever commits adultery with a woman lacks understanding; he who does so destroys his own soul."[10] Solomon's example is a lesson to avoid the lie that asserts, "What someone does in his or her private life is of no concern. It has no bearing on how that person does his or her job."

SEX ON THE INTERNET

Philip Yancey, in his book *Disappointment With God*, relates the tragedy of Solomon, who began well but did not finish well. "In one generation, Solomon took Israel from a fledgling kingdom dependent on God for bare survival to a self-sufficient political power. But along the way he lost sight of the original vision to which God had called them. Ironically, by the time of Solomon's death, Israel resembled the Egypt they had escaped: an imperial state held in place by a bloated bureaucracy and slave labor, with an official state religion under the ruler's command. Success in the kingdom of this world had crowded out interest in the kingdom of God. The brief, shining vision of a covenant nation faded away, and God withdrew his sanction. After Solomon's death, Israel split in two and slid toward ruin."[11] As I read his words, I could not help but think of where America is today and what our original vision was for our nation. We are following the way of Solomon in many ways.

We live in a technology age that makes the discipline of passion even more challenging, especially for men. According to statistics compiled by the National Coalition for the Protection of Children and Families (NCFPCF), the median age of boys for the first exposure to pornography is eleven.[12] And 70 percent of men aged eighteen to twenty-four visit pornographic sites in a typical month, with 66 percent in their twenties and thirties reporting they are regular users of pornography.[13]

Easy access to sex on the Internet is having a huge impact on our culture. To realize the magnitude of the problem and its impact on the culture at large, review the following statistics:

- Seventy-two million Internet users visit pornography websites each year.[14]

- Sex is the number-one topic searched on the Internet.[15]

- In 2004, there were 372 million pornographic Web pages,[16] more than 2.5 billion pornographic e-mails,[17] and 100,000 websites offering illegal child pornography.[18]

- Child pornography generates $3 billion annually.[19]

- Eleven thousand adult movies are produced each year.[20]

- For every ten men in church, five are struggling with pornography.[21]

In June 2009, *Time* magazine published an article entitled, "Cheating 2.0: New Mobile Apps Make Adultery Easier." Several new websites make it easy for men and women to commit adultery through the convenience and privacy of the Internet. The most popular site has doubled its customer base to 4 million in the last twelve months. One consultant explained the site this way: "It's in the business of rebranding infidelity, making it not only monetizable, but adding a modicum of normalcy to it." A forty-five-year-old Florida woman who uses the site regularly now says she's been married for twenty years but started using the site four months ago because her husband constantly turned down sex and refused marriage counseling. "It's like the seven-year itch, but twenty years later," she says. "My husband never throws me a compliment. Now I meet guys who say, 'You're so hot,' or 'You have great eyes.'"[22]

UNDERSTANDING THE ROOT ISSUE
OF SEXUAL ADDICTION

One of the greatest theologian change agents in Christianity was Augustine. Augustine struggled with a sexual addiction. He discovered that his real battle was not in his inability to control his sexual passions but to enjoy God more than sex by experiencing His love. His freedom came when he encountered God personally. In his book *Confessions* he states, "I shall now tell and confess to the glory of your name how you released me from the fetters of lust which held me so tightly shackled and from my slavery to the things of this world."[23]

The public shame of sexual failure can be so great that it keeps many in bondage for a lifetime. Yet, in order to gain freedom we must recognize the root cause of this addiction. Henry Wright, author of a booklet titled *Addictions*, provides insights into the root cause of all forms of addictions. He defines any addiction as follows:

Addiction is anything that you cannot lay down by an act of your will. It does not matter what it is. It might be pornography; it might be drugs; it might be an ungodly soul tie; it might be anything. That which controls you and rules you is your master. The Father is not your master. The Lord is not your master. It has become your Lord. Something in the physical creation is your Lord. *The core issue of any addiction or addiction tendency is rooted in a person's inability to believe they are loved by God.*[24]

If you struggle in this area, I encourage you to begin meditating on scriptures that relate to the love of God. When you live in compromise, you lose confidence in the faith dimension of your life. The Bible says we are to confess our sins one to another. The very act of bringing your struggle into the light brings healing. My friend Ford Taylor often says, "What we cover, God uncovers. What we uncover, God covers." If we try to hide our sin, Satan has a legal right to humiliate us—and he will do so publicly. The more public a figure you are, the greater the humiliation. If you choose humility by initiating repentance, God will cover you by His grace, and your restoration will be quicker.

Start with Ephesians 3:18. Ask God to help you receive His love and believe that you are loved by your heavenly Father. Why not start now to believe and receive God's love for you by praying the prayer David did when he repented for his sin with Bathsheba:

Have mercy upon me, O God,
According to Your lovingkindness;
According to the multitude of Your tender mercies,
Blot out my transgressions.
Wash me thoroughly from my iniquity,
And cleanse me from my sin.

For I acknowledge my transgressions,
And my sin is always before me.
Against You, You only, have I sinned,
And done this evil in Your sight—
That You may be found just when You speak,
And blameless when You judge.

Behold, I was brought forth in iniquity,
And in sin my mother conceived me.
Behold, You desire truth in the inward parts,
And in the hidden part You will make me to know wisdom.
—Psalm 51:1–6

RECOGNIZE THE
TRAP OF POSITION

A good name is to be chosen rather than great riches, loving favor
rather than silver and gold.

—PROVERBS 22:1

Let me ask you if you would like to work for the man who said these words:
"In my own case I grew up the son of a Baptist minister. From this background, I was fully exposed to not only legal behavior but moral and ethical
behavior and what that means from the standpoint of leading organizations
and people. I was, and am, a strong believer that one of the most satisfying
things in life is to create a highly moral and ethical environment in which
every individual is allowed and encouraged to realize their God-given potential."[25] Probably not.

His name was Kenneth Lay, chairman and CEO of Enron. He was convicted on May 25, 2006, on ten counts of securities fraud and related charges.
He would have gone to prison for ten to twenty years if he had not had a heart
attack and died before he was sent to prison. At one time Kenneth Lay had a
spiritual foundation in his life. Something happened as he scaled the mountain
of business. Instead of becoming a change agent for God on this mountain, he
became a casualty of war. Larry Crabb states, "Satan's masterpiece is not the
prostitute or the skid-row bum. It's the self-sufficient person who has made
life comfortable, who is adjusting well to the world and truly likes living here,
a person who dreams of no better place to live, who longs only to be a little
better—and a little better off—than he already is."[26] We are all susceptible to
the same fate were it not for the grace of God in our lives.

The business world is lined with casualties who sought position at the
expense of their integrity: Jeff Skilling, ex-CEO of Enron; Bernie Ebbers,
CEO of WorldCom; Dennis Kozlowski, former Tyco International CEO; Mark
Swartz, Tyco's ex-CFO; and Richard Scrushy, former CEO of HealthSouth to
name a few. All of these men have served or are currently serving prison time
for their ethical failures.

In the fall of 2008 I had the opportunity to participate in a Bible study
at the White House. The room where the study took place was the former
office of President Richard Nixon. We were told that it was the office where
the infamous Watergate tapes were discovered and where he wrote his resigna-
tion letter. I was in college when this was taking place in the early 1970s, but I
remember it as if it were yesterday. As I stood in this office, I was struck with
the history that had taken place in that room. I was saddened to think how this
leader allowed position to so rule his life that he was willing to engage in crim-
inal conduct to maintain his power and control over his office.

When you get to the top of a mountain, the power is intoxicating, and the need to remain on the top of that mountain can drive you to make choices you would never think you were capable of when you were not holding such a position. There is something about power and the need to maintain it that drives leaders to make really bad choices for fear of losing it.

The Companion Trap of Possessions

Possession and position often go hand in hand. The lust of the eyes represents the need to possess, while the pride of life is the need for position. Position, or the pride of life, says, "I must be seen and respected." The lust of the eyes says, "Whatever I see I want." It is the ultimate consumptive lifestyle.

Sometimes your talent takes you beyond where your integrity can keep you. Prosperity is the place where many do not have a spiritual foundation that can keep them from the tremendous temptations that accompany such a place. Prosperity is often a much greater temptation than adversity will ever be.

Dietrich Bonhoeffer, in describing temptation, wrote: "In our members there is a slumbering inclination towards desire which is both sudden and fierce. With irresistible power desire seizes mastery over the flesh. All at once a secret, smoldering fire is kindled. The flesh burns and is in flames. It makes no difference whether it is sexual desire, or ambition, or vanity, or desire for revenge, or love of fame and power, or greed for money, or, finally, that strange desire for the beauty of the world, or nature. Joy in God is in the course of being extinguished in us and we seek all our joy in the creature. At this moment God is quite unreal to us, we lose all reality, and only desire for the creature is real; the only reality is the devil. Satan does not fill us with hatred of God, but with forgetfulness of God....The lust thus aroused envelops the mind and will of man in deepest darkness. The powers of clear discrimination and of decision are taken from us....It is here that everything within me rises up against the Word of God."[27]

How to Avoid Entrapment

How do we avoid the traps of performance, passion, position, and possession?

Humility

God places a high value on change agents who exhibit humility. He often takes great pains to build humility into His change agents. Moses was described by God as the most humble man on the face of the earth.[28] God used thirteen years of preparation to ensure that Joseph had no pride in his life. Humility is a characteristic highly valued by God:

The humble He guides in justice,
And the humble He teaches His way.

—Psalm 25:9

The Lord lifts up the humble;
He casts the wicked down to the ground.

—Psalm 147:6

Generosity

The opposite spirit to possessions is generosity. The demonic spirit of mammon is what motivates us to a greedy and consumptive lifestyle. There are more than two thousand scriptures on money in the Bible. Each of us must evaluate our lifestyle before the Lord. The Lord is a generous God. He desires to bless His people. In Deuteronomy 8 He tells us He gives us the ability to produce wealth in order to establish His covenant. It is also our primary means of provision as we fulfill the calling in our lives. It is the *love* of money that affects the heart. "For the love of money is a root of all kinds of evil, for which some have strayed from the faith in their greediness, and pierced themselves through with many sorrows."[29]

Do you want to destroy a mammon spirit in yourself? Start giving generously. Nothing destroys it more than living a disciplined life materially and investing in the kingdom. "So let each one give as he purposes in his heart, not grudgingly or of necessity; for God loves a cheerful giver. And God is able to make all grace abound toward you, that you, always having all sufficiency in all things, may have an abundance for every good work."[30]

Accountability

Change agents that want to be used in the kingdom of God to reclaim culture must model servant leadership. To avoid the pitfalls of success, accountability needs to be in the equation. Find some trusted friends with whom you can share your life, and be accountable to them in the tough questions in life. One leader who fell was asked why he felt he had fallen. His answer: "I didn't give anyone permission to tell me about my blind spots; I only gave them permission to tell me what I wanted to hear."

Why not set up a group of people in your own life who can ask the tough questions? This will be insurance against falling to the deceit of your own heart that could lead to the sins of performance, possessions, position, and power, and it will foster a life that finishes well.

QUESTIONS FOR REFLECTION

1. Name four traps that Satan uses to ensnare change agents.

2. What causes a person to be motivated by performance?

3. What is the root sin and unmet need of unbridled passion?

4. Is your life defined by position and possessions? If not, how do you avoid these traps?

Chapter 10

UNDERSTAND YOUR SPIRITUAL AUTHORITY AND RESPONSIBILITY

And I will give you the keys of the kingdom of heaven, and whatever you bind on earth will be bound in heaven, and whatever you loose on earth will be loosed in heaven.

—MATTHEW 16:19

HEN ADAM AND Eve were created, God gave them authority to manage all matters on the earth. "The heaven, even the heavens, are the LORD's; but the earth He has given to the children of men."[1] Their sin in the garden represented a rebellious heart that enticed them to move from manager to owner. Satan convinced them that God was holding out on them, and he appealed to their pride to be all knowing like God.[2] Each of us has an innate sin nature that wants to be the boss, not just a steward of what God has entrusted to us. However, stewardship is man's role, to represent God's interests and to execute His will on earth.

When man sinned in the Garden of Eden, that authority was transferred to Satan. He was given free rein over the earth because of man's disobedience. It was not until Jesus came to earth and reclaimed that authority through His death and payment of sin that man could stand against the power of Satan. "For it pleased the Father that in Him all the fullness should dwell, and by Him to reconcile all things to Himself, by Him, whether things on earth or things in heaven, having made peace through the blood of His cross."[3]

GOD ENTRUSTS MAN WITH AUTHORITY

God made a very calculated risk when He decided not to exercise full authority over the earth. He refused to require His children to love Him. God is ultimately responsible for what happens on Planet Earth, but He is not to blame for all that happens, because of man's free will. Unless man exercises his authority to prevent Satan's attack, Satan will exercise his right to steal, kill, and destroy.

There are other things that happen on earth that are a result of man exercising the authority God entrusts to him. We are here to enforce the covenants, what God and Jesus have spoken on the earth. This is done through inter-cessory prayer. God is looking for those He can partner with to accomplish what He wants to do on the earth. "For the eyes of the LORD run to and fro throughout the whole earth, to show Himself strong on behalf of those whose heart is loyal to Him."[4] "So I sought for a man among them who would make a wall, and stand in the gap before Me on behalf of the land, that I should not destroy it; but I found no one."[5] This verse is not just a reference to prayer; it is also an admonition that believers are to stand for righteousness in the culture so that those in that culture will not be destroyed for their sins.

Evil still exists on the earth through Satan, but God has given the *lease* to earth back to us through the blood covenant of Jesus. However, it must be exer-cised to see the manifestation of the covenant promises. God is waiting on His people to exercise our authority to bring these things into being. One of Jesus's last instructions to the disciples related to His authority and His passing of that authority to those of us on earth: "And Jesus came and spoke to them, saying, 'All authority has been given to Me in heaven and on earth. Go therefore and make disciples of all the nations, baptizing them in the name of the Father and of the Son and of the Holy Spirit, teaching them to observe all things that I have commanded you; and lo, I am with you always, even to the end of the age.'"[6]

We are to enforce and teach what Jesus has instructed us to do and what He has said. Jesus came to defeat the works of the enemy.[7] *Our role is to enforce His will through prayer by claiming His promises and defeating the works of the enemy.* We too are called to defeat the works of the enemy on earth. We do not have to ask what His will is in many situations, because He has already stated His will. As God's representatives, we enforce His will through interces-sory prayer, which activates the covenantal blessings of God on earth.

Intercession involves a legal appeal process in heaven by those (you and me) who are interceding for a ruling to be enforced by the landlord (God) for what has already been stated (God's covenant promises). What are some of God's covenant promises? Anything that Jesus modeled while He was on earth can be expected to be realized through us, because He said that the works He did would also be done by us. These include a right to physical provision, health, peace, and a life without fear.

Jesus lived as a man

While He was here on earth, Jesus lived with the same limitations that we live with. However, He appropriated what He needed on earth through His heavenly Father. He always did what He saw the Father doing through Him. He carried out the will of the Father. We are called to do the same. That is how His kingdom is manifested on the earth through each son and daughter. This is why it is so important that we each have a prayer life devoted to praying what we see the Father wanting to pray through us.[8] Jesus is our high priest and intercessor before the Father to enforce His covenants when we pray.[9]

As change agents, we must make this prayer discipline part of our strategy to displace principalities over cultural mountains and repel Satan's activity in our own lives. We have been given the *power of attorney* on earth to act on His behalf until He returns.

Jesus said we have the keys to release His will upon the earth in matters of which He has already spoken. "And I will give you the keys of the kingdom of heaven, and whatever you bind on earth will be bound in heaven, and whatever you loose on earth will be loosed in heaven."[10]

Death and life are in the power of the tongue

Another area we can exercise authority in is our words. God *spoke* the world into existence. God is known as *God the Word* and *Jesus the Word*. "For He spoke, and it was done; He commanded, and it stood fast."[11] When God told Moses to speak to the rock, He was telling Moses to move in the same dimension as God—through the spoken word. When you pray, pray aloud. This allows your words to be heard by principalities and spirits, and as you speak the words, they will be imprinted in your brain. When you read the Word, read it aloud. There is power in the spoken Word of God. In the New Testament, Jesus tells us to speak to the mountain: "For assuredly, I say to you, whoever says to this mountain, 'Be removed and be cast into the sea,' and does not doubt in his heart, but believes that those things he says will come to pass, he will have whatever he says. Therefore I say to you, whatever things you ask when you pray, believe that you receive them, and you will have them."[12]

One time God led me to speak to a mountain of books in my basement and tell them to "leave!" That afternoon I received an order for three hundred books from a ministry I had no prior relationship with, and this was on a Saturday! I have other friends who have been led by the Holy Spirit to do similar things. The key is to be led by the Holy Spirit to use the authority He gives us. God is not a genie in a bottle. We are led as we have fellowship with His Son and are directed by His Spirit in us. There IS power in your words.[13] Faith is what activates the power of God on the earth.

Do you need to see God move on your behalf? Find out what He said in His Word, His covenant, and begin to pray and agree with God that whatever has been done in heaven will be done on earth. Speak aloud what you need God to do on your behalf. Declare His covenant over your situation. As you do this, you will begin to see your prayers manifested in the physical realm.

Each of us should pray, "Cause me to hear Your lovingkindness in the morning, for in You do I trust; cause me to know the way in which I should walk, for I lift up my soul to You."[14]

UNDERSTANDING YOUR RESPONSIBILITY

When the children of Israel committed the grievous sin of making the golden calf for an idol, Moses had to play a new role. That role was priest. He stood in the gap on behalf of the people in order to *stay the execution* of his own people. God was very angry and was going to wipe them off the planet, just as He did in the time of Noah. Sometimes God is looking for an individual to stand in the gap for a situation that requires judgment, which can only be averted by one who is willing to stand on behalf of the offender. Moses was willing to risk his own salvation to thwart a mass judgment. "Now it came to pass on the next day that Moses said to the people, 'You have committed a great sin. So now I will go up to the LORD; perhaps I can make atonement for your sin.' Then Moses returned to the LORD and said, 'Oh, these people have committed a great sin, and have made for themselves a god of gold! Yet now, if You will forgive their sin—but if not, I pray, blot me out of Your book which You have written.'"[15]

Would you be willing to lose your own salvation for the benefit of another? What an amazing level of sacrifice on behalf of the people by Moses. His intercession kept the people from being destroyed. It did not forgive their sin, but it did give them time to repent themselves. This is known as *identificational confession*, when one person pleads before the throne on behalf of another. We identify with and confess before God the corporate sins of one's nation, people, church, or family.

Every marketplace believer has a calling to be both king and priest. Like Melchizedek who was also a king and priest, we too are called to both assignments.[16] Moses operated as both a king and priest. He operated as a king as the leader of an entire nation. His role as a king was a very public one with the people. But he also operated as priest, going before God and interceding on behalf of the people. This does not mean we are called to vocational *priestly* pastorate ministry; it means we are to intercede for those we serve. We are called to lay down our lives for that worker next to us in the cubicle, that CEO who operates at the top of your cultural mountain, or that government leader who wants to change your values in your state or nation. We are called to rebuild the ancient ruins.[17]

JESUS IS OUR PRIESTLY ADVOCATE

Jesus is our intercessor before His heavenly Father. The word *intercessor* comes from the phrase *to intercede*—to intervene or mediate on behalf of another. It is a higher form of prayer on behalf of others. When Jesus was on the cross, He said, "Forgive them, for they do not know what they do."[18] He became sin for us and the payment for our sins. "Seeing then that we have a great High

Priest who has passed through the heavens, Jesus the Son of God, let us hold fast our confession. For we do not have a High Priest who cannot sympathize with our weaknesses, but was in all points tempted as we are, yet without sin. Let us therefore come boldly to the throne of grace, that we may obtain mercy and find grace to help in time of need. For every high priest taken from among men is appointed for men in things pertaining to God, that he may offer both gifts and sacrifices for sins."[19]

When Jesus, the world's greatest change agent, was in the Garden of Gethsemane, He asked the disciples to pray with Him and to intercede on His behalf, but they fell asleep. In many ways this is a picture of the marketplace church. We want to see victories without doing the intercessory work.

The tabernacle was a movable house of worship that involved three distinct sections—the outer court, the inner court, and the holy of holies. The ark of the covenant housed the Ten Commandments.

The outer court was for the offering of public sacrifices by the priests for Israel. It was a very public form of ministry unto the Lord. Our work lives are our outer court expression. It is where we work unto the Lord in our calling. It is where people see and experience what we do. It is where we publicly offer what we have to the Lord through the gifting and calling upon our lives.

The inner court was called the holy place. The altar of incense was placed in the inner room of the tabernacle, the holy of holies, and was located directly in front of the ark of the covenant, where God's presence resided. A veil at the entrance of the holy of holies separated the holy of holies from the rest of the tabernacle. Once a year the high priest went into the holy of holies to atone for the sins of the nation of Israel. Our spiritual walk with God is about living in the inner court with God as opposed to the outer court of performance, posturing, and striving. It is there that we carry out our responsibility as intercessors for others.

Oswald Chambers explains:

> In intercession you bring the person, or the circumstance that impinges on you before God until you are moved by His attitude towards that person or circumstance. Intercession means filling up "that which is behind the afflictions of Christ," and that is why there are so few intercessors. Intercession is put on the line of—"Put yourself in his place." Never! Try to put yourself in God's place.[20]

The apostle Paul understood what it meant to intercede sacrificially for those he was called to minister to: "For I could wish that I myself were accursed and cut off and banished from Christ for the sake of my brethren and instead of them, my natural kinsmen and my fellow countrymen. For they are Israelites, and to them belong God's adoption [as a nation] and the glorious Presence

(Shekinah). With them were the special covenants made, to them was the Law given. To them [the temple] worship was revealed and [God's own] promises announced."[21]

Paul was willing to stand in the gap for others as their ambassador. Paul was more than a change agent. He understood he had to sacrifice his life for others in order for them to receive from God. Are you prepared to sacrifice on behalf of those God has called you to impact for His name? It starts in the inner court.

When Jesus died on the cross and took His last breath, the veil of the temple was torn.[22] There was no longer a barrier to God. He became the bridge. And now He is our high priest who intercedes on our behalf.

If we are weak in prayer, the strongman will come into our homes and our workplaces and take what is rightfully ours.[23] A tree best illustrates the outer court and the inner court of our lives. The tree limbs represent the outer court; intercession represents the roots. The fruit represents the degree of abiding in the vine. Intercession in the inner court allows the roots of our tree to go deep into the soil so that we can withstand the winds that are sure to come. Our tree can only grow bigger if we have a root system to support it. The more influence we have, the greater the storms and the greater the need for deeper roots.

God will lead and be with each of us in our times of intercession. "Likewise the Spirit also helps in our weaknesses. For we do not know what we should pray for as we ought, but the Spirit Himself makes intercession for us with groanings which cannot be uttered. Now He who searches the hearts knows what the mind of the Spirit is, because He makes intercession for the saints according to the will of God."[24]

Intercession is not substitution for sin. Only Jesus, the Son of God qualifies to pay for sin. However, the intercession so identifies the intercessor with the suffering that it gives him a prevailing place with God. He moves the heart of God. He can even cause Him to change His mind, as in the case of Moses and the people of Israel.

The inner court represents the work you and I must do in intercession on behalf of those we are called to serve. We fight the spiritual battle on behalf of those who would never make it without our intercession. When I came to an awareness of this fact, I was very convicted of my own prayerlessness for the marketplace I am called to serve. I realized I had spent much time during my years of ministry operating from the outer court. I asked God to help me learn to be His intercessor for those I am called to redeem. If we are going to reshape cultural mountains, it will only happen if we do our inner court ministry of intercession as a priest to our marketplace.

God asks us if we are willing to stand in the gap for another. Do you need to stand in the gap for a spouse, a coworker, a politician, a business leader, a city leader? Why not identify now whom God may call you to intercede for on their behalf.

Our commitment to intercession allows us to accomplish three things:

1. Intercession allows us to internalize and deepen our ownership of the assignment.

2. Intercession forces us to sit quietly before God to clarify what we are called to.

3. Intercession catalyzes the actions needed for fulfillment of the vision by depending on the Holy Spirit to reveal our action steps.

When Nehemiah heard that the wall in Jerusalem had been torn down, it affected him at a passionate heart level. He mourned along with his people. He fasted and prayed for several days in an effort to gain understanding of what he was to do. He was led to appeal to his king to go and repair the wall. He developed a detailed plan from his prayer time and his professional expertise. He accomplished the task by being aware of the enemy's schemes to thwart his efforts by having his men work with one hand on the wall and a weapon to defend themselves in the other.

We cannot influence culture through the acquisition of worldly power or through a political spirit. This is the world's way of influence. This would be seeking to use the flesh to bring about a spiritual change, which is contradictory to the nature of God.

Are you called to reclaim a cultural mountain as a change agent? Are you called to a specific group of people? If so, make intercession a strategic part of your focus to impact that cultural mountain. Interceding for those who control the mountain is important if you expect to gain victory.

QUESTIONS FOR REFLECTION

1. We lost authority in the Garden of Eden. How are we to reclaim it?

2. Why do we see evil on the earth? What has man failed to do?

3. Explain the concept of identificational confession and its relevance for you and your calling as a change agent.

4. Name the three reasons prayer must be a vital part of our ability to change culture.

Chapter 11

GET READY TO EXPERIENCE
SPIRITUAL WARFARE

For we do not wrestle against flesh and blood, but against princi-
palities, against powers, against the rulers of the darkness of this age,
against spiritual hosts of wickedness in the heavenly places.
—Ephesians 6:12

In C. S. Lewis's book *The Screwtape Letters*, Screwtape writes to his nephew Wormwood, "I wonder if you should ask me whether it is essential to keep the patient in ignorance of your own existence. That question, at least for the present phase of the struggle, has been answered for us by the High Command. Our policy, for the moment, is to conceal ourselves."[1] In the front of the book C. S. Lewis said, "There are two mistakes the church makes when dealing with the devil: to blame everything on him or to blame nothing on him."[2] Research by the Barna Group found that only 26 percent of the general population believe that Satan is a real spiritual being. Belief in the personhood of Satan appears to be gradually dissipating.[3] Only 52 percent of born-again Christians expressed belief that Satan was real.[4] It's no wonder we have a weak church.

Satan wants to kill you and your destiny, which is rooted in God. "Be sober, be vigilant; because your adversary the devil walks about like a roaring lion, seeking whom he may devour."[5] He tried to kill Moses at birth and tried to shut his mouth through a stuttering spirit. He tried to kill Jesus at birth and then tempted Him during His forty-day fast. He tries to kill all babies through abortion.

If he cannot kill at birth, he will try to kill your destiny through childhood wounds. Whether we are rejected as children through a lack of emotional affirmation, sexually abused, or loved only for our performance, our lives become defined by the wounds we receive when we are young. Satan tries to immobilize humans by wounding them, so they spend a lifetime trying to cope with the consequences created by their wound. This is how generational strongholds take root in our lives. Because of childhood wounds, we develop a belief system designed to meet our needs *outside* God, and we protect ourselves from getting hurt by setting up defense mechanisms.

Satan will always attack you in the place of your spiritual inheritance. Israel was attacked because of their land—the Promised Land from God. Abraham was attacked in his relationships, because a people more numerous than the sands in the desert would come through him. That is why Abraham let his nephew Lot choose the land he was to go to. Jesus was tempted by Satan to receive power instead of laying His life down for the salvation for mankind. Entrepreneurs are attacked by choosing *good* and a consumptive lifestyle versus *God*. Their inheritance lies in creating businesses to create wealth to establish God's kingdom on earth. I've always been attacked in the area of close relationships because my inheritance is in relationships. Each of us must have a heightened awareness of how Satan will seek to derail our destinies and develop a greater sensitivity to Satan's ploys.

In my own journey I discovered early wounds that kept me from an intimate relationship with my heavenly Father and those close to me. Satan tried to shut me down early in childhood, by shutting down my emotions and verbal ability. Over many years God showed me where the early wounds originated in order for me to become healed from those wounds. These wounds developed a stronghold of shame, rejection, insecurity, fear, and control, which led to an inability to share at a heart level. As healing took place, Satan could no longer make me believe a lie about myself, and I was able to enter into my destiny.

We must recognize the influence the enemy has had in our lives through generational iniquity. In many cases we may need to revisit early childhood wounds in order to gain healing and victory in our lives where the sins of our fathers may have gained an entry point to our lives. It may require trained counselors to help us. However, we cannot remain a victim to these wounds once we become aware they are influencing us. Christ paid the price for any sins brought into our life, whether through us or our parents. It is our job to stop it from passing to other generations.

The apostle Paul understood the spiritual warfare that we are all in, no matter how spiritual we are. He describes this in Romans 7:15: "For what I will to do, that I do not practice; but what I hate, that I do." When he wrote these words, he had been in the faith twenty years!

In Revelation 12 we find the three primary strategies that Satan employs against humans. He tries to kill,[6] deceive,[7] and accuse.[8] Most of the time he uses other humans to do it. Take a moment and think about these three areas. Think about the times you have felt you were at the point of great despair. Think about the times when you were so totally deceived about God. Beware of the strategies of the enemy to kill, deceive, accuse, and destroy you, your relationships with others, and, most importantly, your relationship with God.

The apostle Paul speaks of strongholds in 2 Corinthians 10:4–6: "For the weapons of our warfare are not carnal but mighty in God for pulling down strongholds, casting down arguments and every high thing that exalts itself against the knowledge of God, bringing every thought into captivity to the obedience of Christ, and being ready to punish all disobedience when your obedience is fulfilled." Although Satan is the source of these strongholds, God's grace will enable us to see the consequences of our own behavior and motivate us to find the root causes. We are still responsible for the behavior our stronghold causes and must repent of it. Jesus said the truth will set us free. As you learn the truth about your childhood wounds, God will provide healing that allows you to move forward with Him in your relationship with God and those close to you. Your behavior must begin to change to align with the truth.

Jesus Came to Redeem All That Was Lost

There is an interesting story in Luke 10 that describes one of the first examples of Jesus sending out the seventy as part of His discipling process. He had trained them in spiritual warfare and equipped them with the tools to fight the schemes of the enemy. Listen to their report back to Jesus after their adventures in kingdom life: "Then the seventy returned with joy, saying, 'Lord, even the demons are subject to us in Your name.' And He said to them, 'I saw Satan fall like lightning from heaven. Behold, I give you the authority to trample on serpents and scorpions, and over all the power of the enemy, and nothing shall by any means hurt you. Nevertheless do not rejoice in this, that the spirits are subject to you, but rather rejoice because your names are written in heaven.'"[9] I want you to notice that Jesus saw what happened in the spiritual dimension when they used the authority He had given them. They were able to defeat the work of the enemy through the authority entrusted to them.

Nehemiah is a great example of a marketplace change agent who had an assignment from God to rebuild the wall of Jerusalem. Political leaders opposed to the work of God opposed Nehemiah at every turn. It is a lesson of how we must deal with spiritual forces that come against us and want to keep us from fulfilling our God-appointed assignments. In Nehemiah's case you find spirits of accusation, discouragement, deception, and lying being used against Nehemiah in hopes of killing the project. "Now it happened, when Sanballat, Tobiah, the Arabs, the Ammonites, and the Ashdodites heard that the walls of Jerusalem were being restored and the gaps were beginning to be closed, that they became very angry, and all of them conspired together to come and attack Jerusalem and create confusion. Nevertheless we made our prayer to our God, and because of them we set a watch against them day and night."[10]

One particular verse sums up Nehemiah's approach to spiritual warfare, and we can all apply this approach in our lives: "Those who built on the wall, and those who carried burdens, loaded themselves so that with one hand they worked at construction, and with the other held a weapon. Every one of the builders had his sword girded at his side as he built."[11] We are to keep the spiritual weapons of warfare close to our vest as we are in the battle. That means being in prayer, using the authority He has given us, and remaining in constant awareness of the enemy's attempts to destroy us and our work. If we operate from a place of disbelief or casualness toward spiritual warfare, we are sure to be taken out by him.

The problem for many in the body of Christ today is that we live as if we are not living in a war. We live more like tourists passing through to our destination of heaven. We are not concerned about the casualties of this war, only getting to our final destination as pain-free as possible. John Piper once said, "You will not know what prayer is for until you know that life is war."[12] Prayer is the tool of this warfare.

GOD FIGHTS FOR US THROUGH HIS PEOPLE

One night I received a particular hateful e-mail from someone close to me. It brought me very low. I could feel Satan trying to bring me into despair through a spirit of accusation. Within five minutes of receiving that e-mail, I got a phone call from a prayer group meeting in Chicago. They had never called me before. They said, "The Lord prompted us that you were going through something very difficult, so we felt we should call and pray for you." They shared a scripture verse that spoke directly to my situation.

I was reminded of a verse from Isaiah that describes God's ability to fight off any weapons or words that are formed against us if we are in the will of God: "No weapon formed against you shall prosper, and every tongue which rises against you in judgment you shall condemn."[13] When people speak against us with lies, and there is agreement with others, that is a curse being spoken against us. Our response must be to forgive them and pray for them. That is our defense.

The greater the calling, the greater warfare and suffering you will experience, but there will be greater revelation of God as well. The apostle Paul understood that his thorn in his flesh was a direct result of the greater call and revelation he was experiencing. "And lest I should be exalted above measure by the abundance of the revelations, a thorn in the flesh was given to me, a messenger of Satan to buffet me, lest I be exalted above measure."[14]

The greater the influence, the greater the warfare. There is a target on the back of anyone who is seeking to impact the kingdom of darkness for the kingdom of light. I am convinced there are many posters in hell with my picture on it that read: "Wanted: Os Hillman, Dead or Alive." I have inflicted serious damage to the kingdom of darkness for the last fifteen years, and

I believe that Satan's measured assaults have intensified to the very core of what is most important to me. He may have won some battles, but he won't win the war!

QUESTIONS FOR REFLECTION

1. Have you ever considered the role spiritual warfare plays in your spiritual journey? If not, why?

2. Jesus was tempted to negotiate with the devil. In what ways might the devil tempt you to negotiate?

3. Where are the greatest temptations for you, and how might you fight the battle against them?

RECLAIMING THE SEVEN MOUNTAINS OF CULTURE

Chapter 12

CHANGE AGENTS ARE PROBLEM SOLVERS

They went out and immediately got into the boat, and that night they caught nothing. But when the morning had now come, Jesus stood on the shore; yet the disciples did not know that it was Jesus. Then Jesus said to them, "Children, have you any food?" They answered him, "No." And He said to them, "Cast the net on the right side of the boat, and you will find some." So they cast, and now they were not able to draw it in because of the multitude of fish.
—JOHN 21:3–6

JESUS MODELED A philosophy that loved people into the kingdom by accepting them where they were and solving their core problem. He often concluded His encounter with the words "Now, go and sin no more." Many Christians withhold blessing until they see a change in a person's life. Jesus shocked His disciples by speaking to the Samaritan woman at the well.[1] That would be like the most conservative Christian hanging out with and blessing the most liberal politician. This encounter led to many coming to faith in Jesus. The leaders of the city invited Jesus to stay and hang out with them, and He did.[2]

How Did Jesus Become the Ultimate Change Agent in Culture?

Most efforts to change culture (even within conservative Christianity) lead to manipulation, domination, and control. When God told the Israelites in Deuteronomy 8 that they would be the head and not the tail, this would be the *fruit of their obedience* by fulfilling the first and greatest command to love and obey God. It was not a goal to try and achieve dominion in culture. Rather, it was the fruit of their obedience that would influence culture.

Jesus came to earth to solve a problem:

1. To be payment for sin and to extend an invitation to salvation through His death on the cross[3]

2. To reclaim all that was lost in the garden[4] and to reestablish His kingdom on earth[5] by giving man authority as His representative[6]

Jesus became a problem solver by listening to and doing the will of the Father. He only solved problems the Father told Him to solve—healing the sick, multiplying five loaves and two fish, telling Peter to cast his net on the other side of the boat, and so on. Jesus solved problems in people's lives. The more He did this, the more His reputation spread and the more influence He had among the people and the culture. His core method was through extravagant servant leadership and being led by His Father as a son. He lived to please the Father. This is the model we are to emulate. The more we are like Jesus, the more influence we will have. It will happen naturally.

We live in a very transactional culture. Jesus, often only having short times of personal encounters, engaged through relationship before moving to transaction. He built a level of trust by serving the person first. This does not mean that Jesus did not confront issues that needed to be confronted. It is worth noting that Jesus got the angriest at the religious community—those selling doves in the temple and the Pharisees for their hypocritical living. He seemed to address sinners as people who didn't know better. We need to stop getting so upset with unbelievers who act like unbelievers. We should *expect* ungodly behavior from sinners, but there should be a higher standard among those of us who know the truth.

Mother Teresa gained an international voice for the poor and down-and-outs of society by serving them. I'll never forget the speech of this ninety-pound woman standing before the United Nations rebuking them for their failure to care for the poor.[7]

There is a time to stand as God's representative once you've earned the right to speak. The same could be said for South Africa's Nelson Mandela, who spoke words of forgiveness and reconciliation to a people who had been ill-treated. No one had been more ill-treated than he after spending twenty-seven years in prison. That became his authority to solve a major problem in his country.

Change agents are men and women who solve societal problems. Young David went from delivering lunch to delivering a nation by solving a major problem for King Saul when he volunteered to fight Goliath. There have been many such change agents in history.

Daniel is a perfect example of a change agent in government who affected change at the highest level as a result of his relationship with God. God worked through Daniel in visions and dreams. Daniel was also very good at what he did. "And in all matters of wisdom and understanding about which the king examined them, he found them ten times better than all the magicians and astrologers who were in all his realm."[8] Are you ten times better at your job than other workers? If we are going to change culture through the marketplace, we must be better than our ungodly counterparts. Daniel was also a part of a network of other believers. Hananiah, Mishael, and Azariah (later renamed Shadrach, Meshach, and Abed-nego) were prayer and covenant partners.

All four of their lives were threatened when King Nebuchadnezzar threatened to kill all the magicians, including Daniel and his friends if they were not able to interpret the king's dream.[9] When Daniel heard of the death decree, he asked for more time. He immediately went to his "network" to pray and seek God's mind on the matter. Daniel acknowledged that God indeed answers prayer when he proclaimed, "He reveals deep and secret things; He knows what is in the darkness, and light dwells with Him."[10] And God answered and saved Daniel and his friends; the ungodly magicians were also saved.

As a result of Daniel solving the king's problem, not only were his and others' lives spared, but also he and his friends were elevated and gained more influence in the government. This same scene happened a few more times with two other administrations that both Daniel and his friends were serving. Their faith was tested to live out an absolute faith that did not compromise. They also used wisdom in knowing how to relate to their superiors without condemning but providing solutions to their superior's problem. God raised up Pharaoh in order to demonstrate His power to him, his nation, and the people of Israel.[11] This is how we change culture. We gain influence by being better and by providing solutions to culture's leaders and their problems.

Johannes Gutenberg was a German goldsmith and inventor best known for inventing the Gutenberg press in 1455. He was a Christian inventor. God gave him the skill to create what may well be the most important invention of all time, when you measure the impact of his invention on culture. Listen to the passion of this man God used to change the world through his invention:

> Religious truth is imprisoned in a small number of manuscript books which confine instead of spread the public treasure. Let us break the seal which seals up holy things and give wings to Truth in order that she may win every soul that comes into the world by her word no longer written at great expense by hands easily palsied, but multiplied like the wind by an untiring machine.[12]

It appears that some people questioned the value of his invention, which is nothing new for those whose ideas often have significant impact on the world. But Gutenberg understood the value of the gift God had allowed him to create, and he stated:

> Yes, it is a press, certainly, but a press from which shall flow in inexhaustible streams the most abundant and most marvelous liquor that

has ever flowed to relieve the thirst of men. Through it, God will spread His Word; a spring of truth shall flow from it; like a new star it shall scatter the darkness of ignorance and become a cause of light hitherto-fore unknown to shine among men.[13]

I find the timing of Gutenberg's invention extraordinary. It seems God pre-ordained this invention for what was to come fifty-seven years later. That would be the year 1517, when Martin Luther would nail his ninety-five theses to the Wittenberg door that would usher in the Protestant Reformation. It would be Gutenberg's press that would print and circulate Luther's writings throughout Europe and print a Bible in their native language of German. Truly, this was God's invention for man but created by a businessman.

No other invention has had as great an impact on mankind as the printing press. The Word of God began to reach the common man for the first time because of his press.

Billy Graham was recently asked where he saw God moving today. "Back when we did the big crusades in football stadiums and arenas, the Holy Spirit was really moving—and people were coming to Christ as we preached the Word of God. But today, I sense something different is happening. I see evidence that the Holy Spirit is working in a new way. He's moving through people where they work and through one-on-one relationships to accomplish great things. They are demonstrating God's love to those around them, not just with words, but in deed."[14]

Today we live in a culture that wants to *see* what you are, not *know* what you say you are. They want to see if you care about culture, not just want to change it to the way you think it should be.

George Washington Carver Solved a Problem for Farmers

I think of George Washington Carver, who was born during the height of racial discrimination in America. He became a Christian early in his life and had an inventive mind. The southern farmers were suffering from a land that had been overused by the planting of cotton. Carver encouraged them to plant peanuts and sweet potatoes.

However, the market was too weak for these crops, and Carver was severely persecuted for encouraging farmers to make such a drastic change in what they planted due to lack of demand. Carver went into the fields early in the morning and cried out to God: "God, why did you make the peanut?" At the age of sixty-three he wrote: "Man, who needed a purpose, a mission, to keep him alive, had one. He could be…God's coworker.…My purpose alone must be God's purpose.…As I worked on projects which fulfilled a real human need, forces were working through me which amazed me. I would often go to sleep with an apparently insoluble problem. When I woke the answer was there."[15]

Over time God answered that prayer with more than three hundred invented products that came from the peanut and one hundred from the sweet potato. Carver was credited for reviving the southern economy. Presidents confided in him, and Henry Ford wanted him to work for him. He refused and continued to fulfill his calling as a change agent and problem solver through invention.[16]

Transforming a Cultural Mountain From the Ground Up

Rarely do I find a story that so demonstrates what it means to influence a cultural mountain as the story of Lynne Ruhl. In the early eighties her seven-year-old daughter participated in gymnastics, just as most American children do at one time or another. However, Lynne's daughter showed particular promise, according to some competitive gymnastics coaches. She was invited to put her daughter in a competitive gymnastics program that would require her to train for eleven hours a week.

Lynne's first thought was, "I need to get to know anyone who is going to have eleven hours of my daughter's life each week." So she visited with the gym that wanted her to participate. What she found deeply disturbed her. She learned that the environment of competitive gymnastics was so damaging to young girls that she could not let her daughter participate. The girls were ridiculed, shamed, and treated like robots. The environment fostered very negative and competitive attitudes between the gymnasts. She hunted for other gyms that did not model such a culture. However, she could not find one.

Her only answer was to buy a gym. After consulting with her husband, they found a gym that they felt they could purchase. It was in disrepair, but they felt it was the one they were to buy. However, something happened just before she was to finalize the deal that prevented the purchase. This led to her being retained to develop the culture within the very gym they felt they were to be involved with. While at the time this was seen as a devastating roadblock, it was a divine interruption to her plans.

Lynne identified a trainer named Mary Lee Tracy who she felt could understand and implement a healthy culture that valued the girls and built up their self-esteem. Lynne prayed with the girls and invested into their lives emotionally and spiritually. She developed a detailed program for the girls. Mary Lee Tracy was not a follower of Christ at the time and "sort of put up with me," as Lynne says. However, the tragic death of Lynne's brother led to Mary Lee, along with fifteen others, accepting Christ at the funeral. Mary Lee would now not only embrace the emotional but also the spiritual culture Lynne was creating for the Cincinnati Gymnastics Academy.

It took six full years before culture changed for the now two hundred girls who were enrolled in her training program. The real evidence that they not only changed a culture but were also extremely successful as a result was two of their girls—Amanda Borden and Jaycie Phelps—making the 1996 US Olympic Women Gymnastics team and winning the gold medal for team combined exercises for the United States, the first ever for a US Women's Olympic gymnastics program.

The notoriety and news value that this created put Lynne's gym on the national map for Olympic gymnast's training. She would be called upon to speak and explain why changing the culture in training young girls was so vital, primarily for the health of the girls but also to lead to a successful program. The Olympic trainers listened, and Cincinnati Gymnastics Academy became a model for training Olympic gymnasts. Gymnastic organizations from around the world began to send their coaches to Lynne's gym to learn her secret. The gym became known as the "hospital" for competitive gymnasts. Head coach Mary Lee Tracy became the assistant coach for the 1996 and 2000 US Olympic Women Gymnastics teams.

Truly, Lynne and her team had transformed a cultural mountain in a highly developed and competitive industry.

Change Agent at Hewlett Packard

We host regular teleseminars on the topic of the seven cultural mountains. After one of these calls I received the following testimony from a businessman from Hewlett Packard.

> Os, this is the first time I have heard about the seven mountains message. I thought before this meeting it was just certain Christians trying to impose their morals on the country, but after listening to the discussion, you have changed my mind. Now I realize the enemy has lied to me and pretty much told me I can't change all of society. With God's help I can influence my sphere with help of my brothers and sisters. But after the last three years, now I see what God is preparing me to do.
>
> > We started the HP Christian Fellowship to bring us together as one (as described in the call).
> >
> > Then I submitted to management through our VP of sales a proposal to change our corporate culture (problem-solving). I even proposed EDS should be more like HP.
> >
> > One year later we were merged with HP (what a surprise or was it a prophecy).

Now just last month our CEO was released from HP and our Christian Fellowship is meeting weekly in intercessory prayer for selection of our new CEO and wisdom for our board. We are boldly proclaiming, "Lord, give us your selection for CEO, a strong Christian believer."

Now, the Lord is speaking to me about corporate culture and influence. Then I heard this seminar, and I feel led by the Lord to move into a bigger position of influence inside HP.

Thank you for the seminar. My eyes have been opened to the fact that our mission in this earth is to give God the glory (like Daniel) by being problem-solvers, prophets, and influencers in this world.
Dale

Rick Warren, pastor and author of *The Purpose-Driven Life*, says change only happens when we solve problems: "I'm looking for a second reformation. The first reformation of the church 500 years ago was about beliefs. This one is going to be about behavior. The first one was about creeds. This one is going to be about deeds. It is not going to be about what the church believes, but about what the church is doing."[17]

QUESTIONS FOR REFLECTION

1. In this chapter we featured many men and women who impacted culture significantly. What were some of the common denominators?

2. Cite some problems that were solved through the change agent's life.

3. What are two things you gained from this chapter you will apply to your own life?

Chapter 13

CHANGE HAPPENS WHEN A SMALL NUMBER OF CHANGE AGENTS BAND TOGETHER

I do not pray for these alone, but also for those who will believe in Me through their word; that they all may be one, as You, Father, are in Me, and I in You; that they also may be one in Us, that the world may believe that You sent Me.
—JOHN 17:20–21

REAL CHANGE HAPPENS when networks band together for change. Changing culture rarely happens without the cooperation among other like-minded change agents pooling their resources and influence capital to make change. This is what happened in the first Reformation. The role of the nobility in Germany was crucial to the success of the Reformation. Their economic and political capital made the difference. Luther would likely have been executed if Frederick of Wise had not removed him and taken him to Wartburg Castle after the Edict of Worms.

James Hunter states, "The key actor in history is not individual genius but rather the network, and the new institutions that are created out of those networks. This is where...cultural change is produced. World-changing is most intense when the networks of elites and the institutions they lead overlap."[1]

WILLIAM WILBERFORCE AND THE CLAPHAM GROUP

William Wilberforce was a British politician and philanthropist who lived in the late 1700s and was a leader of the movement to abolish the slave trade. A native of Hull, Yorkshire, he began his political career in 1780 and became the independent Member of Parliament for Yorkshire (1784–1812) and a close friend of Prime Minister William Pitt the Younger. In 1785 he underwent a conversion experience and became an evangelical Christian, resulting in changes in his lifestyle and in his interest in reform. He was twenty-eight years old at the time and wondered whether he could stay in politics and remain a follower of Jesus Christ. His good friend John Newton, who was a converted slave trader and author of the famous hymn "Amazing Grace," convinced him to stay in politics to model his faith in the public sector. His life was dramatized in a 2007 movie production from Walden Media entitled *Amazing Grace*.

Wilberforce was part of a small band of influential leaders in England called the Clapham Group. Its members were chiefly prominent and wealthy evangelical Anglicans who shared common political views concerning the liberation of slaves, the abolition of the slave trade, and the reform of the penal system. The group's name originated from Clapham, then a village south of London (today part of southwest London), where both Wilberforce and Henry Thornton, the sect's two most influential leaders, resided and where many of the group's meetings were held. They were supported by Beilby Porteus, Bishop of London, who sympathized with many of their aims.

After many decades of work both in British society and in Parliament, the group saw their efforts rewarded with the final passage of the Slave Trade Act in 1807, banning the trade throughout the British Empire, and, after many further years of campaigning, the total emancipation of British slaves with the passing of the Slavery Abolition Act in 1833. They also campaigned vigorously for Britain to use its influence to eradicate slavery throughout the world. It was not a large group. It consisted of less than twenty leaders. However, these leaders were passionate about their faith, their causes and their commitment to them.

OPERATING THROUGH UNIFIED NETWORKS

In John 17 Jesus prayed the following prayer: "I do not pray for these alone, but also for those who will believe in Me through their word; that they all may be one, as You, Father, are in Me, and I in You; that they also may be one in Us, that the world may believe that You sent Me."[2] Notice the key phrases in this passage: "that they all may be one" and "that the world may believe." That is the fruit from standing together in unity for a common cause.

I have realized in my own calling that I can accomplish certain things through my obedience in my individual calling. However, when I align myself with others whereby my gifts and talents can be leveraged and I can support others' efforts, we together can multiply our fruit. I believe that is what Jesus is saying in this verse. I have entered a covenant relationship with others that allows me to do this in a very practical sense to walk together at a deeper relational and ministry level.

Jesus encouraged believers to be unified with one another for the common cause we are fighting for—the kingdom of God on earth. We don't lose our identity or our unique calling; we simply leverage it with other like-minded change agents. We become more effective and reach more people as a result. Our goal is to model this verse: "Let nothing be done through selfish ambition or conceit, but in lowliness of mind let each esteem others better than himself.

Let each of you look out not only for his own interests, but also for the interests of others."³

Here are more reasons Scripture tells us to join hands with others:

> How could one chase a thousand, and two put ten thousand to flight…
> —DEUTERONOMY 32:30

> Behold, how good and pleasant it is for brethren to dwell together in unity!
> —PSALM 133:1

> Five of you shall chase a hundred, and a hundred of you shall put ten thousand to flight; your enemies shall fall by the sword before you.
> —LEVITICUS 26:8

I want to encourage you to form your own network group. Do you have a vision to impact one or more of the cultural mountains? Identify those you can walk with and begin to relationally support one another to impact that mountain. You will be much more effective than trying to go it alone.

Below is a chart showing the six unique stages some of God's change agents went through to becoming His change agent in culture.

David's Six Stages

1. Divine circumstance	1. Anointed by Samuel; Goliath encounter
2. Character development	2. Fleeing Saul's sword
3. Isolation	3. Cave of Adullam
4. Personal cross	4. Betrayal by Saul; living under authority; refused deliverance
5. Problem solver	5. King of Israel; built temple through Solomon
6. Networks	6. David's mighty men

Moses's Six Stages

1. Divine circumstance	1. Saved at birth; burning bush
2. Character development	2. Forty years in the desert; most humble man on the earth
3. Isolation	3. Forty years in the desert
4. Personal cross	4. Willing to sacrifice salvation for the people; stood in the gap

5. Problem solver	5. Deliverance of Israel from slavery; birth of a nation
6. Networks	6. Twelve tribes

Joseph's Six Stages

1. Divine circumstance	1. Thrown in pit
2. Character development	2. Thirteen years of adversity
3. Isolation	3. Being a slave; prison
4. Personal cross	4. Four tests—betrayal; sexual; perseverance; stewardship
5. Problem solver	5. Dream; famine solution
6. Networks	6. Brothers; nation

Daniel's Six Stages

1. Divine circumstance	1. Exiled to Babylon
2. Character development	2. Served wicked king
3. Isolation	3. Isolation from family, nation
4. Personal cross	4. Interpret dream or die!
5. Problem solver	5. Tells and interprets dream
6. Networks	6. Shadrach, Meshach, Abed-nego

Esther's Six Stages

1. Divine circumstance	1. Chosen by the king
2. Character development	2. Leaving her family and people
3. Isolation	3. Isolated from her family
4. Personal cross	4. Chose to risk death
5. Problem solver	5. Saves a nation
6. Networks	6. Mordecai and her people (who prayed three days)

THE ROLE OF MARKETPLACE MINISTRIES

The role of marketplace ministries plays an integral role for the influence of culture. However, a major shift must take place if marketplace ministry organizations are going to have an impact on those they serve. We must move away from a narrow focus of the gospel of salvation to helping our people become change agents of culture. Salvation is important, but we must help constituents integrate their faith life into the way they go about their work life calling.

The International Christian Chamber of Commerce (ICCC) operates in more than one hundred nations and has been instrumental in impacting nations through economic initiatives at the highest governmental levels. This network of marketplace entrepreneurs has impacted nations through several nation-impacting initiatives. One is worth particular note.

ICCC network solves a problem for the Chinese government.

In the early 1990s, when the Berlin Wall came down, communism sealed the fall of the Soviet Union. At that point China began to realize that if communism was not successful in Russia, it would not be successful in China. As a result, China began to selectively allow what they called *socialistic capitalism* to emerge.

In an effort to break into China, Microsoft and IBM joined together, offering to provide a television series on entrepreneurship due to the high rate of unemployment in China. After lengthy deliberation, the government turned down their offer and then came to ICCC about a year later to ask ICCC to provide such a program. After seeking the Lord through their network of intercessors, the international leadership of ICCC made the decision to accept the challenge.

This initial series has been a phenomenal success. According to government figures, the series has now been viewed by more than forty million people, and government figures state that more than 1.2 million small businesses have started since the launch of the series in 1999. The government asked for the project to be expanded from ten episodes to thirty episodes. The second ten-part series, titled "Developing a Leading Business," has been completed.

This project has now expanded well beyond the borders of China. The series is also available in English, Chinese Mandarin, Russian, French, Spanish, Farsi, Turkish, and Arabic.[4]

Are you part of a network of believers seeking to impact one or more of the cultural mountains? If not, let me encourage you to join a network where you can serve and use your gifts and talents to impact culture for Jesus Christ.

QUESTIONS FOR REFLECTION

1. Why are networks important to changing culture?

2. What character changes are needed to allow God to use you?

3. Are there any areas that you have overlooked, as Moses did, that need to be addressed?

Chapter 14

RECLAIMING THE FAMILY MOUNTAIN

The thief does not come except to steal, and to kill, and to destroy
—JOHN 10:10

WHEN JOSHUA LED the Israelites across the Jordan to take possession of the land, he reminded them of the choice they must make: "Now therefore, fear the LORD, serve Him in sincerity and in truth, and put away the gods which your fathers served on the other side of the River and in Egypt. Serve the LORD! And if it seems evil to you to serve the LORD, choose for yourselves this day whom you will serve, whether the gods which your fathers served that were on the other side of the River, or the gods of the Amorites, in whose land you dwell. But as for me and my house, we will serve the LORD."[1]

WHAT IS FAMILY?

Family is an institution created by God. When the love and commitment of humans to the moral and biblical covenant of family are broken, it leads the way to almost every other societal problem imaginable.

The family mountain is where either the blessing or curse of God is passed on to successive generations. As the Israelites were getting ready to cross the Jordan and enter the Promised Land, Moses told them, "Behold, I set before you today a blessing and a curse: the blessing, if you obey the commandments of the LORD your God which I command you today; and the curse, if you do not obey the commandments of the LORD your God, but turn aside from the way which I command you today, to go after other gods which you have not known."[2]

We live today in a time when there is unprecedented breakdown in the family structure. Broken homes are major contributors to drug use, illegal sexual activity, inability to secure gainful employment, jail sentences, and many other problems facing society today. For so many, the choice that is being made is bringing the curse of God upon their lives and on the lives of their children and children's children. According to the National Institute of Mental

Health, about one in four adult Americans "suffer from a diagnosable mental disorder."[3] Satan doesn't want people to be emotionally healthy.

OUR FOUNDATION IS CRACKED

If the foundations are destroyed, what can the righteous do?
—PSALM 11:3

The family, like every cultural mountain, has been deeply affected by the current values of culture. In the last several decades we have seen marriage move from unions born from a basis of covenant (the way it used to be) to a basis of contract. But what do I mean when I say covenant?

Covenant is a unilateral, irrevocable, indissoluble commitment valid until death; it does not depend on the performance of either party. Covenant is represented all throughout the Bible. God made a covenant with Abraham, and circumcision was a physical sign of this covenant.

Jesus made a covenant promise with those He died for when He said, "I will never leave you nor forsake you."[4] This was His covenant promise to His bride. Despite His bride not fulfilling God's command to love and obey, Jesus loves His bride unconditionally. He models faithfulness in the face of unfaithfulness. Marriage is to reflect this level of commitment and faithfulness. Husbands are to model this toward their wives as a prophetic statement to the world.

Today, however, marriage is often lived out as a contract. A contract is between two parties that is based upon the performance of the parties involved. "As long as you love me and meet my needs, I will stay with you." When difficulties come, one partner decides it's too tough and abandons the marriage. It's easier to move on. The only remedy for divorce in the New Testament was the death of one partner. Marriage was for life. If adultery happened, the adulterer was stoned to death, not divorced! Contrary to what some believe, even adultery is not an acceptable reason for divorce. God often illustrated this in Scripture. Hosea the prophet was told to marry a prostitute as a prophetic picture of an unfaithful Israel. Hosea was to model faithfulness in the face of unfaithfulness as a prophetic picture of the heart of God. This is covenant love. It is not dependent on what the other party does or does not do.

The breaking of covenant in marriage is *the* source of the breakdown in the family today. This breakdown is the source of the bad fruit we are now experiencing worldwide, namely the four As, as Craig Hill of Family Foundations cites: adultery, addictions, abuse, and abandonment.[5] This fruit has further manifested into epidemic rates of divorce, gender confusion (gay and lesbian growth), and same-sex marriage.

The trend we are experiencing is a snowball that is gaining speed down the slippery slope of greater and greater aberrant behavior that will continue to grow until it finally destroys the nation, just as it happened in the Roman Empire. Without a tipping point in the opposite direction, *this is our fate!*

SATAN WANTS TO KILL YOU

We have established that Satan has attempted to kill human beings and families from the foundations of the world. When Moses was born, Satan tried to kill him, because he knew that Moses was a chosen leader to bring freedom to an entire people and nation. When Jesus was born, Satan tried to kill Him through King Herod. In America, Satan has killed unborn babies through abortion since 1973 due to the Supreme Court decision of *Roe v. Wade*. There have been more than forty-eight million abortions in this country since 1973.[6]

If Satan cannot physically kill, he will inflict heavy damage to children in order to enslave them to their wounds, which results in dysfunctional families and causes generational iniquity that keeps families from fulfilling their purposes on the earth from generation to generation. Divorce is one of the primary tools Satan uses to accomplish his destructive plans.

ONE MAN'S CHOICE

One family's choice stands out! Tim Tebow was the Heisman Trophy winner for 2007, recognized as the best college football player for that year. However, he became better known because of a controversial thirty-second commercial, sponsored by Focus on the Family, that ran during the Super Bowl in February 2010. The soft-message ad showed his mother describing the joy of having Tim as her son, but his birth almost did not happen. His parents lived as missionaries in the Philippines, with four children already. When his mother conceived at thirty-seven, the doctors said the baby was simply a mass of fetal tissue and that she needed to abort immediately. She rejected this counsel and moved forward with the pregnancy. Tim became a miracle baby.

Without any effort from Focus on the Family, the commercial suddenly became the most talked-about ad to run during the Super Bowl—by far! Hyped by some as the most controversial ad in Super Bowl history, women's groups and pro-abortion advocates protested to CBS, attacked the ad, and accused Focus on the Family of spewing hate. All this, even though until the actual airing during the first commercial break Sunday, no one in any of those groups had even seen the ad! There was incredible spiritual warfare over this ad, which had provoked much more attention than any normal Super Bowl ad. Curiosity grew enormously. The net result was that more than ninety-two million viewers watched the ad, and a million and a half people visited the Focus on the Family website to learn the full story about Tim's miracle birth and his parents' decision to reject the counsel of doctors to abort their pregnancy. Here was a great example of God allowing the media mountain and the family mountain to combine efforts to make a kingdom impact on the culture.

Orphans Lead the World

Dysfunction and abandonment has lifelong consequences in our lives. Recently I came across a little-known fact that demonstrates this dramatically.

In a book entitled *Creative Suffering,* Paul Tournier cites an article written by Dr. Pierre Rentchnick of Geneva, which appeared in a periodical in 1975 under the surprising title "Orphans Lead the World." He went on to explain: "When President Pompidou died, my colleague found himself wondering what might have been the political repercussions of disease in the case of other statesmen, such as for example President Roosevelt at the end of the war. So he set about reading the life-stories of the politicians who had had the greatest influence on the course of world history [not always positive influence]. He was soon struck by the astonishing discovery that all of them had been orphans!...

"Dr. Rentchnick compiled a list of them. It contained almost three hundred of the greatest names in history, from Alexander the Great and Julius Caesar, through Charles V, Cardinal Richelieu, Louis XIV, Robespierre, George Washington, Napoleon, Queen Victoria, Golda Meir, Hitler, Stalin, Lenin, to Eva Peron, Fidel Castro, and Houphouët-Boigny [to name just a few]. All of these leaders suffered in childhood from emotional deprivation. So we are giving lectures on how important it is for a child's development to have a father and a mother performing harmoniously together their respective roles toward him. And all at once we find that this is the very thing that those who have been most influential in world history have not had! From this surprising revelation my colleague deduced 'a new theory of genesis of the will to political power': the insecurity consequent upon emotional deprivation must have aroused in these children an exceptional will to power, which drove them into a career in politics with the aim of 'transforming the world' and succeeding in so far as they were able. Thus an unconscious will to power seems to play an important part in the lives of the most eminent men."[7]

Culture truly is shaped positively or negatively by early childhood experiences.

The Sexual Revolution

Playboy magazine ushered in a sexual revolution when the first issue came off the press in 1953. A new *anything goes* mind-set about sex was introduced. This sexual revolution gained more and more acceptance in the sixties and seventies, during the Woodstock generation and the Vietnam War. More and more people began living together, and premarital sex was no longer considered taboo but actually an accepted practice. Dysfunction in families began to grow as the numbers of divorces rose, unrestrained sexual liberties were expressed, and fathers abandoned their families, opening the door to sexual identities being confused.

As a result, near the turn of the century we began to see the gay lifestyle become legitimized in mainstream culture through two of the major mountains—arts and entertainment and media. When actress Ellen DeGeneres kissed another woman on a national television sitcom in 1997, it became a tipping point in culture. This led to more open expression of gay-themed movies, including the recent *Brokeback Mountain*, featuring two gay cowboys, and the 2008 movie *Milk*, which honored the gay rights movement and one of its pioneers in an attempt legitimize gay rights as the civil rights movement did for civil rights. Even kids were not immune to the new onslaught of the gay agenda, when in October of 2007 the major character in the Harry Potter books and movies, Albus Dumbledore, master wizard and headmaster of Hogwarts, was revealed to be gay.

This is how the frog in the kettle gets hotter and hotter, until one day we wake up and realize we have totally lost the culture. Deception has taken root and become mainstream in the gay movement, convincing even churchgoers that maybe people are actually born gay. Today attempts to legitimize this way of living are being pursued through government legislation by legalizing same-sex marriage.

This battle for the family is heating up with one of the most important issues that could cause a huge tipping point in culture—the redefining of marriage. Can marriage be defined only as a legal relationship between one man and one woman, or can it exist between two consenting adults of the same gender? In 2008, California voters defeated a proposed amendment that would redefine marriage.[8] However, the battle will not stop at the state level. Gay activists want the US government to redefine marriage, which would make it mandatory in all states.

A 2009 report on the state of marriage in America was published by the Institute for American Values in America. In this report we get a snapshot of the health of families and marriages in America.

Over the last forty years, marriage has become less common and more fragile, and the proportion of children raised outside intact marriages has increased dramatically. Between 1970 and 2008 the proportion of children living with two married parents dropped from 85 percent to 66.7 percent, according to census data. About three-quarters of children living with a single parent live with a single mother.[9]

These important changes in family structure stem from two fundamental changes in US residents' behavior regarding marriage: increases in unmarried childbearing and high rates of divorce. More than a third of all US children are now born outside of wedlock (39.7 percent), including 71.6 percent for African American babies and 27.8 percent for whites and other ethnic groups.[10]

> Divorce rates, by contrast, after increasing in the 1960s and 1970s, appear to have declined modestly in recent years. The small decline in divorce after 1980, however, seems to have been offset by increases in unwed childbearing, as the percentage of children living with one parent increased steadily between 1960 and 2000 with only a small drop after 2000. Overall, divorce rates remain high relative to the period before 1970. Today's young adults in their prime childbearing years are less likely to get married, and many more US children each year are born to unmarried mothers.[11]

The divorce rate in America is 45–50 percent of first marriages, 60–67 percent of second marriages, and 70–73 percent of third marriages, according to Jennifer Baker of the Forest Institute of Professional Psychology in Springfield, Missouri.[12] Comparative divorce rates in other countries include Canada, 48 percent;[13] Singapore, 10 percent;[14] UK and Wales, 13 percent;[15] Japan, 27 percent;[16] and Australia, 40 percent.[17] Some of these figures can be misleading based on the high percentage of couples who may live together but do not report when they split up. In the case of the UK, a large number of couples live together, which has become the trend compared to marriage.

"Sixty-five percent of young adults whose parents divorced had poor relationships with their fathers (compared to 29 percent from non-divorced families)," according to a study on family life released by sixteen of the top scholars on the importance of marriage.[18] The *Washington Times* described the impact of divorce on children. "More than half of American teens have grown up with parents who 'rejected each other,' which bodes ill for the nation's future leadership, productivity, wealth, and well-being, says a new national report on American families. Only 45 percent of teens, aged 15–17, have grown up from birth with their married, biological parents, says the new US Index of Belonging and Rejection."[19]

THE IMPACT OF THE GAY AGENDA ON THE FAMILY

In February 1988, a meeting was held with 175 gay activists in Warrenton, Virginia. Marshall Kirk, a Harvard-educated researcher in neuropsychiatry, and Hunter Madsen, who holds a doctorate in politics from Harvard and is an expert in persuasion tactics and social marketing, were the conveners of this meeting. In that meeting they said, "AIDS gives us a chance, however brief, to establish ourselves as a victimized minority legitimately deserving of America's special protection and care. It generates mass hysteria of precisely the sort that has brought about public stonings and leper colonies since the Dark Ages and before.... How can we maximize the sympathy and minimize the fear? How, given the horrid hand that AIDS has dealt us, can we best play it?"[20] This was the beginning of a public relations multiyear plan. They developed a public relations bible of the gay movement. They outline the key strategies for the movement in their book. Their goals include:

- Break current negative associations with our cause and replace them with positive associations.

- Change what people actually think and feel.

- Reframe the terms of the debate.

- Seek desensitization and nothing more (until it doesn't matter any more).[21]

Public perception of the gay agenda

Seventeen Magazine has been doing a survey about the gay lifestyle for several years. To get an idea how effective the gay rights movement has been with public relations, one only needs to look at this survey of its readers compared to earlier years. Consider their 1991 survey, which revealed that 17 percent of their readers accepted homosexuality as appropriate. However, in their 1999 survey, after eight years of PR, the same survey said 54 percent accepted homosexuality as appropriate.[22]

Recently I was talking with a director of a Christian teen ministry that operated in public schools. I asked her what she saw as the greatest problem among teens today. Her answer nearly knocked me down. "Teen girls are experimenting with same sex. They are not necessarily gay, but they are experimenting with same-sex affections. And what is worse, the teen boys think it is cool." I almost could not believe my ears. However, that is how the media make social issues normative. Teens see things on TV and think it's cool. They have no idea they are playing with fire that could consume them.

In 2010 ABC News did a poll on the public's view of gay marriage. In 2006 only 36 percent were in favor of gay marriage, while 53 percent opposed it. However, in the August 2010 poll, 53 percent supported the gay marriage amendment and 46 percent opposed it.[23] This is clearly further evidence of the success of the gay agenda using the media for their cause and the public's increased acceptance of an ungodly lifestyle. Gradually even those in the church begin to succumb to public persuasion and pressure and begin to rationalize sin. This has led to an entire Episcopal denomination to not only embrace the lifestyle as acceptable but also to even ordain them as priests. This has spread into parts of the Lutheran church.

Divorce is the entry point of dysfunctional and wounded lives that often leads to aberrant behaviors in human beings in each new generation. Unless there is a stopgap somewhere in the cycle, more and more expressions of aberrant behavior will be the result until we end up like the Roman Empire and disintegrate from within.

Not born gay admission

Most of us hear the rationale of gay activists that they are born gay rather than their sexual preference being an influence of how they were raised and what exposure they had to societal factors and childhood wounds that predisposed them to this lifestyle. Kirk and Madsen made an amazing admission in their book: "We argue that, for all practical purposes, gays should be considered to have been born gay, even though sexual orientation, for most humans, seems to be the product of a complex interaction between innate predispositions and environmental factors during childhood and early adolescence."[24]

What is their ultimate goal? It isn't just to get acceptance. It is far more than that. David Kupelian explains: "The end game is not only to bring about the complete acceptance of homosexuality, including same-sex marriage, but also to prohibit and even criminalize public criticism of homosexuality. In other words, total jamming of criticism with the force of law. This is already the case in Canada and parts of Scandinavia."[25]

The battle over gay rights and the church

The gay rights movement is exploiting media to convince mainstream that the gay lifestyle is an acceptable lifestyle and should be acceptable to all people.

Scripture is very clear about the gay lifestyle, that it is sin and not a biologically born behavior. God still loves the sinner, but no matter what the sin, whether it is the gay lifestyle, adultery, murder, greed, or even gluttony, God is absolute about sin. He loves the sinner, but He does not love or endorse the sin. There is no question about what the Bible says about the gay lifestyle. "Therefore God also gave them up to uncleanness, in the lusts of their hearts, to dishonor their bodies among themselves, who exchanged the truth of God for the lie, and worshiped and served the creature rather than the Creator, who is blessed forever. Amen. For this reason God gave them up to vile passions. For even their women exchanged the natural use for what is against nature. Likewise also the men, leaving the natural use of the woman, burned in their lust for one another, men with men committing what is shameful, and receiving in themselves the penalty of their error which was due."[26]

God loves all people, no matter what lifestyle a person has been in. He created us in His image. His grace is always there to redeem us from any lifestyle that is contrary to His ways. Although there are many factors that can lead to a gay lifestyle, it is yet another physical manifestation of a wayward baby-boomer generation that often failed in their parenting and their ability to love and care for their kids from a godly foundation. Their failure led to voids in role identities for an entire segment of this generation. As the sexual revolution took root, families became more and more exposed to aberrant role models, which impacted a new generation. There was a disconnect from our spiritual roots. We need to understand that any addiction is merely a reflection of a failure to feel loved and receive the love of God in our lives, and it is Satan's ploy to sell us a counterfeit form of love.

The evangelical church has taken a very judgmental posture on the gay lifestyle issue. The church must recognize our own sins of condemning those who are a product of our failures in upholding godly family foundations. The church must learn to love those who are different but not love the sin. Part of the reason we don't have influence in culture is that we struggle with loving those who are different from ourselves. A survey cited in the book *UnChristian* revealed that 87 percent of young people outside the church feel that Christians look down their noses at anyone different from them.[27]

Danny Wallace, a former homosexual and victim of abuse who now speaks across the country on how the church must view this issue, says, "The real change will come forth in the generation we are raising up, a generation of now, tender babes. As we open up this topic into the church and remove the trembling of fear that has existed by pulling back the curtain and expose this attack on innocent hearts, while encouraging responsible adults to step forward and bathe this new generation in unconditional love and heal marriages, we will begin to turn the tide on this issue."[28]

When Jesus dealt with the harlot in the public square, He did not utter one word of condemnation to her. She already knew what she was doing was wrong. He said to her, "I do not condemn you. Go and sin no more." He also told the accusers who had no sin to cast the first stone. They all left.[29] The question we need to ponder is this: How judgmental have we been for our gossip, gluttony, and materialism inside the church? We all have our own sins we must deal with before we can cast stones. Until we can deal with the marriage crisis effectively, we need to stay away from making the gay agenda the core issue. The failure of marriage in the church is the core issue today.

We've defined certain sins, especially sexual sin, as the unpardonable sin. When leaders fail, we are often the first to pile on instead of helping those who fall when they are repentant. God says all sin is unacceptable—including gluttony—a sin few want to confront in the body of Christ. God lists the works of the flesh in Galatians 5: "Now the works of the flesh are evident, which are: adultery, fornication, uncleanness, lewdness, idolatry, sorcery, hatred, contentions, jealousies, outbursts of wrath, selfish ambitions, dissensions, heresies, envy, murders, drunkenness, revelries, and the like; of which I tell you beforehand, just as I also told you in time past, that those who practice such things will not inherit the kingdom of God."[30] There is plenty of sin to go around for all of us without trying to place a hierarchy on sin, which God never did. Before you get on the bandwagon of condemnation, ask yourself if there is any sin you are still walking in or struggling to gain freedom from. We should all love the sinner but hate the sin—just as God does.

It is important for us to recognize that the church may be being duped into focusing on the wrong family issue when it comes to the gay rights movement. Gay marriage might directly affect no more than 3–5 percent of the entire population. However, divorce is affecting at least 55 percent of the population and has lasting damage for generations to come. When we fail to focus on the root issue behind divorce and remarriage in and outside the church, we are swatting a flea when a giant is standing in front of us. The giant is causing much more havoc than the flea. The gay agenda is merely a symptom of the divorce issue we are facing in our nation. I have personally experienced the devastation caused by divorce. It goes far beyond the two people and affects many generations. We need to focus our attention on helping couples find the root issues of problems that lead to the divorce/remarriage cycle. If the divorce rates were 5 percent, there would be no gay issue.

Craig Hill, founder of Family Foundations International, explains: "Divorce and remarriage in one generation deeply wounds the hearts of children and sows the seed of insecurity, shame, and performance orientation into the next generation. When these wounded children grow into adulthood, such seed then frequently reproduces in marriage the fruit of one or more of the four 'big As': adultery, abuse, abandonment, or addictions. These symptoms then in turn result in divorce in the second generation. If core issues are not dealt with in marriage, and true healing is not brought to the deep wounds of the heart, but rather we continue to accept divorce and remarriage as an appropriate solution to these four 'big As,' we can expect an intensification and proliferation of ever-increasing deviant sexual sin in each succeeding generation. Gay marriage is just the tip of the iceberg of things to come. History records that just such a cycle ultimately led to the downfall of the Roman Empire. If we hope to avoid repeating Roman history ourselves, our priority must be the authentic healing and transformation of hearts in this generation, and the restoration of the family in our nation and in the world."[31]

BECOME A CHANGE AGENT FOR THE FAMILY MOUNTAIN

Healthy Christian families lead to producing positive change agents in culture. Conversely, a poor family history often leads to producing destructive change agents. Noel and Phyl Gibson, in a book entitled *Evicting Demonic Squatters and Breaking Bondages*, compared the family history of two families over a two-hundred-year period. One family, the family of Max Jukes, was an atheistic, nonbelieving family, while the other family was that of Jonathan Edwards, a committed Christian leader. Here was the difference between the two families over the two hundred years in what each family produced.[32]

Max Jukes	Jonathan Edwards
Married an atheist woman	Married a godly woman
Had 560 descendants	Had 1,394 descendants
310 died as paupers	295 graduated from college
150 criminals	13 college presidents; 65 professors
7 murderers	3 US senators
100 drunkards	3 state governors
One-half of the women were prostitutes	30 judges
Cost the US government $1.25 million in 19th century dollars	100 lawyers
	56 doctors
	75 military officers
	100 missionaries, preachers, authors
	80 held public office
	3 mayors
	1 comptroller of the US Treasury

Generational iniquity can pass through to the third and fourth generations. "For I, the LORD your God, am a jealous God, visiting the iniquity of the fathers on the children to the third and fourth generations of those who hate Me, but showing mercy to thousands, to those who love Me and keep My commandments."[33]

The conditions of life that generated the family form have changed. Yet the one thing that has not changed through all the years and all the family transformations is the need for children to be raised by mothers and fathers. Indeed, in modern, complex societies in which children need an enormous amount of education and psychological security to succeed, active and nurturing relationships with adults may be more critical for children than ever. We must fight for the family and marriage in our culture.

What can I do as one individual to make an impact for God on the family mountain?

This chapter has highlighted several steps that any individual can take that will impact the family mountain for God. Consider each of these as an action point for you.

1. Tim Tebow and his mother found a way to partner with individuals from the media mountain for a large-scale impact on culture through their Super Bowl commercial. Is there a way for you to partner with someone from another mountain to double the impact you can have in a way similar to that of Tim Tebow and his mother?

2. One of the primary breakdowns in the family is the failure of some husbands to meet the emotional needs of their wives by "laying down their lives" as Christ did for the church. Are you a husband? Are you doing everything you can to meet the emotional needs of your wife and family?

3. We learned in this chapter that most addictions are rooted in an individual's failure at feeling loved. Are you showing godly, unconditional love to all the significant people in your life? Are you helping your loved ones to be open to receiving God's love in their lives?

4. One thing that has not changed since the beginning of time is the need children have to be raised by a mother and a father— together. Are you a parent? Are you providing your children with the love and nurture of *both* mother and father?

5. In a culture that targets the family for destruction, we must recognize our need to fight for our families and our marriages. What steps are you taking to enter this fight? If you are a father, are you caring for your children?

6. We must focus our attention on what we are for, not what we are against. We must invest in strategies to heal and build strong marriages.

What would success look like on the family mountain?

- The divorce rate would go down dramatically. Families would be stronger.

- There would be less dysfunction and fewer tendencies for people to move into abnormal sexual expressions due to the pain in their lives because they would be coming from healthy families.

- Businesses would be more successful because more families would be healthy and emotionally whole.

- There would be less political issues surrounding gay marriage and other societal ills affecting the family.

- Mothers would value their unborn children, resulting in fewer abortions, and fathers would take responsibility in the home and love their wives as Christ loves the church.

- Fathers would love and nurture their children.

- There would be less discrimination among the races.

- Abuse in the home would disappear.

- Healthy and whole marriages and individuals would mean no adultery, which means no divorces.

- There would be a huge decline in families in the incidence of the four big "As": adultery, addictions, abuse, and abandonment.

- The incidence of teenage rebellion would dramatically decline.

- The incidence of teenage pregnancy and children born out of wedlock would dramatically decline.

- There would be a great reduction of the incidence of teenage suicide.

- There would be a reduction of the overall crime rate.

- A culture of blessing would be established in the families of believers, resulting in parents naturally blessing their children in the critical times of life.

- Self-esteem and self-confidence would increase in children, who would then know a strong sense of destiny and purpose for their lives.

- There would be much higher overall SAT scores among students in schools.

- There would be an increase of entrepreneurial businesses started as confidence and creativity are released in children through the blessing of parents.

Chapter 15

RECLAIMING THE MOUNTAIN OF GOVERNMENT

For unto us a Child is born,
Unto us a Son is given;
And the government will be upon His shoulder.

—Isaiah 9:6

THE YEAR IS 2076. It is the three hundredth anniversary of the birth of America. The nation is preparing for a celebration on July 4. John Birkshire is a thirty-year-old reporter for the *New York Times* preparing to write a story on the Founding Fathers of the nation.

America has changed a lot, especially in the last sixty-five years. Just sixty-five years ago America was the leading nation in the world—today we are no longer the leading nation. We are not a third-world nation, but we are ranked forty-fifth in GDP among nations, where we were number one and far above any nation just forty-five years earlier. We were a nation that was known for our generosity, but now we are no longer prosperous enough to give to other nations. Years ago someone once said, "When America ceases to be good, it will cease to be great."[1] We have seen this prophecy fulfilled in the last seventy-five years. Back then we had 40 percent of the population that claimed Christianity as their religion. Today, less than 3 percent of our nation claims to be "Christian."

China, Russia, and Japan are the dominating nations of the world, and we are subject to many of their trade laws, because our livelihood, and now even our security, is tied to these nations. Their defense budgets are now almost twice the size of ours, and we live in constant fear of these nations invading us. Israel has been in the news lately, recently falling to outside invaders in the Middle East with support from Russia. We no longer can come to their defense. We are too weak. And our government no longer sees the need to support this little nation that seems to be in conflict with every other nation in the Middle East.

WHAT IS GOVERNMENT?

Government exists in many, many arenas. In this book we are considering government to be *the political institutions that rule a land*. They administrate civil righteousness and justice at multiple levels. The top of the mountain is occupied by only a small handful of people. Our national leader is one of those at the top of the mountain.[2] When this nation was founded, the Founding Fathers were also positioned near or at the top of the mountain of government.

John Birkshire has an assignment from his employer, the *New York Times*, to write an in-depth article on the Founding Fathers of America. It was an unusual assignment for John. He knew little about the Founding Fathers. He grew up being taught that the Founding Fathers were secular men who were not unlike the liberal leaders in government today. He often bristled at the mention of these political leaders because of their self-serving policies that seem to have gotten the nation into more debt and resulted in a reduced standard of living compared to the distant memory of days when life would have been considered prosperous by any world standard. Frequently he wondered how America lost its prosperity as a nation. Senior executives at the newspaper told him it was because of corrupt politicians and business leaders over the last several decades that took America off track. Somehow that didn't quite satisfy his curiosity. There had to be more to this story.

FOUNDING FATHERS MUSEUM

Birkshire heard about a museum created by a small group of Christians in Virginia Beach, Virginia, called the *Founding Fathers Museum*. Supposedly this museum archived every major Founding Father's role in the formation of America with documents that cite their statements and intent for the new nation. He decided this was a must visit for his assignment. He arrived in Virginia Beach and made his way to the museum. It was a massive museum, with many statues and statements attributed to the Founding Fathers displayed on the walls. There were video excerpts of notable speeches. George Washington was the first bigger-than-life statue that greeted John when he walked through the impressive entrance. There was also a display that described the most amazing story about George Washington's early years as a soldier before he became president.

> George Washington, our first US president, was a public servant for forty-five years. In the French and Indian war in 1755, George Washington commanded thirteen hundred troops against the Indians in a woodland battle. Washington's officers (on horseback) and most of his troops were cut down. At the end of the battle Washington was the only officer that remained still on horseback. Afterward, he found four bullet holes in his jacket, later writing to his wife that "God had protected him."
>
> Fifteen years later the Indian chief that fought against Washington traveled a good distance to meet him when he heard that he was in

the area of the battleground. This chief stated that he had commanded his braves to concentrate on killing Washington, and had personally shot at him seventeen times. He wanted to meet the man that "God wouldn't let die."

George Washington was president of the convention that gave us the Constitution. He called for the First Amendment and Bill of Rights. After two terms as president, he gave a farewell speech, which was heralded as the most significant political speech ever given to the nation. It has since been removed from American history books, and it would be rare to find it in any from the last thirty years.

John wondered why this was so. While he was not a religious person, he was not against it. He felt that whatever a person feels is good for them should be allowed as long as it does not require others to believe the same way. After all, relativism had been the mantra for the last fifty years in America. John continued reading the display, focusing particularly on Washington's farewell address.

"Of all the dispositions and habits which lead to political prosperity, religion and morality are indispensable supports. In vain would that man claim the tribute of patriotism, who should labor to subvert these great pillars."[3] John had never read that part of the speech before. A comment on the display stated, "Apparently the people writing the history books wanted to change what children are taught about the connection between political prosperity and religion and morality."

"Hmm, that does not seem right to me," John said to himself. "If that is the real history, then that is the history. Who are we to change history? We need to be true to what actually took place."

John came to another display that posed a question about Washington's faith: "So what was George Washington's faith? Historians have long debated the extent of his faith. 'Washington's own step-granddaughter, Nelly Custis, thought his words and actions were so plain and obvious that she could not understand how anybody failed to see that he had always lived as a serious Christian.'"[4]

John read further on the encased display: "The form of government established by the founders of the United States has lasted 300 years. Some other countries have undergone many different forms during this same period—such as France, seven forms, and Italy forty forms."[5] "Wow," John thought to himself. "Imagine that, one form of government all these years. I know how hard it is to write one major article without the need for ten changes to my story. These guys got it right the first time! That's pretty remarkable."

John walked to the next display and found another interesting piece of history. "Political science professors at the University of Houston wondered if there was something unique about the government of the United States. They gathered 15,000 quotes from the founders and located where all of them came from. They then boiled that down to 3,154 quotes that had significant impact on the founding of America. It took them ten years to finish the project, but they found that the three men most quoted by the Founding Fathers were William Blackstone, Charles Montesquieu, and John Locke. They also found that the Bible was quoted four times more often than Montesquieu, twelve times more often than Blackstone, and sixteen times more often than Locke. Additionally, 34 percent of all quotes were from the Bible, and another 60 percent of the quotes were from men who were using the Bible to arrive at their conclusions. Added together, 94 percent of all the quotes of the founders had their origin in the Bible."[6]

"Wow," he thought to himself. "The Bible seems to have been a major reference point for many of these guys."

At another display John learned that *William Blackstone's Commentary on the Law*, introduced in 1758, became the law textbook for lawyers for 160 years and that the Supreme Court quoted from it to settle cases. It gave Bible verse references as to the source for our laws. For instance, the display stated that the three branches of government were based on Isaiah 33:22, the separation of powers was based on Jeremiah 17, and the tax exemption for churches on Ezra 7:24. Neighboring countries to the United States—Canada and Mexico—didn't have tax exemption for churches.

A separate display showed a picture of a famous preacher named Charles Finney, a well-known evangelist in the 1800s. It stated he was studying to become a lawyer and became a Christian primarily because he saw the truth of the Bible references in *Blackstone's Commentary*. John thought that was very interesting, as he had studied pre-law before he decided to go into journalism. "Strange that someone could find religion studying a law book," he pondered.

John continued his walk through the museum and came upon the bust of Patrick Henry. Below his name were the following quotes: "Give me liberty or give me death!"[7] and "It cannot be emphasized too strongly or too often that this great nation was founded not by religionists, but by Christians, not on religion, but on the gospel of Jesus Christ."[8] "Well, its pretty clear where Patrick Henry stood on his religious beliefs," John concluded.

VIEW OF AMERICA FROM A FRENCHMAN

John entered another room with the headline on the wall, "A View of America From a French Journalist." Under the headline were the following words: "Alexis De Tocqueville wrote a book entitled *Democracy in America* in 1835. This was a result of a trip he took to American in 1831. He and Gustave de Beaumont were sent by the French government to study the American prison system. They arrived in New York City in May of that year and spent nine months traveling the United States, taking notes not only on prisons but also on all aspects of American society, including the nation's economy and its political system. However, De Tocqueville was surprised at what he found: 'Upon my arrival in the United States, the religious aspect of the country was the first thing that struck my attention; and the longer I stayed there the more did I perceive the great political consequences resulting from this state of things, to which I was unaccustomed. In France I had almost always seen the spirit of religion and the spirit of freedom pursuing courses diametrically opposed to each other; but in America I found that they were intimately united, and that they reigned in common over the same country....Religion in America...must nevertheless be regarded as the foremost of the political institutions of that country....From the earliest settlement of the emigrants politics and religion contracted an alliance which has never been dissolved.'"⁹

BENJAMIN FRANKLIN AND HIS FAITH

A few steps later John came across a beautiful white granite statue of Benjamin Franklin. He had always heard that Franklin was an atheist and had not believed in God. Yet, here were some actual words from Franklin supporting Christian education: "We need God as our friend not our enemy. We need him to be our ally not our adversary. We need to make sure that we keep God's concurring aid." According to the display, Franklin called for regular daily prayer to be sure God was kept alongside what was being done in the nation. The display then questioned: If this was needed by our leaders, why would it not be good for children to be able to pray in school and learn and prepare for this important facet of life?

John saw other public statements made by Franklin that were even stronger examples of his belief in God, including one he made at the Constitutional Convention of 1787: "...how has it happened, Sir, that we have not hitherto once thought of humbly appealing to the Father of lights to illuminate our understandings? In the beginning of the Contest with G. Britain, when we were sensible of danger we had daily prayers in this room for divine protection. Our prayers, Sir, were heard, and they were graciously answered....And have we now forgotten that powerful friend? or do we imagine that we no longer need his assistance? I have lived, Sir, a long time, and the longer I live, the more convincing proofs I see of this truth—*that God Governs in the affairs of men*. And if a sparrow cannot fall to the ground without his notice, is it probable that an empire can rise without his aid? We have been assured, Sir, in the sacred writings, that 'except the Lord build the House, they labour in vain that build it.' I firmly believe this; and I also believe that without his concurring aid we shall succeed in this political building no better, than the Builders of Babel: We shall be divided by our little partial local interests; our projects will be confounded, and we ourselves shall become a reproach and bye word down to future ages....I therefore beg leave to above—that henceforth prayers imploring the assistance of Heaven, and its blessings on our deliberations, be held in this Assembly every morning before we proceed to business."[10]

John sighed after he read these words. "If only some of our politicians believed and acted that way today, how different things would be."

SEPARATION OF CHURCH AND STATE

John continued his walk through the museum and came across a big headline across the wall: "Separation of Church and State." Now, that statement he had heard a lot. It seemed every time someone wanted to talk about religion in his office or write an article about religion that statement was brought up. He had always heard religion had no place in the public arena based on this statement. He wondered where it originated. Some people thought it was in the Constitution. Others were not sure. An elaborate display told the complete history of this well-known statement.

"Many people think the separation of church and state is part of the First Amendment, but it is not. The First Amendment reads: 'Congress shall make no law respecting an establishing of religion, or prohibiting the free exercise thereof.'

"What the founders did not want was any one denomination of the Christian religion to run the nation. They wanted to stay away from what they had left in England, where the king was the head of the church. However, the Founding Fathers and the Supreme Court were quite clear that Christianity was the established religion and WAS to be involved in the government. This is evident in the Supreme Court decision of 1796, and many other writings."[11]

"Well, now, that makes sense to me," thought John. "It wasn't that they didn't want religion in the public arena; they simply didn't want one religious tradition or denomination to be ruling the government. The fathers clearly felt religion was important to the success of any government." The light was shining brighter and brighter for John.

He walked a few steps to his right and found another example of a Supreme Court ruling and a copy of a letter from Thomas Jefferson that further explained the reasoning behind the separation of church and state reference.

THOMAS JEFFERSON'S FAMOUS LETTER

On January 1, 1802, President Thomas Jefferson wrote a letter to Danbury Baptist Church of Connecticut. In 1801, the Danbury Baptist Church heard a rumor that the Congregationalist denomination was going to be made the national denomination. This disturbed them, as it well should. Jefferson answered in his letter:

> To messers. Nehemiah Dodge, Ephraim Robbins, and Stephen S. Nelson, a committee of the Danbury Baptist association in the state of Connecticut.
>
> Gentlemen,
>
> The affectionate sentiments of esteem and approbation which you are so good as to express towards me, on behalf of the Danbury Baptist association, give me the highest satisfaction. My duties dictate a faithful and zealous pursuit of the interests of my constituents, and in proportion as they are persuaded of my fidelity to those duties, the discharge of them becomes more and more pleasing.
>
> Believing with you that religion is a matter which lies solely between Man and his God, that he owes account to none other for his faith or his worship, that the legitimate powers of government reach actions only, and not opinions, I contemplate with sovereign reverence that act of the whole American people which declared that their legislature should "make no law respecting an establishment of religion, or prohibiting the free exercise thereof," thus building a wall of separation between Church and State. Adhering to this expression of the supreme will of the nation in behalf of the rights of conscience, I shall see with sincere satisfaction the progress of those sentiments which tend to restore to man all his natural rights, convinced he has no natural right in opposition to his social duties.
>
> I reciprocate your kind prayers for the protection and blessing of the common father and creator of man, and tender you for yourselves and your religious association, assurances of my high respect and esteem.
>
> TH. JEFFERSON
JANUARY 1, 1802[12]

GOD IN THE PUBLIC SQUARE

John now walked to a different room with the title "God in the Public Square." In this area the displays dealt with the various places where public examples of faith could be seen on public government buildings. It began with the US Capitol.

The religious imagery in the Capitol rotunda is significant. Eight different historical paintings are on display, all with a religious connotation to them. The first is the painting *The Landing of Columbus*, depicting the arrival on the shores of America. Second is *The Embarkation of the Pilgrims*, showing the

Pilgrims observing a day of prayer and fasting led by William Brewster. Third is the painting *Discovery of the Mississippi by DeSoto*. Next to DeSoto in the painting is a monk who prays as a crucifix is placed in the ground. Finally, there is the painting *Baptism of Pocahontas*.

Throughout the Capitol, there are references to God and faith. In the Cox Corridor, a line from "America the Beautiful" is carved in the wall: "America! America! God shed His grace on thee, and crown thy good with brotherhood, from sea to shining sea!"[13]

In the House chamber is the inscription "In God We Trust." Also in the House chamber, above the gallery door, stands a marble relief of Moses, the greatest of the twenty-three lawgivers (and the only one full-faced). At the east entrance to the Senate chamber are the words *Annuit Coeptis*, which is Latin for "God has favored our undertakings." "In God We Trust" is also written over the southern entrance.

In the Capitol's chapel is a stained-glass window depicting George Washington in prayer under the inscription "In God We Trust." Also, a prayer is inscribed in the window that says, "Preserve me, God, for in Thee do I put my trust."

The Washington Monument

The tallest monument in Washington DC is the Washington Monument. From the base of the monument to its aluminum capstone are numerous references to God. This is fitting, since George Washington was a religious man. When he took the oath of office on April 30, 1789, he asked that the Bible be opened to Deuteronomy 28. After the oath, Washington added, "So help me God" and bent forward and kissed the Bible before him.

In a ceremony on December 6, 1884, the aluminum capstone was placed atop the monument. The east side of the capstone has the Latin phrase *Laus Deo*, which means, "Praise be to God."

The cornerstone of the Washington Monument includes a Holy Bible, which was a gift from the Bible Society. Along with it are copies of the Declaration of Independence and the US Constitution.

If you walk inside the monument, you will see a memorial plaque from the Free Press Methodist Episcopal Church. On the twelfth landing you will see a prayer offered by the city of Baltimore. On the twentieth landing you will see a memorial offered by Chinese Christians. There is also a presentation made by Sunday school children from New York and Philadelphia on the twenty-fourth landing.

The monument is full of carved tribute blocks that say: "Holiness to the Lord"; "Search the Scriptures"; "The memory of the just is blessed"; "May heaven to this union continue its beneficence"; "In God We Trust"; and "'Train up a child in the way he should go, and when he is old, he will not depart from it.'"

The Supreme Court

The Supreme Court has often issued opinions that have stripped religious displays from the public square. It is ironic that public expressions of faith have been limited when all sessions of the court begin with the Court's marshal announcing, "God save the United States and this honorable court."

In a number of cases the Supreme Court declared the posting of the Ten Commandments unconstitutional (in public school classrooms and in a local courthouse in Kentucky). But this same Supreme Court has a number of places in its building where there are images of Moses with the Ten Commandments. These can be found at the center of the sculpture over the east portico of the Supreme Court building, inside the actual courtroom, and finally, engraved over the chair of the Chief Justice and on the bronze doors of the Supreme Court itself. Nevertheless, the Supreme Court has often ruled against the very kind of religious expression that can be found in the building that houses the court.[14]

GOD ON CURRENCY

John moved down the hallway to a sign that stated, "Congress adopts new motto of the United States: 'In God We Trust.'" He read the statement below: "The United States Congress passed in 1956 H.J. Resolution 396, adopting In God We Trust as the official motto. However, the seeds of the nation moving toward the adoption of this motto began much earlier and was a result of the Christian influence from the Civil War. In God We Trust first appeared on the 1864 two-cent coin. In 1865 gold and silver coins also had the inscription added to them."[15]

John recalled seeing that statement on some of his currency. He pulled out his wallet and looked at a five-dollar bill. He read the words "In God We Trust." He pulled out a one-dollar bill. The same statement was there. In fact, he discovered this statement is on every currency of the United States, including all the coins. He wondered if that statement would ever be put there today intentionally. Probably not. "How ironic," he thought, "that the nation's motto is *In God We Trust*, and yet politicians, schoolteachers, and public prayers cannot mention God in them." He also realized this is further evidence of the original intent of the forefathers. Truly they were men who had a faith in God.

John walked out of the museum totally transformed about his view of the founding of America. He was disturbed. He had been told lies his whole life about America. Here it is in black and white with actual documents of their statements. Somehow he thinks he will not be around long at the *New York Times* after he writes his story. He started on his way back to New York.

WHY AMERICA NO LONGER NEEDS GOD

Could John's story become a reality in America? There is a reason America is moving further and further away from discussions about God in the public arena. History and the Bible tell us that the more prosperous a people are, the less they need God. Humility and prosperity rarely coexist. God warned the people of Israel not to forget God. If they did, there would be consequences. "Beware that you do not forget the LORD your God by not keeping His commandments, His judgments, and His statutes which I command you today, lest—when you have eaten and are full, and have built beautiful houses and dwell in them; and when your herds and your flocks multiply, and your silver and your gold are multiplied, and all that you have is multiplied; when your heart is lifted up, and you forget the LORD your God who brought you out of the land of Egypt, from the house of bondage; who led you through that great and terrible wilderness, in which were fiery serpents and scorpions and thirsty land where there was no water; who brought water for you out of the flinty rock; who fed you in the wilderness with manna, which your fathers did not know, that He might humble you and that He might test you, to do you good in the end—then you say in your heart, 'My power and the might of my hand have gained me this wealth.'"[16]

God then proceeded to explain what happens when Israel, or any nation forgets God: "And you shall remember the LORD your God, for it is He who gives you power to make wealth, that He may establish His covenant which He swore to your fathers, as it is this day. Then it shall be, if you by any means forget the LORD your God, and follow other gods, and serve them and worship them, I testify against you this day that you shall surely perish. As the nations which the Lord destroys before you, so you shall perish, because you would not be obedient to the voice of the LORD your God."[17]

BECOME A CHANGE AGENT FOR OUR GOVERNMENT

As you can see in this chapter, our nation has come a long way—a long way from the foundations established by those who founded our nation. How do we return? Can we return? It starts with one leader at a time. It starts with one student who believes in absolutes and has a backbone to not be swayed by public opinion. It starts with a man or woman who says, "Enough is enough. It is time for *godly change*, not just change!"

Abraham Kuyper was one of those leaders. He was prime minister in the Netherlands from 1901 to 1905 and was the first to formulate the principle of *common grace* in the context of a Reformed worldview. Most important has been Kuyper's view on the role of God in everyday life. He believed that God continually influenced the life of believers, and daily events could show His workings. Kuyper famously said:

> Oh, no single piece of our mental world is to be hermetically sealed off from the rest, and there is not a square inch in the whole domain of our human existence over which Christ, who is Sovereign over all, does not cry: "Mine!"[18]

It is time to begin to raise up a new kind of political leader whose only loyalty is to Jesus Christ and His government.

What can I do as one individual to make an impact for God on the government mountain?

There were several examples from our nation's founders that demonstrated how strongly they believed our nation should be linked to godly righteousness and integrity. Which of the following foundational planks from our founders can you strengthen by actions you take today?

1. *Awareness of the need for God's protection.* George Washington bowed in prayer before his greatest battle.

2. *A foundation on the Word of God.* From a total of fifteen thousand quotes from our Founding Fathers, an amazing 94 percent were based on God's Word.

3. *Freedom of religion.* Patrick Henry took a stand by stating strongly that "this great nation was founded...on the gospel of Jesus Christ."

4. *The Importance of prayer in school.* Benjamin Franklin called for daily prayer in both school and government.

5. *The laws of man are to be established on the laws of God.* There are numerous places on the Supreme Court building where the Ten Commandments are engraved, yet the Supreme Court itself has ruled against the same kind of display in the public square.

We cannot write a chapter like this and not acknowledge that although the Founding Fathers had a faith in Jesus Christ, their actions regarding slavery were anything but Christian. More than 70 percent of the founders were against slavery; however, the evidence of the failure to remove this from our nation is self-evident. It reveals how deeply deceived the human heart can become around tradition and mammon-centered strongholds.

We could say the same thing about our nation regarding Native Americans.

We could cite the failure of Christians in Germany during the Nazi regime when Christians failed to stand up for what was obvious ethnic cleansing but somehow turned their heads. There have been many things done in the name of Christ during dark periods of history that Christ would consider an abomination. Nevertheless, that does not change the root foundations by which our nation was formed and what the founders sought to establish.

We are all capable of being deceived with an inability to see the forest for the trees. We are capable of the worst atrocities were it not for the grace of God. "The heart is deceitful above all things, and desperately wicked; who can know it? I, the LORD, search the heart, I test the mind, even to give every man according to his ways, according to the fruit of his doings."[19]

Will the bright light of American influence grow dimmer and dimmer? The Bible speaks of what happens when light no longer illuminates: "Remember therefore from where you have fallen; repent and do the first works, or else I will come to you quickly and remove your lampstand from its place—unless you repent."[20]

May God have mercy on America.

What would success look like on the government mountain?

- Any nation operating from a foundation of righteousness and justice shall be blessed.

- Mud-slinging political campaigns would be a thing of the past.

- Politicians would lead based on truth and absolute values.

- Unselfish leadership qualities would emerge with leaders not caring who got the credit if their city or country benefited.

- Political parties could work together without regard to who gets more power or credit.

- Decisions would not be made based on whether the decision would determine their reelection or affect opinion polls as opposed to being the right decision for the issue based upon a Christian worldview.

- The US Congress would understand the ungodly nature of *Roe v. Wade*. The Supreme Court would overturn abortion law in the land and repent of their sins of killing millions of unborn children.

- New leaders would emerge who model servant leadership using wisdom and discernment to rule just as Solomon modeled in his earlier years before pride and sexual sins overtook him.

- Leaders would not rule from a basis of fear, intimidation, or public opinion but a basis of the needs of the people and the nation from a godly perspective.

- The nation would be a strong ally and protector of Israel, because all nations that bless Israel shall also be blessed. Those who curse Israel shall be cursed.[21]

Chapter 16

RECLAIMING ARTS AND ENTERTAINMENT

He rested from all His work which God had created and made.
—GENESIS 2:3

I WAS SITTING IN the VIP box in the opera house in downtown Singapore awaiting the start of a magic show performance. It was unusual for me to attend such an event, but even more unusual was the identity of the performing magician I was there to see. It was a pastor, with his daughter assistant, who pastored one of the largest local megachurches on the island of Singapore. As a young boy growing up, Pastor Lawrence Khong had loved to perform magic tricks. Today he is the pastor of the ten-thousand-plus-member Faith Community Baptist Church (FCBC) in Singapore. Earlier that day I had spoken at the three services at this dynamic church.

The Lord gave Lawrence Khong a burden for the arts and entertainment mountain. "Every time someone mentioned television, theater, movies, or the media, I would burst into tears," he had told me as he explained his call to the arts and entertainment while continuing to be the local pastor of this megachurch. He continued by telling me what the Lord had said to him: "I have called you to the pulpit ministry. Do you know that the real pulpit of the world is not found in the churches? The church has lost the means to speak to the millions."[1]

WHAT IS THE ENTERTAINMENT MOUNTAIN?

The arts and entertainment mountain includes all forms of celebration; for example, art, music, sports, and entertainment. It is a societal arena where values and virtue are celebrated or distorted. This mountain has so thoroughly been captured by Satan and his demons that many view it as totally corrupt and lost to God. But we will see in this chapter that there are some change agents today who are making an impact for righteousness in this area.

Bryan Hickox is a former producer of more than one hundred movies and now serves as vice president of Mastermedia, a Christian ministry serving the film industry. During a lunchtime presentation hosted by our organization,

Bryan explained how tipping points can occur from movies: "In 1934, in the movie *It Happened One Night*, popular star Clark Gable performed without an undershirt to better display his physique, and thereafter undershirt sales dropped dramatically. In 1942, when *Bambi* premiered, deer hunting in America dropped from a $5.7 million business to barely $1 million. More recently, the international news services reported that after Afghanistan was invaded by Coalition forces in the search for Osama bin Laden, the first public buildings in that country to reopen were not hospitals, schools, or government agencies, but movie theaters showing American movies."

Hollywood, Ronald Reagan and Communism

If we were to be transported into the heavenly realm and we heard the demons vying over which cultural mountain they would be salivating over the most, it would be arts and entertainment, and specifically Hollywood. Why? Because there is no other cultural mountain by which culture is most defined as Hollywood films. Cultural messages about lifestyles, beliefs, and trends are portrayed through stories released through Hollywood into mainstream American homes and theatres.

Even the Communists knew the power of Hollywood when they strategically positioned themselves to infiltrate Hollywood in the 1930s. "Of all the arts, the cinema is the most important for us Communists, to keep the people under control," said Vladimir Ilyich Lenin (from Lenin's instruction to Dzerzhinsky, the founder of KGB). "The prize will be the complete control of the greatest medium of communication in history," said Herb Sorrell, Communist Party activist in 1946.

The Communists believed that if they could capture Hollywood labor unions, they could influence the type of pictures being produced. So they sought to take leadership in intellectual groups—directors, writers, and performers. "One of the most pressing tasks confronting the Communist Party in the field of propaganda is the conquest of this supremely important propaganda unit, until now the monopoly of the ruling class. We must wrest it from them and turn it against them," said Willie Muenzenberg, Comintern boss, 1946.

Ronald Reagan's legacy will always be tied to his famous statement at the Berlin Wall on June 12, 1987: "If you seek peace, if you seek prosperity for the Soviet Union and Eastern Europe, if you seek liberalization: Come here, to this gate. Mr. Gorbachev, open this gate. Mr. Gorbachev, tear down this wall." This became the tipping point for the collapse of the Soviet Union and Communism.

In a book entitled *Reagan's Wars*, we learn about his first encounter with the Communist Party. Reagan's battle with Communists began some forty years earlier in the 1930s when he almost single-handedly defeated their infiltration of Hollywood. When Ronald Reagan began to develop as a major film star, he was shocked to discover that by the end of World War II, more than six hundred prominent film producers, writers, actors, and directors had become members of the Communist Party—actors like Lloyd Bridges, Edward G. Robinson, and Fredric March to name just a few.

When the Communists tried to control the labor unions and began to strike against the studios, Ronald Reagan crossed the picket lines at his own risk. He was threatened and had to carry a gun for protection. He lost his first wife, Jane Wyman, over this issue. Reagan joined the Screen Actors Guild (SAG) in 1937. Here he gained a leadership position in SAG and was able to introduce a rule that you could not be a member of the Communist Party and SAG. This passed and was the first turning point against the Communists. Reagan took his fight all the way to Washington and appeared before the Un-American Activities Committee of the US Congress. This too became a turning point for removing the Communists from their influence in Hollywood.[2]

THE CHURCH EXITED HOLLYWOOD IN THE 1930S

The attitude that the church should isolate itself from culture instead of influence it has been around for a very long time. Dr. William Dyrness, professor of theology and culture at Fuller Seminary, tells of a producer at Twentieth-Century Fox in the 1930s. The producer wrote letters to several evangelical colleges, asking them to send their graduates to become screenwriters, to help make good, wholesome movies. The response was alarming. One college president wrote back saying he'd rather send their young people to hell itself than send them to Hollywood.[3] As a result of this withdrawal, we have allowed the enemy to come in and take this cultural mountain.

Recently I had a meeting with the CEO and owner of a privately held Hollywood studio. He is a follower of Jesus but is careful whom he shares this with. The industry would blackball him if he were vocal about his faith. When I shared with him what God was doing in the seven mountains and affirmed his own calling to moviemaking, his face lit up. "I wish I knew you twenty-five years ago! The church has looked down on me for decades. I never knew where I fit. What you are saying is so refreshing." We spent the next several hours together. I was like a long-lost friend he never had but wished he'd had when he wrestled with his faith and calling to make movies.

HOLLYWOOD IS CORRUPT

My friend went on to share just how corrupt the system is in Hollywood:

> Distribution is a nasty business filled with liars and thieves dressed in expensive pinstriped suits that feed off the unsuspecting film producer at every turn in the road. Like the jungle leach they suck every bit of

strength from your project along with any profit that was rightfully yours. Welcome to Hollywood.

The reason you never see one story in print about profits made from a motion picture is because there isn't any. (Not to be confused with a film's highly publicized box office gross). The entire system is designed to seize creative control from the producer and steal every cent of profit. To the major Hollywood Distributor, it's a game. To the film maker, it's their life.

They steal because they are supporting a corrupt system motivated by greed. The film maker produces movies because it's an art form which has captivated every part of their being. This immoral system continues because it has never been challenged by our government, like they did with Enron, or heaven forbid…what would happen if the IRS checked their system of accounting with multiple sets of books? The film maker makes their "deal with the devil" because they believe it's the "only game in town."

If you are part of mainstream Hollywood and think the major studios are your reason for life, read no further. I don't worship their golden idols and you won't like what I have to say. I started my own studio twenty-eight years ago and have been living in rebellion ever since. I believe in treating people with love, dignity, and respect. A foreign language in this business, and one that allows me to sleep well at night.[4]

Films as Tipping Points for Cultural Issues

Several recent tipping points in culture have occurred through the arts and entertainment mountain. Earlier I described how the gay rights movement experienced a tipping point when Ellen DeGeneres kissed Laura Dern in a 1997 episode of *Ellen*. This event became a tipping point for the gay rights movement. Gays and lesbians have long been prominent in the arts and entertainment worlds, but this event encouraged famous gays and lesbians to come out of the closet. Issues about gay life worked their way into story lines in television, movies, and plays. Hollywood films have become one of the primary propaganda machines for their cause, which is designed to legitimize their lifestyle.

Changing culture

Randall Collins, a sociologist and author of *Discovery of Society*, has stated that culture is defined by the adoption of values and beliefs in seven spheres, but that four of these spheres have the greatest influence: military, economic, political, and cultural. The cultural network is the most important of the four. It is made up of education, arts and entertainment, and media. These three define values and beliefs.

As values are expressed through education, arts and entertainment, and the media, they are adopted, often subconsciously, by those who view the messages on an ongoing basis. If the messages that are being communicated are anti-biblical in nature, it is only a matter of time before the *frog in the kettle* realizes that the temperature is too hot and dies. The viewer does not recognize the subtle change in temperature until one day it is too late. Unless those in the culture understand the messages that are being communicated and seek to alter those messages, then culture will be changed by whoever chooses to influence the media avenues available to them.

In his book *Hollywood Worldviews,* Brian Godawa says that most Christians hold two extreme views when it comes to pop culture: "They are either 'culture anorexics,' cut off from culture completely, or 'cultural gluttons'; who uncritically consume anything that comes along."[5]

Tyler Perry is a change agent who has successfully penetrated the culture and provided a product that moviegoers want to see within a very specific niche. In October 2009, Perry was featured on *60 Minutes*. They opened their segment on Tyler with the following question: "What movie producer has had five opening number-one box office hits in the last five years?"[6] It wasn't Spielberg or another famous movie producer. It was Tyler Perry. His films had grossed $418 million at that time. He caters largely to the African American audience of women, with films that are inspirational stories mixing God, love, faith, and forgiveness as part of every movie. He uses the comedic characters in his movies as bait to deliver his message.

Perry grew up as a physically and emotionally abused child by his father in New Orleans, but today he is a very successful movie producer. He tried to get funding through the Hollywood route but was turned down. He made it the unconventional way, first writing and producing plays. He then turned those plays into movies after he raised his own capital, and he maintained control, something he says was always a requirement for him. Perry now has a thirty-one-acre movie production set and studios in Atlanta. He produces two sitcoms for TBS and plans to release two films a year. He recently partnered with Oprah Winfrey on one film. He candidly shares his faith in Christ but does so in the context of who he is and where he has come from in his life.

It's hot at the top

The higher you go up the arts and entertainment mountain, the more demons are assigned to you, and the more spiritual warfare you will encounter. The apostle Paul understood this principle when he said, "For a great and effective door has opened to me, and there are many adversaries."[7] You won't need to convince Whitney Houston, Britney Spears, Jessica Simpson, or even Amy Grant of this spiritual principle. Each of these successful artists began from a spiritual foundation before they moved away from their early Christian roots, as witnessed by their very visible lives in the tabloids. Grant has probably weathered the storm best among those listed above. Whitney Houston rededicated her life to the Lord in 2007 after her career took a nosedive, due to drug influence and husband Bobby Brown's negative influence, with her marriage ending in divorce in April 2007.

Believers seeking to live and influence others at the top of this mountain need to understand the great temptations that are waiting to derail their Christian faith. *Sometimes your talent takes you beyond where your integrity can keep you.* Many do not have a deep enough spiritual foundation to keep them from yielding to the tremendous temptations that accompany success and prosperity. Prosperity is often a much greater temptation than adversity will ever be.

However, there are great opportunities to impact many lives if their faith can remain strong. Carrie Underwood made history at the Academy of Country Music Awards when she became the first woman to win entertainer of the year twice. Carrie got her start on *American Idol* and has been one of the most successful of all *American Idol* winners, topping the charts with successful hit after hit. Underwood has bridged a successful country music career with her public faith quite well. She grew up on a farm in the small Oklahoma town of Checotah, where she sang at the First Free Will Baptist Church.

POSITIVE TIPPING POINTS

The Passion of the Christ caused its own tipping point in Hollywood by breaking down a barrier that has existed for a long time there. That barrier involves Christian-themed movies produced by major studios. Mel Gibson had to fund and distribute the project himself. It was such a huge success that it caused a proliferation of Christian-themed movies to be released over the next several years. Movies such as the Lord of the Rings trilogy, *Matrix Reloaded*, *X-Men 2*, *Bruce Almighty*, the Chronicles of Narnia series, and *Amazing Grace* are just a few of the Christian-themed movies that have been box office hits.

Then came two surprising hit movies made on shoestring budgets by none other than a local church in south Georgia—*Facing the Giants* and, in 2008, *Fireproof*. *Fireproof* was the highest-grossing independent film of 2008, more than *Milk* and *Slumdog Millionaire*. ABC's *Nightline* did a segment on their Friday evening show that dealt with the rise in faith-based films. *Fireproof* starred former teen idol Kirk Cameron and even beat out the Academy Award–winning *Slumdog Millionaire*, which opened in mid-November.

The film was written and directed on a shoestring budget by brothers Alex and Stephen Kendrick, who are pastors in Albany, Georgia. Other than Cameron, the entire cast was made up of church members—and everyone worked for free.[8]

Ralph Winter is a successful Christian Hollywood film producer. He would love for more Christians to become involved in Hollywood. However, he cautions many young people who want to do films to strive to produce films of quality. Although *Facing the Giants* and *Fireproof* have been box office hits with a very limited budget, he believes we must be careful about the quality of product that is presented under the banner of *Christian* to make sure it is not synonymous with poor quality. "People come to a movie to be entertained first," he said in an interview at a conference I attended. "We have to master the art of filmmaking and create a powerful story before we think about how we're going to put some kind of Christian message in the film. Most Christians fail in the film business today because even though their intentions are admirable, they haven't learned the art and skill of making a great movie. We have to earn the respect of the viewer if we're going to succeed."[9]

Barbara Nicolosi, founder of Act One, a nonprofit organization founded to train Christians of all denominations for careers in mainstream film and television, agrees with Winter. In a telephone interview with her, she said she was very leery of the recent Christian films and their poor quality and fears what it might say about Christians and their failure to model excellence. My own view is there is a place for both. After all, Jesus did say He would use the foolish things of this world to confound the wise. We don't want to use that as an excuse for poor work, but we also must recognize God likes to show Himself strong through foolish things. The recent success of *Fireproof* is living *proof* of this principle. Yes, the acting could have been better. However, God used that film to positively impact many marriages.

More faith-based films are on the horizon. Samuel Goldwyn Films is the first major studio to embrace Christian films. *Fireproof* was their release in collaboration with Sherwood Pictures (the Christian film company) and Provident Films. In 2006 the home-entertainment division of Rupert Murdoch's movie studio started *Fox Faith*, a new film division. Murdoch is also owner of Zondervan Publishing, which published Rick Warren's book *The Purpose-Driven Life*, which has more than thirty million copies. That book got Murdock's attention, and he recognized the sheer number of people in the evangelical audience. Fox describes Fox Faith titles as "morally-driven, family-friendly programming," and requires them to "have overt Christian content or be derived from the work of a Christian author."[10]

Pixar Animation Studios, creators of the entirely new form of animation that came out in the 1990s and now best known for movies such as *Toy Story* (1–3), *Monsters, Inc.*, *Cars*, *The Incredibles*, and *WALL-E*, has a number of believers in key creative positions. Andrew Stanton (*WALL-E, Finding Nemo*) is a director, screenwriter, producer, and occasional voice actor who won two Oscars for the above-mentioned films and has discussed his Christian faith and its role in filmmaking.

Stanton explained his singular vision for *WALL-E*: "What really interested me was the idea of the most human thing in the universe being a machine because it has more interest in finding out what the point of living is than actual people. The greatest commandment Christ gives us is to love, but that's not always our priority. So I came up with this premise that could demonstrate what I was trying to say—that irrational love defeats the world's programming. You've got these two robots that are trying to go above their basest directives, literally their programming, to experience love."[11]

Pete Docter, the writer and director of *Monsters, Inc.* and director of *Up*, commented on how his faith affects his work: "Years ago when I first spoke at church, I was kind of nervous about talking about Christianity and my work. It didn't really connect. But more and more it seems to be connecting for me. I ask for God's help, and it's definitely affected what I'm doing. It's helped me to calm down and focus. There were times when I got too stressed out with what I was doing, and now I just step back and say, 'God, help me through this.' It really helps you keep a perspective on things, not only in work, but in relationships."[12]

USING A WINSOME STRATEGY

Earlier in the book I mentioned that Christianity has become a subculture that is more known by what we don't like than what we believe. In the eyes of the secular world, we have become a right-wing political action group instead of a loving, caring church of our Lord Jesus Christ seeking to solve societal problems. Our message has been shut out because of the *way* of the messenger. We still have the right message, but we have failed to deliver it in a manner consistent with the gospel of Jesus Christ. Jesus modeled love and mercy and sought to change the hearts of people before He expected to see change in their behavior. Few people are attracted to Christ through a boycott.

In 2008 our organization held our international "Reclaim 7 Mountains Conference." One of our speakers was Dr. Larry Poland, founder of Mastermedia International, a nonprofit organization that provides professional consulting and personal counseling to media professionals. Mastermedia maintains a prayer bulletin that features Hollywood executives in the industry who are being prayed for. Mastermedia also hosts an annual prayer breakfast for those in arts, entertainment, and media in Hollywood. During Dr. Poland's presentation he made some very insightful observations about the church's approach to influencing Hollywood.

Hollywood is mostly controlled by media moguls who operate in Hollywood and New York City. These change agents are largely Jewish in their makeup, but from a secular worldview more than from an orthodox one. Their orthodox brothers are actually as upset with them as many evangelical Christians are.

They do not reflect our values for one simple reason: they are lost. They are simply modeling and reflecting the worldview of lost people. What more can we expect? Poland said, "At Mastermedia we try to *catch* them, then let the Lord *clean* them. You catch more flies with honey than you do with vinegar."

He explained, "Some people think that it is the actors who make decisions, but that is not correct; it is the executives in the movie studios who make the important decisions about what movies will be produced. In fact, only 5–6 percent of all actors in Hollywood make $50,000 or more annually. There is a very small group of very successful actors."

Dr. Poland said that Hollywood's relationship to Christianity has gone through four distinct phases:

1. 1900–1950: During this phase the church isolated ourselves from Hollywood completely and condemned all movies. We called anything that came out of there *evil.*

2. 1950–1970: During this phase we were *separate but equal.* The church began producing Christian movies with Christian themes, and Christian merchandising arose. We did little to change Hollywood through these initiatives.

3. 1970–2000: During this phase we demonstrated *anger* more than anything else. The gay and lesbian agenda took root in Hollywood by a multiple of ten. We began to see more boycotts and hate mail being sent to studio executives. One studio executive, in response to the postcard responses that came in protest of one campaign, said, "These don't impact us at all. They are just Christian fund-raisers." (Poland cited that genuine letters that are grace-filled but share their concern do much more good than these kinds of campaigns.)

4. Since 1980: Poland has been building genuine caring relationships with entertainment and media executives in Hollywood and New York. He becomes their friend in an effort to demonstrate the love of Christ personally to them. He has seen many powerful men and women in the industry come to Christ, and he says, "You know, it is an interesting thing. When someone's heart changes, their behavior changes." He has seen this show up in the type of product these people begin to put out. There are now more than twenty-five ministries in Hollywood that are seeking to impact Hollywood through a strategy of praying and loving those in this industry. "We all work together and we all have a unique contribution," said Poland.

HOLLYWOOD PRAYER NETWORK

As a TV producer in Hollywood entertainment and as a Christian, when Karen Covell first started pursuing a career in Hollywood, she found it very difficult to live out her faith and pursue her career without a body of solid believing friends around her. So, twenty-eight years ago, Karen and eight other very young Christian professionals started praying together. That group, called Premise, still meets monthly today. Karen and her covenant group have grown to hundreds of Christian Hollywood professionals who now see themselves as marketplace ministers and artists sharing their faith; praying together; doing works of truth, beauty, and grace; and keeping their eyes on Jesus all along the way.

Ten years ago Karen realized another need—the church outside of Hollywood had to understand what God was doing there and needed to support the Christians in this mission field—the world's most influential mission field! Most of the "church" at large hated Hollywood, boycotted its films, and kept young creative people away from this place. That's when Karen started the Hollywood Prayer Network (HPN). "I felt the need to bridge the gap between the church and Hollywood through prayer," said Karen.

HPN has three goals: to pray for the Christians in Hollywood as "entertainment missionaries," to pray for the nonbelievers as children of God who just don't know Him yet, and to encourage talented Christians to come to Hollywood to live out their lives as creative people who also love God.

Today HPN offers a monthly e-mail that is sent to thousands of Christians around the world; they have their "I to I" prayer partnerships where they match an intercessor on the outside of Hollywood to pray for a Christian who is working in the entertainment industry. They have a monthly kids and teen prayer calendar where young people can download a new list of celebrities to pray for each month who are known on the shows they watch, the movies they go to, and the music they're listening to. HPN has local chapters around the world in order to allow artists and/or prayer warriors from any city across the globe to gather locally and pray for the media and entertainment industries in their part of the world or to pray corporately for Hollywood from wherever they are.

Karen sees firsthand that God is doing miraculous things in their mission field. They are seeing more people become Christians, an incredible growth of committed Christians in the entertainment community, and more and more Christians outside of Hollywood catching the vision that this is not Sodom and Gomorrah, but Nineveh—it can and is being redeemed.

Shawn Bolz came to Hollywood in May of 2007 and launched a ministry with twelve others directed at the arts and entertainment industry of Hollywood as well as inner-city work.

Since 2007 Shawn and his team have raised up a group of people who are believing God wants to impact the arts through film, music, and the other entertainment industries. "There is no faster way to change people than the power of story that is imparted through entertainment," says Shawn. "Every couple has a song, who wrote it? Everyone has their favorite movie that caused them to want to be a hero, who directed it? Every kid has a video game that makes them feel powerful, who designed it? We want to be those people so we can define the principles that cause humanity to soar."

Shawn is raising up teams who pray with the intention to hear God for others and do power evangelism at clubs, in meetings, at music venues, and in tourist areas, and they are experiencing incredible fruit. "It's cool to see people who came to us through having an encounter with one of our teams and God."

Shawn says they now have actors, costumers, makeup designers, and more praying on their sets and intentional God interventions with their coworkers that have changed the environment they work in. Their worship leaders have played for major artists and bands, they have been on *American Idol*, and sing as session singers on the hit show *Glee*. Their leadership has been presented on TV, designed sound for movies, starred on TV shows, etc. It's been an intense ride for all of them as they try and bring the kingdom to every environment they get launched into.

CALLED TO IMPACT CULTURE THROUGH THE ARTS AND ENTERTAINMENT MOUNTAIN

My close friends and pastor Johnny Enlow and his wife, Elizabeth, lead Daystar Church in Atlanta. One evening in 2008 Johnny was teaching on the topic of "The Mountain of Celebration of Arts and Entertainment." That night he gave a general prophecy to his people that God would raise up His sons and take them to the top almost overnight as He would put His "it factor" on them, and that this would begin immediately with a few and then be exponential beginning in 2012.

That night the mother of a teenage want-to-be singer was in his audience. The mother approached Johnny and said, "My son is one of those you speak." This was the mother of Justin Bieber. She and Justin were in the audience that night, and she came forward with Justin, who was thirteen at the time. His mother asked, "Could you pray for us? We are going to be one of those suddenly at the top." This was in 2008, before anyone had heard of him. Johnny explained that they prayed, and at the time of this writing in 2010, he is the number one teen pop star in the world. Both Justin and his mother are strong Christians, and Johnny says they are very "into" the seven mountain message. Johnny and Elizabeth remain in an advisory level with Justin and his mother.

Justin Bieber had just received the American Music Association's (AMA) 2010 Entertainer of the Year Award as I write this story, even though the teenage singer was up against some of music's top stars such as Eminem, Katy Perry, Lady Gaga, and Ke$ha. Justin not only took the top honor, but the teenage sensation also took home an award in all of the other categories he was nominated in—Favorite Male Artist, Pop or Rock; Favorite Album, Pop or Rock; T-Mobile Breakthrough Artist. He was nominated for two Grammys in 2011 but did not win.

God is accelerating His presence among those in the arts and entertainment mountain.

Kong Hee and his wife, Sun Ho, are founding leaders of City Harvest Church, the largest church in Singapore. Sun Ho, a musician and the worship leader in her church, was led by the Lord to make a major shift in her ministry. She moved into the marketplace by entering the pop music field. Those in her church leadership thought she had lost her way. However, today she is the most popular singer in China. I had dinner with one of the pastors from this church. He told me that her greatest persecution has come from within the church, as Christians felt that Sun Ho was selling out her faith when she felt God was leading her to this mountain to influence it for Christ. This is exactly what happens when believers seek to influence secular culture. We are often attacked through a religious spirit that seeks to make judgments about money and power, even when there might be pure motives from those who seek to influence a cultural mountain.

Sun Ho topped the charts twice in the United States and twice in the United Kingdom, the first Asian to do either. Using her wealth and influence, she is building a modern school building in each of China's thirteen largest cities; two are already completed. The Chinese government admires Sun Ho so much that it has issued a commemorative postage stamp honoring her. Sun Ho is an example of a Christian who has achieved great success at the top of the entertainment mountain and impacted the culture at the same time.

Sun Ho represents a new breed of artist that is part artist, part philanthropist and social entrepreneur. These artists are using their gifts to impact culture in practical ways. This new generation will see emerging social entrepreneurs who will put their faith and artistry to use by solving cultural problems.

WALDEN MEDIA: A RAY OF LIGHT IN HOLLYWOOD

Walden Media was birthed in 2001 when three individuals came together— Philip Anschutz, Cary Garnat, and Michael Flaherty. Walden Media has produced several successful family films, such as *The Chronicles of Narnia: The Lion, the Witch and the Wardrobe* and followed that with the *The Chronicles of Narnia: Prince Caspian*, both adaptations from C. S. Lewis's book series. Other films include *Journey to the Center of the Earth, Amazing Grace, Charlotte's Webb*, and *Bridge to Terabithia*.

The company is owned by Philip Anschutz, an oil magnate, media mogul, and the owner of the Regal Entertainment Group—the largest motion picture exhibitor in the world (it operates nearly 20 percent of all indoor screens in the United States)—and a growing force in Hollywood.

Anschutz, a professing Christian, was seeking to change Hollywood by putting more wholesome movies in his theaters. However, he quickly realized he could not change content that way and decided he needed to be in the movie production business. Thus, Walden Media was formed. "We expect movies to be entertaining but also to be life affirming and to carry a moral message," Philip Anschutz told an audience at the conservative Christian Hillsdale College. While "Hollywood as an industry can at times be insular and doesn't at times understand the market very well," he also "saw a chance with this move to attempt some small improvement in the culture."[13]

Walden execs saw The Chronicles of Narnia seven-book series as the cornerstone upon which to build their company. As the company has progressed, they have found it difficult to maintain the spiritual foundation that they are seeking to influence through Hollywood. One former Walden employee told me, "The struggle internally to maintain a spiritual foundation to what we are doing is always a battle. The bottom line is often fighting with the mission."

MAKING AN IMPACT ON THE INDUSTRY

Shun Lee came to Hollywood in 2003 after having a career as a lawyer in Omaha, Nebraska. He grew up in an arts and entertainment family, playing four instruments and playing musical theater. However, God touched him with a burden to impact Hollywood, and he moved there. He is a writer and has a production studio in the heart of Hollywood today. He is also founder and president of a nonprofit organization called Greenhouse that seeks to serve the emotional, spiritual, and professional needs of the arts and entertainment community. Their group holds a monthly meeting the first Sunday of each month in the CBS Studios. He also directs Hollywood Connect, a place for new arrivals of want-to-be actors and talent.

Carey Arban is an another emerging change agent in the arts and entertainment arena. She is founder and director of Actors, Models, and Talent for Christ (AMTC). Her journey in this industry began with her mother, Millie Lewis. Millie was her role model, a former New York cover girl in the late 1940s. Millie opened her first modeling school in Columbia, South Carolina, in 1960 to help instill poise and self-esteem in young people. There are five Millie Lewis modeling agencies still in existence today.

AMTC was founded in 1982 but did not have the Christ focus it has today until Carey had a personal conversion experience between 2005 and 2006. Her daughter and son-in-law, who both work with her in the business, also came to faith in Christ not long after. Carey describes AMTC on their website as a "company, a ministry, and a mission. It is a movement of Christian performers who are rising to be His light in the entertainment industry."[14]

Today Carey wants to use her influence to have an impact on the arts and entertainment mountain. Their agency has helped launch careers for many who have made a successful career in arts and entertainment. Tayla Collins, listed among the top fifty models in the world, got her start with AMTC and is a strong Christian. Veteran actress Andie McDowell got her start through AMTC, and a more recent success story is Megan Fox, the actress who starred in the two box office hits *Transformers*. Certainly not everyone who comes to AMTC is Christian. "All faiths are welcome," says Arban, who wants to bridge their professional expertise with their faith. AMTC provides a safe, family-oriented, and effective path for promising talent to meet with many of the best agents, managers and casting directors in the world.

Reclaiming Hollywood

I first met Bob (not his real name) in 2008 at a Reclaim 7 Mountains conference we hosted. He was deeply impacted by what he experienced at our conference, and a vision for reclaiming Hollywood was birthed in his heart. Bob comes from a life of success in sports, business, and even acting. Living in Hollywood, Bob has rubbed shoulders with the Hollywood elite. However, God took him through his own Joseph pit experience to come into an intimate relationship with Jesus.

Bob and a few other Christian friends in the movie business began to see that Hollywood had become Babylon. They could see that film production and distribution was controlled by a handful of major studios that garnered the lion's share of the money. Actual creators, producers, and theaters got a very small percentage of the revenue. God began to reveal a better way to Bob and his friends. As I write this, a new way of creating movie projects is being birthed that would be distributed through one of the largest distribution networks in the world—the local church. And the lion's share of the money would be shared with producers, local churches, and theaters instead of the movie studios.

Bob and his friends want to remain anonymous, and that is why I am not sharing names. However, when you begin to hear of movies being shown in churches, you will be seeing the fruit of their vision to reclaim Hollywood and become God's change agent on the arts and entertainment mountain.

When you are dealing with people of influence that may have a visible high public profile, it is important to maintain strict confidence. These people want to know if they can trust you. Avoid name-dropping in an effort to impress others of whom you might be working with. The apostle Paul understood this by his comment in his letter to the Galatians: "And I went up by revelation, and communicated to them that gospel which I preach among the Gentiles, *but privately to those who were of reputation,* lest by any means I might run, or had run, in vain."[15]

Become a Change Agent for the Arts and Entertainment Mountain

What can I do as one individual to make an impact for God on the arts and entertainment mountain?

Has God called you to be a change agent in the arts and entertainment mountain? If so, learn from the wisdom of those who are scaling this mountain. How can you take your stand in any of the following areas where others have had a positive impact for God?

1. Lawrence Khong, pastor of a megachurch in Singapore, has stepped into the arts and entertainment culture as a performing magician. What talents do you have that you could use for God?

2. Tyler Perry has had five opening number one box office hits in the lasts five years. He uses the comedic characters in his movies as bait to deliver a godly message. What are the tools you have in your hand that you could use as bait?

3. A Christian "insider" witnessed to CBS office producers and crews when a popular Christian worship song was sung by finalists on *American Idol*. She asked Christians to "pray, pray, pray" for Christians working in Hollywood. Are you praying?

4. The highest-grossing independent film of 2008, *Fireproof*, was written and directed on a shoestring budget with everyone working for free. What can you do at a grassroots level to impact this mountain?

5. Carey Arban, founder and director of Actors, Models, and Talent for Christ (AMTC), provides a safe, family-oriented, effective path for promising talent to get started on careers in this culture. How can you support Christians working in arts and entertainment careers?

6. As we saw in this chapter, boycotts and indignant e-mails do not have the effect the originators intend. How can you pray effectively for individuals involved in the arts and entertainment industries, showing them God's love?

What would success look like on the arts and entertainment mountain?

- Creative people would view the world from a God-based world-view as opposed to a flawed, ungodly view.

- There would be less ungodly and aberrant behavior being shown in entertainment.

- There would be wholesome values-based stories represented in movies and other entertainment.

- There would be less pornographic movies and Internet sites.

- There would be more entertainment reflecting the glory of God and His creativity.

- There would be more creative art reflecting the nature and glory of God and less art on the dark side of life due to brokenness.

Chapter 17

RECLAIMING THE MEDIA MOUNTAIN

How beautiful upon the mountains are the feet of him who brings good news
—ISAIAH 52:7

Os, YOU WOULD be shocked. The entire media are controlled by about one hundred people!" These words came from a friend who has had a career in mainstream media at the highest level.

There is not a week that goes by that I do not hear a Christian conclude—either in conversation, on talk radio, or in sermons—that the national media have a liberal bias. The Christian church has been quite prolific in its critical view of the national media. Is their assessment true? If so, why? If not, how have we mistakenly judged them? In this chapter we will attempt to answer these questions.

WHAT IS THE MEDIA MOUNTAIN?

Media refers to the news outlets that report and establish the news. Therein lies the power of the media—they can actually create the news. We have all been able to observe the worldly skills at work as major media outlets turn a non-story into *the* big story or totally ignore the events that *should* be the big story for our nation to hear.[1]

Francis Schaeffer said, "Whoever controls the media controls the culture. Art and media are the means and the bridge over which the current philosophy of the philosophers reaches the general culture."[2] The national media are the prophetic voice of the nation. Their primary role should be to report what is taking place in the nation and the world from an unbiased perspective. They are to proclaim truth and expose unrighteousness. God also created the media to provide accountability for the leaders. God uses the media as His Holy Spirit posse to vet out things done in darkness.

The media do provide some of these things today. However, because so few in the media have a biblical worldview, Satan has largely operated at the top of this mountain. He does this through a highly professional mix of reporting partial truth but without any redemptive purpose. Instead, the spirit behind

155

the media is often designed to create fear, despair, and hopelessness and can often present situations inaccurately to portray something that is good to be evil or simply shape the viewer's opinion that may not be accurate. National media has great power to persuade public opinion. A friend of mine who works in a national media position in New York City said to me once, "We tell you what you should believe about the world." What a sobering responsibility and power to shape culture. The way in which the media report news shapes our view on what is happening in society, right or wrong.

National media are one of the most important culture-shapers in society. David Kupelian, author of *The Marketing of Evil,* states: "No, the scary fact is that the media—both news and entertainment—are literally the creators and sustainers of what most of us *perceive* as reality, reminiscent of the malevolent computer program in The Matrix film trilogy. In The Matrix, humans are born into a slave state in which what they think of as reality is actually a powerful computer-generated virtual reality program. They live in constant and deep delusion. Without realizing it, these humans have been reduced to the lowest form of servitude, their life energies literally sucked out of them to fuel the insatiable needs of their rulers."[3]

In 2007, the Culture and Media Institute released a National Cultural Values Survey. The results are revealing.

- Seventy-four percent of people surveyed, including majorities of every major demographic group, say they believe moral values in America are weaker than they were twenty years ago.

- Sixty-eight percent, including majorities of virtually every demographic group, say the media—entertainment and news alike—are having a detrimental effect on moral values in America.

- Sixty-four percent agree the news and entertainment media exercise powerful influence over American moral values. In fact, the substantial majority (74 percent), who believes moral values are weaker than twenty years ago, considers the media to be the second greatest influence on moral values after parents and families.

The survey concludes: "Americans have clearly identified the media as primary culprits in the nation's moral decline. If the media continue to singularly promote Progressive values and a secular worldview, while undermining Orthodox faith and values, reversing America's moral decline will be very difficult. Americans who care about the nation's moral condition should insist that the media strive to more fairly represent all views, including those of the Orthodox."[4]

Is there any wonder why our values are eroding?

RULING PRINCIPALITY

In order to view media correctly, we must recognize that there is a spiritual battle taking place in our world. We are not just fighting people in the media; we are also fighting a principality that is in control of that medium. Consider Ephesians 6:12–13: "For we do not wrestle against flesh and blood, but against principalities, against powers, against the rulers of the darkness of this age, against spiritual hosts of wickedness in the heavenly places. Therefore take up the whole armor of God, that you may be able to withstand in the evil day, and having done all, to stand."

The Hittites described in Joshua 1 and Deuteronomy 7 represent the media. Johnny Enlow, in his book *The Seven Mountain Prophecy*, describes it this way:

> Apollyon is the name of the ruling spirit over the Hittites. Apollyon means "destroyer" and "destruction" means to fear, promote terror, especially as it relates to wars like Iraq and Afghanistan. These demonic influences can cause deception, lack of truth telling, manipulation of truth, partial truth, and can become a source to instill fear in society. They can also shape culture to be viewed in an ungodly and humanistic way. They promote doubt, unbelief, and discontent with our national leaders in our government by often focusing on only the negative aspects of the war instead of the positive outcomes being achieved. It is more often the bearer of bad news. Media can serve as a pawn by Satan to deliver and communicate fear and despair to culture.[5]

That is why national media will always end with an upbeat story to counter the twenty minutes of mostly bad news they have already delivered into your home and your spirit.

THE OPRAH PHENOMENON

Oprah Winfrey has become the idol of American women audiences. Her human-interest stories inspire and educate. Her generosity is a model of philanthropy. She started a school for girls in South Africa. She has given away millions of dollars through innovative programs. She has created a huge audience of followers as a result of being the number one show in its category. When a product is mentioned on her program, people run out to buy it. She is her own *tipping point* in culture.

In 2008 Oprah began her own religion, which is consistent with her generous giving and feel-good philosophy but has some very strange, nonbiblical foundations. Many women are being led astray because of the tremendous influence that she yields, regardless of the foundation of the message. This is the power of media. In a 1994 article *Vanity Fair* said: "Oprah Winfrey arguably has more influence on the culture than any university president, politician, or religious leader except the Pope."[6] *Christianity Today* said of Oprah: "To her audience of more than 22 million mostly female viewers, Oprah has become a post-modern priestess—an icon of church-free spirituality."[7]

How Do Spirits Get a Foothold?

Influence from demonic principalities has taken place over several decades since television began. With the advent of broadcast journalism, people have turned to the television for their news. Young people who prepare to become news journalists are more often trained in Ivy League schools. These Ivy League schools, like Harvard, Yale, and Columbia, despite most having a Christian foundation, have now become the primary liberal educational factory of the nation. Those who graduate from these schools have received a steady diet of an anti-Christian worldview. Consequently, when these people take on high-level journalistic positions, they represent this worldview, often without even knowing it.

Journalists are trained to be neutral in their reporting. However, a journalist's views often come through in subtle ways in the manner by which the reporting is delivered. It is unrealistic for Christians to think that the national media will report on something without the journalist's worldview showing up in the reporting. The only way to change this is to impact the individual reporter, who will then adopt a Christian worldview. One of the ways bias shows up is in the way something is actually reported. A journalist may be covering a story and may interview a major leader. However, if that journalist has ever had a bad experience with that person, there might be a particular slant to the way he or she allows the report to get on the air. The reporter might show that person in a negative light or allow a sound byte to be taken out of context. There are a number of ways this can happen.

Are the Media Liberal?

In order to better understand the national news, let's get a profile of typical national news journalists. They are most often educated at an Ivy League school, which largely promotes a liberal worldview. A high majority of journalists will hold a Democratic political view, with the exception being the Fox Network, where more Christians work than at other networks.

Journalists often live in a bubble—they may not drive a car because they live in New York City and work in Manhattan, where only a small minority of the population are Christians. Journalists see what is bad in society every day and often become jaded by what they see. Mac Pier, director of Concerts of Prayer, with whom I participated on a leadership committee in 2007 for the 150th anniversary of the 1857 revival in New York City started by Jeremiah Lanphier, said there are less than 1 percent of Christians on the island of Manhattan, the most influential and powerful city in the world.

The media do have a political viewpoint, and at times they will not hide that fact, though you must be watching carefully to catch it. David Kupelian, in his book *The Marketing of Evil*, stated: "In the 2004 Democratic National Convention, *New York Times* columnist John Tierney asked 153 journalists whether they thought John Kerry or George W. Bush would make a 'better president.' Reports from outside the beltway favored Kerry three to one, while the approximately 50 Washington-based journalists polled favored Kerry over Bush by a stunning twelve-to-one margin! This bias reached absurd levels when Dan Rather and CBS News pathetically stonewalled the entire world— even the rest of the 'mainstream media'—arrogantly defending the obviously bogus documents Rather and *60 Minutes* had featured for the intended purpose of bringing down a U.S. president. We've been lied to so thoroughly and consistently that we no longer perceive the meaning of what we see nor understand what we hear."[8]

How do liberals vote in elections? Let's take a look at some research.

- In a 1999 survey by the American Society of Newspaper Editors (ASNE), 61 percent of newsroom respondents described themselves as Democrats and only 10 percent as Republicans.[9]

- In 1992, 89 percent of the Washington journalists surveyed voted for Bill Clinton and only 7 percent for George Bush.[10]

- In the ASNE survey, 61 percent of the journalists rated themselves as *liberal* or *liberal to moderate*, and 9 percent as *conservative* or *conservative to moderate*.[11]

- In 2007, the Pew Research Center found there were four self-identified liberal journalists for every one conservative.[12]

In June of 2008, I was sitting in my living room watching *NBC Nightly News* with Brian Williams. A profile story was being presented on Doug Coe, the founder of Trinity Forum, a Washington-based ministry to political leaders, both Republican and Democrat. I had met Doug a few years ago as an invitee to the President's Prayer Breakfast held annually in February each year. Doug and his group do a good job of serving the spiritual needs of political leaders.

However, the story cast suspicion about the mission of the organization, criticized some of the work they had done, and left an overall negative impression of an organization that is doing a tremendous job among the Washington elite without bringing any attention to Doug or his organization. It was one of the most blatant misuses by the national media I had seen about an organization with which I was very familiar. I wrote a letter of protest on the story. They never answered my e-mail.

Unfortunately, the view of the secular media about Christians is very negative. The very thing most Christians would like to be known for is the opposite of how we are perceived by the national media. Dick Staub, in his book *The Culturally Savvy Christian*, states: "When the press covers evangelicals, a pattern is emerging: evangelical strength is usually calculated by the size and the number of churches, church attendance, economic clout, or political muscle or by its enviable breadth of distribution outlets and educational institutions; the press does not generally find evangelicalism noteworthy for its spiritual depth, intellectual rigor, aesthetic richness, relational health, or moral purity."[13]

The 2008 presidential election revealed the bias of the media better than any other time. This was proven through several independent studies that measured media stories. The Center for Media and Public Affairs at George Mason University, Virginia, surveyed 585 network news stories from August 23 through September 30, 2008, during the heat of the presidential campaign season. Here were their findings based on the number of favorable stories reported by each network.[14]

Favorable to Obama	Favorable to McCain
65 percent	36 percent
CBS, 73 percent	CBS, 31 percent
NBC, 56 percent	NBC, 16 percent
ABC, 57 percent	ABC, 42 percent
Fox, 60 percent	Fox, 60 percent

Michael Malone, a fourth-generation journalist for ABC News website, recognized the bias in the media and made the following comment: "The traditional media are playing a very, very dangerous game. With its readers, with the Constitution, and with its own fate. The sheer bias in the print and television coverage of this election is not just bewildering but appalling. And over the past few months I've found myself slowly moving from shaking my head at the obvious one-sided reporting, to actually shouting at the screen of my television and laptop computer."[15] There were many, many other examples of bias during the 2008 election. The media could not hide their preference and proactive efforts for getting Barack Obama elected president.

Cable media have become more polarized in recent years with both the Left and the Right giving greater voice to their agendas. The first two years of the Obama presidency resulted in the greatest liberal policies implemented of any prior US president. This awakened a sleeping giant of mainstream America that became increasingly concerned with the liberal direction of the nation. The Tea Party movement, which stood for smaller government and a focus on reducing the national debt, became a catalyst to a landslide midterm election in 2010. Many of those elected to Congress for the first time have a strong Christian faith. However, it's important we don't politicize culture change. God has His representatives in both political parties. We must evaluate policies and leaders based on the Word of God regardless of the party they belong to.

There are usually three types of journalists. One type is the true-blue journalists who want to produce only the truth, no matter what it says. They are true to their profession. Another type is those who operate from middle ground. They allow their worldview to show up from time to time. Finally, there are those who have a clear agenda but try to share it in very discreet ways. Bernard Goldberg states, "For example, the *Atlantic* magazine hired a photographer who *intentionally* shot John McCain to look like a monster. Turns out the photographer was a self-described 'hardcore Democrat.' The magazine didn't use the 'diabolical McCain' picture on the cover, but it did use one that the photographer didn't bother to touch up. 'I left his eyes red and his skin looking bad,' she later admitted, adding, 'Maybe it was somewhat irresponsible for [the *Atlantic*] to hire me.'"[16]

In other cases, all of this is done on a subconscious basis, and their worldview simply slips through the cracks. However, today we are seeing less and less unbiased reporting by certain networks such as CNBC and MSNBC—two of the most liberal cable networks.

Sadly though, as we have said already, less than 19 percent of the Christian population has a Christian worldview, Republican or Democrat. So how can we expect the media to have a Christian worldview if we in the body of Christ do not even have one? We are losing the culture both within and outside the Christian community.

PRAYERS OF REPENTANCE

One of our first responsibilities for reclaiming the media is to repent as believers. As I mentioned in earlier chapters, it was our own disobedience that entitled liberal voices to arise during our watch. As recently as the ASNE Survey of 1999, despite the belief that the media is biased, the viewing public—including those of us who call ourselves Christian—have not protested the obvious media bias. The survey reported: "Despite the belief that the news media are biased, the public does not view that bias as a major hindrance to using the news. Their perception of bias in newspapers does not represent a 'major obstacle' to being able to trust newspapers as a source of news—perhaps because they believe they've built sufficient filtering mechanisms to identify and neutralize it when they think they see it."[17]

Believers in the national media—and Christians in the viewing public—must stand in the gap just as Daniel and Nehemiah did for their nations who had sinned. Christian journalists must repent on behalf of the larger media industry for reporting a worldview that focuses on humanistic foundations without acknowledging God's role in society. We must repent of propagating fear and inaccurate reporting about people and situations—whether we are the journalists who do the reporting or the Christians who do nothing to protest it.

We must pray for the airwaves to be filled with truth in reporting, righteousness in the way reports are prepared, and stories of nobility, justice, truth, virtue, and praiseworthy things. Truth must replace stories that promote fear, anxiety, and an unbalanced view of situations and people. Truthful, accurate reflections of what is taking place and the people involved must be broadcast. We must raise up a new generation of journalists at a national level who are willing to stand up for righteousness when they are confronted with bowing down to the god of power and influence that contradicts our worldview. Yet we must also follow Jesus's instructions to live as sheep among wolves and be wise as serpents and harmless as doves: "Behold, I send you out as sheep in the midst of wolves. Therefore be wise as serpents and harmless as doves."[18]

This is not an easy assignment in such a pressure-packed industry. Consider Shadrach, Meshach, and Abed-nego, who refused to bow down to the god of Nebuchadnezzar. "Shadrach, Meshach, and Abed-nego answered and said to the king, 'O Nebuchadnezzar, we have no need to answer you in this matter. If that is the case, our God whom we serve is able to deliver us from the burning fiery furnace, and He will deliver us from your hand, O king. But if not, let it be known to you, O king, that we do not serve your gods, nor will we worship the gold image which you have set up.'"[19]

The result of their refusal to bow down led to the God of Israel being protected by the Babylonian government. These three men were elevated for their courage. This is the model for influencing culture at the highest level. This will be required of those who operate at the highest levels in the media mountain.

Media Careers

It is very difficult to get a job in the national media. Jobs are often given to family members within the network and to those who know people who run in Ivy League circles. It can be a very closed network. God must open doors for people to get into the media profession. And if they do get in, they will need to work long hours to advance to positions of power. Their families will need to understand the significant warfare that takes place at the top of this mountain and be prepared to face it. Work hours are long, and it often involves a great deal of travel away from the family.

We need to better understand the world a national journalist lives in and how it contributes to their worldview. Consider these facts:

- Journalists are lied to every day by those wanting to manipulate public opinion. "Why should the church be any different?" they conclude. "Who can I really trust?" They are trained to believe that most people are lying to them, and their role is to expose it.

- It's especially hard for Christians in media to recover when a Christian is the source of dishonesty or failure in integrity. It tarnishes their faith, and their secular counterparts use this as ammunition against their own faith.

- Media are seen as a means to an end. Journalists are viewed as a resource to power and influence and as a way for someone to advance his or her own agenda. Consequently, they routinely feel used by society and leaders in society.

- Many Christians hold a narrow and judgmental attitude toward those in the media. Consequently journalists view Christians as narrow and judgmental. They know what Christians don't believe in, but they would like to know what they really stand for and why others should want what they have. They see Christians as critics who fail to provide solutions to world problems such as world hunger and AIDs.

USING MEDIA TO INFLUENCE CULTURE

In the early 1980s a media ministry was birthed called The Graphic Truth. A small band of creative directors came together to create media "ad" campaigns designed to convey the real truth about cultural issues of the days. Issues like abortion, divorce, and sex outside of marriage were just a few of the topics addressed. Commercials and print ads were created that churches could brand with their name. Unfortunately, the only distribution was through paid advertising, which was costly. This was an idea birthed before its time. Now is the time for such a ministry because of the ability to get free airtime on YouTube and the hundreds of other video channels. A good case in point is a commercial known as The Chinese Professor 2030. This controversial sixty-second ad shows a Chinese professor teaching his college students how the greatest nation in the world fell through too much debt, being involved in too many wars, and healthcare reform. The conclusion finds the professor saying, "And now they work for us." The students laugh in delight.

This commercial was created by Citizens for Government Waste. It ran over national TV but had greater circulation through the thousands of views on the Internet. Christians should use the media creatively to create dialogue about important cultural issues.

Become a Change Agent for the Media Mountain

Are the national media liberal? Well, *yes* is the answer to that question. Do they always report in a liberal fashion? *No.* Not all journalists have an agenda. However, what we must realize is they are simply expressing their own personal worldview, without an agenda attached. A person without Christ should operate like a person without the love of God in his or her heart. That person has no motive to live a righteous life. So we cannot expect much more, unless we become the source of the solution. Let's begin to think differently about how we should view those working in the national media. Let's strategically find a way to love them into the kingdom.

What can I do as one individual to make an impact for God on the media mountain?

Francis Schaeffer said, "Whoever controls the media controls the culture." In today's culture, there is no question but that the media are currently controlled by liberals who have strayed far from the beliefs of our Founding Fathers. How can you have an impact in the following areas?

1. Most college graduates today are graduating from schools that have fed their students a steady diet of an anti-Christian worldview.

2. I told of writing a letter of protest when *NBC Nightly News* presented a blatantly untruthful, negative report about a Washington-based ministry with which I was familiar. Have you protested misuses of media you have seen?

3. I stressed that we must pray for the airwaves to be filled with truth in reporting stories of nobility, justice, virtue, and praise-worthy things. Are you praying?

4. How can you help to "raise up" a new generation of journalists at a national level who are willing to stand up for righteousness?

What would success look like on the media mountain?

- News reporting would be balanced without bias.

- There would be less posturing of positions taken by media and their representatives.

- There would be respect for the media.

- Media would be seen as valuable resources for news, information, and accountability for leaders.

- Positive stories would be profiled to represent the best in human nature instead of the worst.

Chapter 18

RECLAIMING THE MOUNTAIN OF BUSINESS

And whatever you do, do it heartily, as to the Lord and not to
men, knowing that from the Lord you will receive the reward
of the inheritance; for you serve the Lord Christ.
—Colossians 3:23–24

I WALKED INTO THE boardroom and was greeted by several over-fifty marketplace leaders from the community of Oklahoma City. Each one had achieved a significant level of professional success in his or her life. One man was a former attorney general, another founded a company that taught ethics and character in public schools, another was a former Miss America and TV anchorwoman, another was a successful businessman in the hair care business, another was a former mayor, and another was David Green, founder and CEO of Hobby Lobby. We were meeting in the headquarters of Hobby Lobby, a company that David Green began with $600. Today it is a $1.3 billion per year enterprise. Green opened his first retail store in 1972 and today has three hundred stores in twenty-seven states. He is a committed follower of Jesus Christ and uses his influence to impact culture, nationally and internationally.

The purpose of the small gathering was for me to spend a full day to review with the group the concept of what it means to reclaim culture from a city perspective. We spent the day walking through concepts and stopped along the way to take questions and discuss the core premises. These were men and women who had succeeded in life professionally, but now they wanted to invest in others and pass on a spiritual heritage to the next generation of leaders.

I was particularly impressed as David Green shared a little of his story. He began to tear up as he shared how the past weekend he had been "in awe of God and how He had blessed him so much." He shared how his business was increasing during one of the worst recessions in recent history. He believed it was simply the grace of God. I was impressed with the humility of such a successful businessman.

WHAT IS THE MOUNTAIN OF BUSINESS?

The business mountain holds the power over economy, resources, and power that are either consecrated for the kingdom of God or captured for the powers of darkness. It is a mountain that is often ruled by the spirit of mammon and pride. Satan rules at the top of this mountain. Take this mountain, and all others will fall. In recent months and years, we have all watched as the world of business—nationally and globally—began to face negative economic realities.

HISTORY OF BUSINESS

Nations in Europe and North America that became prosperous through business can attribute their prosperity to the reformers of the 1500s. Martin Luther and John Calvin made the greatest impact. Before this time Geneva, Switzerland, was a poor, weak nation. Today we associate Geneva, Switzerland, with economic activity, prosperity, international summits, and the banking center of the world.

History reveals that Geneva was transformed from a poor nation into a prosperous nation through the teaching of John Calvin, who taught the importance of individual responsibility and seeing work as a form of worship. He helped abolish the "sacred-secular" dichotomy that existed among the people. He taught a holistic gospel that involved God in all aspects of life.

Calvin studied the Bible to learn economic principles that could be applied in business in nations. He taught bankers not to charge high interest rates in order to avoid the sin of usury and was credited for instituting the maximum interest rate of 4 percent so the lender could still make some income, but the rate was low enough for borrowers to finance their projects. This 4 percent interest principle was used for four centuries in Switzerland and was adopted by other Western nations. So, you can see that the prosperity that transformed a poor nation into a prosperous nation was rooted in a scriptural foundation of work and economy.

In Zechariah 4:6 we learn that we must combine our natural abilities with the manifestation of the power of God in the area of our calling: "This is the word of the LORD to Zerubbabel: 'Not by might nor by power, but by My Spirit,' says the LORD of hosts."

I am often interviewed by the secular media about faith and work. They ask me, "So what makes a Christian any different than a non-Christian when it comes to their work?"

Over the past several years I have observed four key qualities exhibited by workplace believers who are transforming their workplaces, cities, and even nations for Christ through their work life calling. I devoted an entire chapter to these four attributes in my book *The 9 to 5 Window*. I believe these attributes are God's ideal for the Spirit-led worker today. Let's take a look at them. These attributes are:

1. *Excellence:* If we fail to do our work with excellence, we fail to earn the right to be a leader others will look up to.

2. *Ethics and integrity:* Psalm 51 says God desires truth in the inward parts. Are you the same person in private as in public?

3. *Extravagant love and service:* Jesus said we must be servants just as He was. Serving others tangibly models the humility of Jesus.

4. *Signs and wonders:* Experiencing God's presence and power is what distinguishes you as a follower of Jesus. Are you manifesting His life in the area of your calling?

When a change agent exhibits these traits, he will experience transformation at many different levels.

THE STRONGHOLD OVER THE MARKETPLACE

The spiritual stronghold that rules over the marketplace is mammon and pride. Mammon is actually a demonic principality. It motivates men and women in the marketplace to operate based on greed and pride. The economic crisis that began with the mortgage crisis in 2008 in America is clearly the work of these two spirits operating in men and women. The marketplace decided they wanted to write more business in the form of subprime mortgages. In order to do that, they decided to change longstanding rules that were used for qualifying a person for a loan. These rules made it easier for people to get a loan. However, these people were high risk, because they really could not afford these loans.

Some consumers saw the opportunity to acquire the American dream of home ownership in spite of their inability to afford such loans. Presumption became the rule of thumb, and this was multiplied throughout an entire mortgage and banking industry. Cracks in this foundation began to surface, and before we knew it, we were in one of the most devastating market downturns in our history as a nation, one that is affecting the entire world. Why? Because mammon and greed infiltrated the minds of marketplace people.

This began a series of bailouts, the likes of which we have never seen in our history. The problem is that the nation has not recognized its spiritual failure or the source of the problem. Until America, and business leaders in particular, repent for the wrong, the Lord may allow America to stay in this place for a long time. How much pain do we need before we decide to get on our knees and cry out to God?

God gave us His instruction for solving such problems. It is found in 2 Chronicles 7:14:

> If My people who are called by My name will humble themselves, and pray and seek My face, and turn from their wicked ways, then I will hear from heaven, and will forgive their sin and heal their land.

God is looking for righteous business leaders who will turn our nation back to a righteous form of commerce. He is looking for men and women of integrity. He is looking for the *Josephs* in the land.

THE RISE OF SOCIAL ENTREPRENEURSHIP

In May of 2004, advertising executive Kennan Burch challenged twenty trustworthy, like-minded, passionate Christian men on a journey to pursue God's waterfall of grace together and, secondarily, God's dreams for their lives. The plan was to meet once per month, early in the morning (6:00–8:00 a.m.) for a time of grace, fellowship, and dream building. It was designed to be a safe place to show up and express the deepest dreams/yearnings/desires that God had placed within all of them. Using Ephesians 2:10 as their primary verse, Kennan asked the men the question, "What promise(s) did God make the world when He made you?" Or, "Whose hero did God create you to be?" Their mutual belief in a big God and His calling on their lives has led them to see hundreds of dreams come true.

To focus their thoughts, they developed the following creed: *The glory of God is man fully alive. We come fully alive when we pursue God and His dreams that use our uniqueness to love others. By the grace of God we will pursue His dreams for our lives by listening for Him to say, "Let there be . . ."* At this writing they have now met for eighty consecutive months. The stories these men can tell are almost beyond belief. Among some of the dreams are: publishing books, making movies, starting companies, adopting orphans from foreign countries, building orphanages in Mongolia, dramatic rescues (from Haiti), large-scale (city-wide) events, evangelistic media campaigns, starting churches, writing screen plays, hosting retreats, creating radio programs, expanding organizations, etc. This process resulted in one man's dream to produce movies that led to the production of box office hits *Facing the Giants*, *Fireproof*, and *Letters to God*. Today this has become a website where others share their dreams: www.DreamBuildersNetwork.com.

Doug Holladay is the founder of PathNorth, a very high-end gathering for executives to "broaden their definition of success." It is not overtly a Christian event, but it is a place where very high-end business leaders and government leaders show up to hear many different speakers on current relevant topics. But there is definitely an underlying Christian message. PathNorth was created as a place where church and cultural leaders could come together to collaborate and explore ideas about how the gospel can be expressed within our cultural context. PathNorth's method of learning is based upon three keys: exposure, conversation, and collaboration. The members don't want to create just another conference, but instead, they make an intentional effort to platform the best and the brightest ideas that are shaping our world and interact with them.

Gabe Lyons, author of *The Next Christians*, hosts an annual event called Q Ideas each year in a new city, carefully chosen to reflect a unique context of Western culture so that leaders are continually challenged and exposed to the changing landscape of a post-Christian setting. By bringing together leaders from the channels of media, education, politics, arts and entertainment, business, the social sector, and the church to learn from one another, it instigates lively interaction and learning that seldom take place in other environments.

Gabe believes that inherent in Christian faithfulness is the responsibility to create a better world, one that reflects God's original design and intention. Q is a place leaders can explore what that might look like and how God's intention is showing up in the lives of their peers and the cultural projects they create.

Their scope continues to grow, but they strive for their gatherings to remain intimate and intentional, a small environment designed to draw together innovators and the best ideas through which we can embody the gospel in public life. Over the course of three days at Q, you will encounter short, powerful presentations from over twenty-five dynamic presenters.

New wealth, created by a new generation of technology artists, is fostering a new brand of social entrepreneur. *The Ultimate Gift* movie (2006) portrays this new brand of social entrepreneur. The synopsis reads:

> Jason thought his inheritance was going to be the gift of money and lots of it. Was he ever in for a big surprise. Based on the best-selling book *The Ultimate Gift* by Jim Stovall, the story sends trust fund baby Jason Stevens on an improbable journey of discovery, having to answer the ultimate question: "What is the relationship between wealth and happiness?" Jason had a very simple relationship with his impossibly wealthy grandfather, Howard "Red" Stevens. He hated him. No heart-to-heart talks, no warm fuzzies, just cold hard cash. So of course he figured that when Red died, the whole "reading of the will" thing would be another simple cash transaction, that his grandfather's money would allow him to continue living in the lifestyle to which he had become accustomed. But what Red left him was anything but simple. Red instead devised a plan for Jason to experience a crash course on life. Twelve tasks, which Red calls "gifts," each challenging Jason in an improbable way, the accumulation of which would change him forever.[1]

Today God is preparing His Josephs who can be trusted to steward His resources and purposes on the earth. One of the hallmarks of the emerging generation, both Christian and non-Christian, is to use business to make a positive impact upon the great needs in culture.

MODERN-DAY CYRUSES

There will also be another emerging group who we are already seeing take their place in culture today. They are the *Cyruses*. In the Book of Isaiah we find a description of Cyrus. He was a nonbelieving king whom God raised up to rebuild Jerusalem. God used his wealth and power for His purposes.

> I will raise up Cyrus in my righteousness:
> I will make all his ways straight.
> He will rebuild my city
> and set my exiles free,
> but not for a price or reward,
> says the LORD Almighty.
>
> —ISAIAH 45:13, NIV

Cyruses are social entrepreneurs who identify underutilized resources—people, buildings, equipment—and find ways of putting them to use to satisfy unmet social needs. Social entrepreneurs are driven, ambitious leaders with great skills in communicating a mission and inspiring others to join them. In the last ten years there has been a growing trend toward social entrepreneurship throughout the world and especially in the United States.

Blake Mycoskie was vacationing in 2006 and playing polo. The polo fields were near some very poor areas of the community, where he was exposed to 250 children in the Argentina village who had no shoes to protect them during long walks to food, water, and school. Upset by what he saw, he created TOMS Shoes. He returned to Argentina with 250 pairs of shoes for the kids. Today, Blake's business model includes with every pair purchased, TOMS gives a pair of new shoes to a child in need. Blake is one of many leaders in business to give back as a social entrepreneur who uses his for-profit venture to serve traditionally nonprofit ends. TOMS has given away 1,000,000 pairs of shoes as of the fall of 2010 since the business began in 2006. In December 2009, TOMS Shoes was awarded the State Department's Award for Corporate Excellence by Secretary of State Hillary Rodham Clinton. Between business ventures, Mycoskie competed in the CBS primetime series *The Amazing Race*. With his sister, Paige, he came within minutes of winning the million dollar grand prize.

A graduate of Texas Christian University, Blake was asked about his mission in life. "I believe each of us has a mission in life, and that one cannot truly be living their most fulfilled life until they recognize this mission and dedicate their life to pursuing it. Sometimes a mission lasts for two weeks or two months, or possibly twenty years. I have given my life to several over the past thirty-three years, but none of them have resonated so deeply with my soul as the one I am currently pursuing. This mission is not singular in its track, but consists of several evolving pursuits interconnected by the TOMS movement."[2]

Blake has followed a biblical principle of giving that has blessed TOMS shoes as they have incorporated their giving as part of their business model on the front end instead of the backend.

BILL GATES AND WARREN BUFFETT

It would be hard to talk about change agents in business without talking about two of the most influential change agents in culture today. Bill Gates's influence on business and the world is easily comparable to the impact that the printing press has had on the world. Gates, now the richest man in the world, had an early interest in software and began programming computers at the age of thirteen. In 1975, before graduation, Gates left Harvard to form Microsoft with his childhood friend Paul Allen. The pair planned to develop software for the newly emerging personal computer market.

These problem solvers came along at the right time and have made a huge impact on culture. Warren Buffett is also one of the modern-day Cyruses in business. Although they may not wear an evangelical armband, Gates and Buffett clearly exhibit kingdom values in their approach to philanthropy. Gates and his wife, Melinda, have endowed the Bill and Melinda Gates Foundation with more than $28.8 billion (as of January 2005) to support philanthropic initiatives in the areas of global health and learning.[3]

In 2006, Warren Buffett gave $60 billion worth of stock to the Gates' foundation. This is the largest ever gift to a foundation. When asked why he chose to entrust Gates' foundation with the gift, Buffett looked at Gates and said, "Because you can do a better job of giving it away than I can."[4] That is quite a statement of faith and trust. They have become very good friends over the last ten years. Since 1994 the foundation has given grants in excess of $21 billion, and in 2008 they gave out grants of $2.8 billion.[5]

Today Buffett is recognized as the world's premier investor in the stock market. He has used his wealth to invest in the needs of mankind through the Gates' foundation. It is clear he loves the hunt, and the money he makes is a mere by-product of his enjoyment of playing the game. This is evidenced by the modest lifestyle he exhibits. I was once in Buffett's hometown. My host drove me through a typical middle-class neighborhood and pointed out Warren Buffett's residence to me. There was no gated community. It was very understated. You would never imagine Buffett would live in such a modest home. As he told young Columbia Business School students, "Do what you love, not what you think will make you a lot of money."[6]

In May 2009 Bill Gates and Warren Buffett organized and presided over a private dinner meeting of billionaires in New York City to discuss philanthropy. The result of the meeting was the formation of a philanthropy-giving campaign called "the giving pledge," which had been made public earlier. The organization doesn't collect any money or require the billionaires to do more than write a letter stating their intention to donate at least half their fortune to charity while they're still alive. The giving pledge is going to expand outside the United States soon, Buffett has said. Carol Loomis wrote, "The crowd at the inaugural event added up to a list that would make any charity— or any conspiracy theorist—swoon. [It included] Bill Gates, Oprah Winfrey, Warren Buffett, Eli and Edythe Broad, Ted Turner, David Rockefeller, Chuck Feeney, Michael Bloomberg, George Soros, Julian Robertson, John and Tashia Morgridge, Pete Peterson."[7]

According to CNN.com, the net worth of the *Forbes* 400 in 2009 was around $1.2 trillion. So if these individuals gave away 50 percent of that net worth either during their lifetimes or at their deaths, the total given would be $600 billion. Looking simply at Internal Revenue Service for both annual giving and estate taxes, we can see that the very rich are far from that $600 billion. Here's an admirable fact about Americans you might not know: the United States annually gives around $300 billion to charities, surpassing all other countries in philanthropic generosity.[8]

In December of 2010 Facebook cofounders Mark Zuckerberg and Dustin Moskovitz pledged to join approximately sixty other US-based billionaires— including Steve Case, Paul Allen, Larry Ellison, Carl Icahn, and George Lucas— to give away a minimum of 50 percent of their fortunes. "People wait until late in their career to give back," Zuckerberg said. "But why wait when there is so much to be done? With a generation of younger folks who have thrived on the success of their companies, there is a big opportunity for many of us to give back earlier in our lifetime and see the impact of our philanthropic efforts."[9]

BECOME A CHANGE AGENT FOR THE MOUNTAIN OF BUSINESS

Deuteronomy 8 tells us that God gives us the ability to create wealth in order to establish His kingdom on earth. That's it! That is why you have been given money! God is raising His change agents in the business mountain today to establish His kingdom on that mountain. God's kingdom on each of the seven mountains of culture will be established by change agents who understand their calling and use their God-given ability to create wealth through entrepreneurship.

What can I do as one individual to make an impact for God on the mountain of business?

This chapter was filled with information about change agents who are having an impact on the mountain of business. How have these examples motivated you to find a way to make your own impact in the marketplace? Will your actions intersect in any of the following areas?

1. We learned that Zechariah 4:6 instructs believers to combine their natural abilities with the power of God, which is being manifested in the area of your calling. How can you follow this instruction?

2. God wants you to let go and let Him work. Have you yielded completely to Him in the area of your goals and purposes for your life?

3. God is looking for righteous business leaders who will turn our nation back to a righteous form of commerce. How can you help in this area?

4. Deuteronomy 8 tells us that God gives us the ability to create wealth in order to establish His kingdom on earth. How are you using your wealth to advance His kingdom?

What would success look like on the business mountain?

- There would be more integrity in business and less opportunity for greed and mammon to rule in the marketplace, making the marketplace and culture more prosperous.

- Special noonday prayer meetings would be held in the workplace, asking God to direct their efforts.

- More inventions that solve societal problems would result as entrepreneurs learn to gain direction from God in their working lives. They would have greater influence as a fruit of fulfilling their calling.

- There would be less corporate scandals.

- There would be less crime in our cities because there would be healthier families producing healthier people spiritually who would do honest work.

- There would be more wealth created as men and women fulfill Deuteronomy 8:18 to have the ability to create wealth to establish God's covenant on the earth.

- Christian CEOs would ban together and commit their corporate profits to philanthropic enterprises and care for the poor. More money would be given to Christian causes.

- More money would be received into the local church as business leaders tithed and gave offerings generously from their increase.

- By acknowledging that God is the source of science and technology, there would be greater innovation and revelation of the world around us.

- Unemployment would be greatly reduced.

Chapter 19

RECLAIMING THE EDUCATION MOUNTAIN

Love the LORD your God with all your heart, with all your
soul, with all your mind, and with all your strength.

—MARK 12:30

C HUCK STETSON IS a change agent who wants to impact the educational system in America. I first met Chuck at a Pinnacle Forum national conference where I spoke in 2007, in Scottsdale, Arizona. Pinnacle Forum is a network of change agents mostly made up of CEOs and entrepreneurs. Chuck is a managing director of PEI Funds, a private equity firm based in New York. He is a graduate of Yale University and Columbia University's Graduate School of Business. He is the author of articles for *Harvard Business Review*, *Pratt's Guide to Venture Capital*, and *The Journal of Corporate Strategy*. He created the *Doubleday Pocket Bible Guide*. His book *Lessons From William Wilberforce* was published in 2007, and *The British Abolitionists and Their Influence* was published in 2009. He is a change agent with a passion to influence culture. And he is doing it on several levels.

One of Chuck's passions involves something called the Bible Literacy Project. In late 2005 he unveiled *The Bible and Its Influence*, a lavishly illustrated 390-page textbook designed to help public school students understand how the Bible has impacted American culture. Instead of the normal two reviewers for a high school textbook, he had it vetted by forty academic, legal, and religious scholars, including Jews, Protestants, and a Roman Catholic bishop. The textbook is meant to be read alongside a Bible in its first year. It was used in eighty-two public high schools in thirty states in its first year and is being considered by over one thousand public high schools. It is now taught in more than three hundred schools in forty-one states.[1]

When Chuck launched his organization's research on April 26, 2005, almost everyone Chuck talked to said, "Oh no, you can't teach about the Bible in public schools." Less than two years later, through a strong media campaign developed on the research, *Time* magazine featured a cover story on its April 2007 cover with the headline: "Why We Should Teach the Bible in Public School." The subtitle said, "But very, very carefully."[2] Stetson provides an example of how Christian change agents must think differently about how to influence culture through thoughtful dialogue versus being religious critics and boycotters of all that is wrong in culture. "There has never been a public high school textbook like this," he said. "It was created to satisfy all constituencies involved in the heated debate about the Bible in public schools. It treats faith perspectives with respect and was examined by forty reviewers for accuracy, fairness, and the highest level of scholarship. At the same time it meets consensus standards for fulfilling First Amendment guidelines in that it informs and instructs but does not promote religion."[3]

According to surveys, "90 percent of high school English teachers said it was important for both college-bound and 'regular' students to be biblically literate."[4] However, the teachers estimated that less than a fourth of their current students were biblically literate.[5]

Four legislatures—Georgia in 2006, South Carolina and Texas in 2007, and Tennessee in 2008—have passed legislation based on the research that Chuck's organization did to encourage high schools to offer courses to their high school students on Bible literacy.

Stetson represents a new breed of change agents who seek to use the media and the existing educational system to present a logical reason to show how Judeo-Christian history has impacted our culture and the value it offers for educators. His strategy has been very effective.

What Is the Education Mountain?

Education is knowledge or a skill obtained or developed by a learning process. Most American educational institutions were meant to serve as places of training and admonition in the fear of God. However, this mountain has been infiltrated and taken over by forces opposed to these foundational principles.[6]

Education in America in 1690

The New England Primer was first published between 1688 and 1690 by English printer Benjamin Harris, who had come to Boston in 1686 to escape the brief Catholic ascendancy under James II. Based largely upon his earlier *The Protestant Tutor, The New England Primer* was the first reading primer designed for the American colonies. It became the most successful educational textbook published in the colonial and early days of United States history. It was used in what would be our first grade for two hundred years.

While the selections in *The New England Primer* varied somewhat across time, there was standard content for beginning reading instruction. Each lesson had questions about the Bible and the Ten Commandments. In fact, most of the entire book taught Bible verses at the same time it taught students how to read.

The ninety-page work contained selections from the King James Bible as well as other original selections. It embodied the dominant Puritan attitude and worldview of the day. Among the topics discussed were respect to parental figures, sin, and salvation. Some versions contained the Westminster Shorter Catechism, others contained John Cotton's shorter catechism, known as Milk for Babes, and some contained both. The primer remained in print well into the nineteenth century and was even used until the twentieth. A reported two million copies were sold in the 1700s. No copies of editions before 1727 are known to have survived; earlier editions are known only from publishers' and booksellers' advertisements.[7]

Supreme Court Challenge

Using Bible verses to teach English and morality in public schools was challenged in 1844. There were three different cases that upheld the use of the Bible for that specific use in public schools, one being a Supreme Court case of 1844, *Vidal v. Gerard*, where a Philadelphia school wanted to teach morals without using the Bible. The Court said, "Why may not the Bible, and especially the New Testament, without note or comment, be read and taught as a divine revelation in the college; its general precepts expounded, its evidences explained, and its glorious principles of morality inculcated?"[8] The court concluded that any book teaching good morality would certainly be teaching what the New Testament teaches, so why not use the original source that doesn't change.

Noah Webster, writing in the *History of the United States* (1832), stated, "The moral principles and precepts contained in the Scriptures ought to form the basis of all our civil constitutions and law.... All the miseries and evils which man suffer from vice, crime, ambition, injustice, oppression, slavery, and war, proceed from their despising or neglecting the precepts contained in the Bible."[9] Daniel Webster, in his July 4, 1800, *Oration at Hanover,* New Jersey: "To preserve the government we must also preserve morals. Morality rests on religion; if you destroy the foundation, the superstructure must fall. When the public mind becomes vitiated and corrupt, laws are a nullity and constitutions are waste paper."[10]

National Education Association (NEA)

The National Education Association (NEA) began in 1857 when forty-three educators from eight states and the District of Columbia attended the first meeting of the National Teachers Association (NTA). In 1870 the NTA changed its name to National Education Association (NEA) and merged with three smaller organizations.[11]

The National Education Association is the largest professional organization and largest labor union in the United States, representing public school teachers and other support personnel, faculty and staffers at colleges and universities, retired educators, and college students preparing to become teachers. The NEA has 3.1 million members and is headquartered in Washington DC. With affiliate organizations in every state and in more than fourteen thousand communities across the nation, the NEA has a permanent, paid, full-time staff of at least eighteen hundred United Service (UniServ) employees. According to its 2007 financial report, the NEA's total receipts for the year were $352,958,087.[12] NEA is incorporated as a professional association in a few states and as a labor union in most states (but it is not a member of the AFL-CIO or other trade union federations). On its website the NEA describes itself as a "professional employee organization."[13] However, it is often categorized as a labor union with strong leftist and liberal leanings, particularly by critics. Today, the NEA is one of the most liberal organizations in existence.

THE MORAL DECLINE IN EDUCATION

There is a direct correlation between the removal of Christianity from public education and the decline in moral behavior among students. Following is a comparison of the top disciplinary problems of 1940 compared to 1990.[14]

1940	1990
Talking out of turn	Drug abuse
Chewing gum	Alcohol abuse
Making noise	Pregnancy
Running in the halls	Suicide
Cutting in line	Rape
Dress code infractions	Robbery
Littering	Assault

Impact of Removal of Prayer in Schools

In 1991, David Barton, in conjunction with Specialty Research Associates, released a report entitled, *America: To Pray or Not to Pray*. This report provides statistical evidence of the impact of the removal of prayer from public schools since 1963 and includes more than one hundred pages of graphs and statistical analyses to prove that crime, venereal disease, premarital sex, illiteracy, suicide, drug use, public corruption, and other social ills began a dramatic increase after the *Engel v. Vitale* Supreme Court decision was made in 1962, which banned school prayer.[15]

It is clear this was a benchmark year from which tipping points began to emerge regarding social ills in our nation. Prayer in schools prior to 1962 was utilized in school districts all over the United States in many varieties. Some teachers used extemporaneous prayers, simply expressing their thoughts and desires; others implemented structured prayers, such as the Lord's Prayer or the Twenty-Third Psalm, or others approved by local school boards. New York students prayed each day: "Almighty God, we acknowledge our dependence on Thee and beg Thy blessing over us, our parents, our teachers, and our nation." It was this simple prayer that came under fire and went to the Supreme Court for the landmark decision.

Says David Barton, "It is impossible to know how many of the thirty-nine million children were involved in daily verbal prayers, but most accounts indicate that a clear majority of the students voluntarily participated in daily school prayer. Is it possible that the prayers that were being offered by these children and their teachers across the nation actually had any measurable, tangible effect?" It was this question that led Barton to uncover the statistical proof that the removal of prayer did indeed take its toll on America.[16]

OUR FIRST UNIVERSITIES

The motto that Harvard University adopted in 1692 was *Veritas Christo et Ecclesiae*, which translated from Latin means "Truth for Christ and the Church." It was later changed to simply say: "Truth (*Veritas*)."[17] Certainly they have removed the true source of truth.

Harvard was first established in America by the Puritans. Early documents reveal such statements: "Let every student be plainly instructed and earnestly pressed to consider well the main end of his life and studies to know God and Jesus Christ which is eternal life (John 17:3) and therefore lay Christ at the bottom, as the only foundation of all sound knowledge and learning."[18] Princeton was founded in 1746. Its founding president, Jonathan Dickinson, stated, "'Cursed is all learning that is contrary to the Cross of Christ.'"[19]

Reclaiming Harvard

In April 2011 I spoke at a conference hosted by students from the Harvard Extension Service & Leadership Society (HESLS). The theme of the conference, which was held on the campus of Harvard, was "Social Transformation by the Power of God." Many of the students attending were greatly impacted by the conference, including a Wiccan, who, when asked why she attended a Christian conference, answered, "Curiosity. I wanted to hear what all the fuss was about. I thoroughly enjoyed myself and felt totally welcomed. I even had someone pray for me. I was amazed at how 'in touch' these people were that were praying. They 'hear' a lot better than we do."

The students who hosted this conference have a vision to restore Harvard to its Christian roots. One of the objectives for the conference was: "To facilitate a shift in the spiritual atmosphere over Harvard that will assist in reestablishing the foundations of faith upon which this university was built."[20] A lofty goal, for sure, given where the school is today. But we must begin somewhere. We need educators and "Joshua" students who see themselves as change agents if we are going to reclaim the education mountain.

Columbia University

Columbia University was founded in 1754 as King's College by royal charter of King George II of England. The motto of the university is, "*In lumine Tuo videbimus lument*," which means, "By Your light we shall see light" (based on Psalm 36:9). It is the oldest institution of higher learning in the state of New York and the fifth oldest in the United States. Controversy preceded the founding of the college, with various groups competing to determine its location and religious affiliation. Advocates of New York City met with success on the first point, while the Anglicans prevailed on the latter. However, all constituencies agreed to commit themselves to principles of religious liberty in establishing the policies of the college.

The American Revolution brought the growth of the college to a halt, forcing a suspension of instruction in 1776 that lasted for eight years. However, the institution continued to exert a significant influence on American life through the people associated with it. Among the earliest students and trustees of King's College were John Jay, the first chief justice of the United States; Alexander Hamilton, the first secretary of the treasury; Gouverneur Morris, the author of the final draft of the US Constitution; and Robert R. Livingston, a member of the five-man committee that drafted the Declaration of Independence. The college reopened in 1784 with a new name—Columbia—that embodied the patriotic fervor that had inspired the nation's quest for independence.[21]

Gouverneur Morris was widely credited as the author of the Constitution's Preamble. Morris enrolled at King's College (now Columbia University) at age twelve. He graduated in 1768 and received a master's degree in 1771. He is credited with saying: "Religion is the only solid basis of good morals; therefore education should teach the precepts of religion, and the duties of man towards God." He was also one of the most prominent speakers in the Constitutional Convention.[22]

Supreme Court, June 25, 1962—*Engel v. Vitale*

This is the landmark case that removed prayer from the public schools. The 1963 *World Book Encyclopedia* refers to this case as the first time that we had separation of religious principles from public education. The amazing thing is that it was done without citing any precedent from other cases, as is the normal procedure. There were no quotes from previous legal cases. Instead, it was a brand-new doctrine, which, according to all the previous legal decisions, was in violation of the Constitution. Nevertheless it took precedent over all the previous interpretations of the Constitution.

John Dewey, regarded as the architect of modern education, instigated early changes to move away from God in education, which led to promoting a belief in no absolute truth: "...faith in the prayer-hearing God is an unproved and outmoded faith. There is no God and there is no soul. Hence, there is no need for the props of traditional religion. With dogma and creed excluded, then immutable truth is also dead and buried. There is no room for fixed, natural law or moral absolutes."[23]

GAY INFLUENCE IN EDUCATION

In 2009 the Obama administration made a controversial appointment as director of the Office of Safe and Drug Free Schools. Kevin Jennings is the homosexual founder of the Gay, Lesbian and Straight Education Network (GLSEN), the nation's largest advocacy group devoted entirely to promoting homosexuality among school kids, even as young as kindergarten age. Under the guise of "safe schools," GLSEN uses its interpretation of "safety" terminology to promote special protections for "sexual orientation, gender identity or expression." This is another example of how a liberal leader like President Obama begins gradually to infiltrate the educational system with appointments that can impact the entire educational system. Gradually his worldview will be expressed in subtle and not so subtle ways, followed by legislation that can mandate beliefs and behavior to the most vulnerable of all people, our school children.

RECLAIMING EDUCATION

There are a number of universities that desire to change this trend away from our biblical foundations in education. There are three that should be noted for their efforts. I have recently had direct involvement with all three of these schools.

Regent University

When Dr. M. G. "Pat" Robertson established Regent University in 1978, he envisioned a high-caliber institution that would attract a leadership team brimming with superior professional experience and extraordinary academic credentials. In just three decades, that vision is being fulfilled. Distinguished faculty and guest lecturers include John Ashcroft, former US Attorney General; Vern Clark, former Chief of Naval Operations; Steve Forbes, president and CEO of Forbes, Inc.; and others.

Regent also exposes students to speakers who are front and center on some of the most important seven-mountain caliber issues of our time. Nationally covered events such as Clash of the Titans, The Ronald Reagan Symposium, and Executive Leadership Series allow students and the greater community to learn firsthand from major world and national leaders about today's most pressing issues.

Just as Loren Cunningham, Bill Bright, and Francis Schaeffer saw in the late 1970s, Pat Robertson also saw that the seven mountains of culture must have Christian leaders operating at their tops. Robertson had a particular calling to the media and started *The 700 Club*. Later he began the Family Channel, which was sold to fund the operations of the school.

Today the graduate school has more than eleven thousand students and has announced the start of an undergraduate program. Regent trains leaders to operate at the tops of the seven mountains of culture who will be able to work with other change agents to reclaim culture from further decline into liberalism.

The King's College

In July 2008 I traveled to New York City with four others for a prayer journey to pray over several key mountains of influence that reside in New York City. I had heard about The King's College, which operates from inside the Empire State Building, renting more floors than any other tenant. The mission of The King's College states: "Through its commitment to the truths of Christianity and a biblical worldview, The King's College seeks to transform society by preparing students for careers in which they help to shape and eventually to lead strategic public and private institutions, and by supporting faculty members as they directly engage culture through writing and speaking publicly on critical issues."[24] That's a seven-mountain mandate! Our team made our way to their offices and were hosted by Dr. Lance Covan, then-president/CEO of The King's College. I asked Dr. Covan where education has failed and what we must do to impact culture through the next generation.

Dr. Covan believes that the goal of education should be "to engage the world and influence culture," something Christian higher education has strayed from recently, in his opinion. "Instead of influencing the public debate regarding important issues, we have become introspective and fallen silent. Now, we have our work cut out for us," he told me.

He outlined for me the specific things that we need to teach our young people to prepare them with the tools they need to influence society. He included the following elements:

Challenge students to leave the holy huddle and the Christian ghetto.

He reminds us that according to the Great Commission, "Our goal as Christians must be to engage culture." He believes Christians have largely abandoned major cities and culture along with them. He stated, "Cities are treated as lepers (get too close and you will contract their diseases) instead of opportunities for engagement. As a result, Christians have begun losing their influence in the public square. We are no longer trading in the marketplace of ideas." Covan knows how dangerous that is. We need to teach our young men and women to engage those who do not think like they do in the most influential places in the world. "Ideas have consequences," he says. "And ideas not influenced by truth will have destructive consequences."

Teach young people to be bilingual—besides speaking Christianese, they also must speak the language of the world, of business, of the public square.

Covan believes that in order to engage those who do not think like them, and in order to be influential, young people must speak to others in a language that those people understand. "Instead of using Christian jargon and abstract, nebulous language," he told me, "young people have to learn how to speak persuasively, with tact and tenacity, on a variety of topics using ideas and terms that have universal appeal."

Young people must embrace the Triple X principle: excellence, excellence, excellence.

Covan stresses, "We must teach young people that respect is earned, not given." He believes that the easiest, most effective way to earn respect is to strive for excellence in all that you do. This goes beyond just giving your best. He says that we must teach young people to go out of their way to help out, put in extra hours if needed, triple check their work when everyone else is only double checking it, and to do the right thing when the wrong thing is accepted, even expected. He says, "Once they earn the respect of their bosses, colleagues, and peers, young people will then earn the right to speak in those people's lives, influencing them, their decisions, and eventually culture."

Baylor University

I first met Dr. Gregory Leman, director of University Entrepreneurial Initiatives, and Curtis Hankamer, chair of Entrepreneurship, at Baylor University in Waco, Texas, over the Internet. Dr. Leman found me when he was researching curriculum for the seven-mountain strategy, which he was beginning to learn about. He was impressed with the practical nature of the seven-mountain strategy and felt it must be taught to his students at Baylor. He invited me to come to Baylor to meet with some of the faculty and speak to his seniors who were part of one of his classes. Dr. Leman later came to our conference and led a breakout session on equipping the next generation.

He shared his thoughts on the approach he is using to raise up a new generation of change agents through college-level education. He believes that although we presume that education is about preparation for impact, in reality it lacks effectiveness in many settings because of two paradigm problems.

1. Its content is focused on deep knowledge within specific topics, whereas breakthrough almost always happens at intersections of bodies of knowledge.

2. Its methods are focused on acquiring the theory for later application, while experiential, mentored learning is often more efficient.

Dr. Leman pointed out how the Baylor design of new programs in technology entrepreneurship will illustrate ways to alter these paradigms so that they have a much higher chance of producing graduates who are well prepared to lead the innovative efforts needed to impact mountains of culture. "The first paradigm we challenge is the *silo learning* paradigm," he said. "We must provide an educational experience for our students that forces teamwork, develops common vernacular, and spurs mutual appreciation across boundaries to simulate the environment they will enter so often dubbed the *real world* after they graduate." Leaders need to possess simultaneous competencies that include using technology to solve complex problems, creating business principles that capture value, and utilizing cultural interactions to solve issues that have global impact.

Recent events also make it obvious that even mastery of global, business, and technical competencies is insufficient without integrity and ethical grounding. So for Baylor's programs they have articulated the goal of infusing these specific skills and savvy in applying them to real-world problems with unswerving commitment to the highest ethical standards.

"How can the classroom produce such an ambitious outcome?" Leman postured. "It is a trick question," he continued. "The traditional classroom simply cannot do so." He believes that a more *Eastern* view of education—one that is experiential rather than theoretical alone—is needed. In order to transform a traditional classroom into more of a learning lab, Leman believes we need to commission student teams to assess actual innovation opportunities in a cross-disciplinary environment. He pointed out that this is effective on campus at Baylor. In order to enhance the global nature of the world of tech-enabled businesses, it was necessary for Baylor to develop a summer program in China to enhance the global nature of the world of tech-enabled businesses, in which half the class is made up of local Chinese students. The opportunity assessments they perform together are for companies operating there.

Leman believes that in the same way that a youth pastor can have huge impact on a student during a two-week *mission trip*, a summer session for students in an unfamiliar culture, where they live elbow to elbow for six weeks with another culture, can accelerate content transfer *and* character transformation. "The intensity of such an experience makes a transfer almost unavoidable," he told me. The result is highly skilled graduates who know how to actually do the real world tasks and how to conduct themselves as culturally sensitive contributors—"in short it means success with the impact mission we started with."

He believes the keys to apply to educational programs of all types are these:

- Design the content to force interaction across disciplinary boundaries that are relevant to the practice of the specific field.

- Develop a learning environment that is enables interactions with seasoned, high-integrity practitioners.

- Invent a cross-cultural, *mission trip* environment for maximum impact.

In order to reclaim the mountain of education, we will need a spiritual renewal among educators in our nation. The god of education today is knowledge that is not based on truth, simply more knowledge without wisdom. The Old Testament describes a conflict between Greece, which represents knowledge-based systems, and Hebraic, which is based on obedience-based intimacy with God.

> For I have bent Judah, My bow,
> Fitted the bow with Ephraim,
> And raised up your sons, O Zion,
> Against your sons, O Greece,
> And made you like the sword of a mighty man.
> —ZECHARIAH 9:13

BECOME A CHANGE AGENT FOR THE EDUCATION MOUNTAIN

What can I do as one individual to make an impact for God on the education mountain?

We must have more mighty men and women in the educational arena who stand for knowledge AND truth and righteousness. What can you do in the following areas of education to reclaim the education mountain?

1. Chuck Stetson developed *The Bible and Its Influence,* a 390-page textbook now taught in more that three hundred schools in forty-one states. What impact can you have in your community's public schools?

2. Pat Robertson envisioned Regent University as a high-caliber institution that would attract a leadership team brimming with superior professional experience and extraordinary academic credentials. How do you envision the institutes of learning in your community? What can you do to raise the standard?

3. Dr. Lance Covan believes that the goal of education should be to equip your young people to engage the world and influence culture. How can you support this vision?

4. What goals have you set personally regarding the education and training of your own children? How are you investing in their lives to assure that they are prepared to make a stand for knowledge AND truth and righteousness?

What would success look like on the education mountain?

- There would be more acceptance of biblical absolutes and recognition of the value the Bible can bring to the classroom.

- There would be less concern about politically correct behavior regarding faith expressed in the public classroom.

- Creationism would be affirmed and taught instead of Darwinism.

- There would be an acknowledgment of our Christian heritage in the founding of our nation.

- We would evaluate and embrace truth based on truth instead of allowing biases to influence what we believe.

- There would be excellence demonstrated in the art of teaching. More people would be in the teaching profession because they are called to it.

- Teachers would model a worldview that reflects a belief that every human being has the potential to become a great person with a unique contribution to offer humanity.

- We could live in a pluralistic society and still honor other viewpoints without the insecurity to conform or defend. Christians would operate in a pluralistic setting from a foundation of truth with confidence and greater impact.

- There would be less time spent disciplining in the classroom and more time learning.

- Education would address both mind and spirit.

- There would be divine insights into the design of creation so science and technology research would yield advances in every arena: technology and science would impact cures, food production, environmental recovery, travel and communication, and so forth—ultimately more creativity and innovation in all fields of education.

Chapter 20

RECLAIMING THE CHURCH MOUNTAIN

And He Himself gave some to be apostles, some prophets, some evan-
gelists, and some pastors and teachers, for the equipping of the saints
for the work of ministry, for the edifying of the body of Christ.
—EPHESIANS 4:11–12

ASTOR SUNDAY ADELAJA is the founder and senior pastor of The Embassy
of the Blessed Kingdom of God for All Nations in Kiev, Ukraine. He
is a pastor who is a change agent in Europe and throughout the world
through his calling as pastor to the largest and fastest-growing church in
Europe. Born and raised in Nigeria, he successfully pastors a congregation
consisting of 99 percent white Europeans in a racially sensitive country. The
church has six hundred daughter churches in different parts of Ukraine and
in more than forty-five countries of the world. Pastor Sunday, as he is fondly
called, came to Eastern Europe more than twenty-one years ago to study journalism but later felt called by God to plant a church that would one day become
a megachurch of more than twenty-five thousand people.

Although he grew up in poverty in Africa, today he plays an active role
in the political and social life of Ukraine and is acknowledged by many world
political leaders for his spiritual and practical leadership across the world.
He is also recognized as an influencing factor in bringing political change to
Ukraine in 2004–2005 during what has been called the Orange Revolution. In
2007 Pastor Sunday opened the US Senate in prayer and has also spoken at the
United Nations. National and international media have reported on his work.

Pastor Sunday authored a book called *ChurchShift*, which describes why
many churches have been ineffective at changing culture. He believes that
the local church is called to change culture in all spheres of society, especially the seven mountains. "God is not terribly concerned with church size
and church ministries. These are all sidelights to His main goal, which is for
all nations to walk after Him in kingdom principles. The church fulfills its
mandate when it changes society, not when it's confined to its sanctuary and
Sunday school classrooms. The church is to build the kingdom of God in a
nation. The kingdom must overflow into streets and workplaces, governments

and entertainment venues. If you try to keep it to yourself, you lose it. And we didn't want to lose it."[1]

Pastor Sunday understands the role of the local church is to equip and release his congregation in a way that impacts culture.

> Too many Christians and Christian leaders spend their energy, creativity, and precious time promoting churches instead of the kingdom. They work for the success of their church, or perhaps for a group of churches in their city, or they work for their ministry or denomination. They believe that by building churches and ministries they are building the kingdom. They think *church* and *kingdom* are practically synonymous. This isolation of the church from the world has led to ineffectiveness and failure to carry out the Great Commission.
>
> But the church is not the kingdom. Jesus said in Luke 17:21, "Nor will people say, 'Here it is,' or 'There it is,' because the kingdom of God is within you." It's not confined to temples and churches. No church can contain or control the kingdom of God. The kingdom is meant to inhabit the entire earth, not just your church sanctuary.[2]

Pastor Sunday believes they are to be proactive about changing the culture. "Because God wanted to do something in the Ukraine that was much bigger than our 'big church' or me, He graciously taught us to take a proactive position in society, to go outside our building and enforce His authority over an ungodly nation and government. Today many people sit in church pews hoping to make it to the kingdom of God, and they don't realize that, according to Jesus, the kingdom is here and now. Nobody has to die to see the kingdom. We are as close as we will ever get. Jesus didn't leave the kingdom of God in heaven when He came to earth. He brought it with Him. The born-again believer is in the kingdom at this moment. We can stop hoping for it—it came two thousand years ago, and it is present with us now," says Pastor Sunday.[3]

What Is the Church Mountain?

People either worship in spirit and truth, or they settle for religious ritual on the church mountain. The church is often referred to as an institution instead of a people who love and serve society for the purpose of influencing culture. We've reduced the "church" to a place where we go on Sunday instead of a people that IS the church spread throughout the marketplace daily.

Dr. Henry Blackaby sees a vacuum in the area of the local church when it comes to equipping men and women in their work life callings. Blackaby speaks to many church leaders every year about equipping those in the workplace. He is personally equipping leaders in the marketplace because he sees this as the only place we will see societal change. In an interview I did with Henry Blackaby, he offered some helpful comments.

"If someone were to ask me right now where do I sense the greatest potential for revival," he said, "I'd say in corporate America." Blackaby relates to about 170 CEOs of Fortune 100 and Fortune 500 companies, most of whom have read his book *Experiencing God*. After reading the book, all of them have requested a conference call with Blackaby to discuss their responses to the book. He has scheduled about ten different conference calls, with eight to ten of them on each call at one time. What is the major concern of these CEOS? Blackaby says, "They are asking me, 'How do we experience God in corporate America?'" He finds it much, much easier to guide corporate America than to guide the church community into fresh, new experiences with God.

Although these CEOs make huge decisions and are personally connected to government leaders and the president's cabinet, they ask, "How can we use our lives?" Some of them have told him, "We're convinced that the way to control TV is to make it family friendly, but this must be done through sponsorship." So the executives said, "We are not going to sponsor any programming that is going to destroy our moral fiber as a nation."

A lot of these changes they are willing to make in philosophy have come out of their studying *Experiencing God*. Blackaby told me, "One of the men in our group is a multibillionaire who already had a deep commitment to have a controlling interest in all the theaters in America, and he controls one major theater chain. He desires to help bring family friendly movies in the theatres in America." Blackaby stressed that these executives want to affect the values system of corporate America.

I asked Dr. Blackaby why the local church has been so ineffective at equipping men and women in the workplace. "We need spiritual leaders to guide them. I find very few spiritual leaders understand the role of the marketplace in the mind of God. I hear leaders speak, and they never address that issue. It is as if they are totally oblivious to the need to equip these leaders. When I preach on this and why they need to equip leaders in the marketplace, I get a tremendous response. If the churches ever caught the ways of God toward the marketplace, everything would be different. Right now they are telling marketplace people to come and help them build their church. They have it backward. They are supposed to be equipping them for their role in the marketplace. When I tell them that, the lights come on. Many pastors repent when they realize they have it backward. Churches totally turn around when they change their focus."

There is no other institution in the world that has leaders in the seven cultural mountains gather weekly in one place together as they do in the local church. Pastors miss a wonderful opportunity if they do not use

that opportunity to equip men and women in the workplace for cultural transformation through their work life callings.

The Local Church as an Equipping Center

In random surveys among people and groups over the last fifteen years of
working in the faith and work arena, I have asked this question: "How many of
you have been intentionally trained at your local church to apply biblical faith
in your work life? That means you have been in a Bible study, heard a sermon
series, or had a training course on applying biblical faith at work." The percentage of hands that go up is consistent—5 to 10 percent. The job to make this
shift among church members and church leaders is still enormous. Thankfully,
this is changing.

One study conducted several years ago by the London Institute of
Contemporary Christianity found that 47 percent of people surveyed say that
the preaching and teaching they receive is irrelevant to their daily lives.[4] Given
these statistics, it is no wonder the average Christian has had no spiritual
impact on their workplace and has been unable to integrate their faith life into
their work life. Relevance is the key word here. The average church member
finds no relevance in their church experience and what they are taught about
their daily work life. Dr. Eddie Gibbs, a Fuller Seminary professor, once made
the following amazing statement in one of our conferences: "I teach students
who spend $40,000 to learn a language no one understands."

Doug Spada's Atlanta-based WorkLife ministry is one of the pioneering
efforts to equip the local church to focus on faith at work issues. Spada's ministry does this by creating the infrastructure for a sustainable work-life ministry. His ultimate vision is that churches will send out members to minister
in the workplace, just as missionaries are sent out to foreign lands. "We help
people launch full-blown work life ministries within their church," Spada
explained. Spada's group has had the most penetration of any group into some
of the largest and most influential churches in America.

Spada has coined a phrase that has helped him relate to local church leaders
in trying to help them see the problem that exists inside the local churches:
"Many churches are *luxury cruise liners* instead of *aircraft carriers* designed to
equip and send out those who are called to impact culture." Spada was a former
nuclear submarine engineer and has found his training helps him identify with
this metaphor with the church leaders. Spada even arranged for one of his pastors to get on an aircraft carrier to learn about what actually happens on a carrier to better relate to his church's ministry.

Spada comments further on the need to equip men and women through the
local church: "Few churches offer anything resembling an ongoing ministry in
this area. Often, the closest they come is an effort focused on the white-collar

business community—a *marketplace ministry* that is often defined as a businessmen's small group, or a 7:00 a.m. executive prayer breakfast. In doing so, they minister to the 5 percent who are leaders in their work environments and ignore the 95 percent who are not." Spada believes that fact is tragic, not only because the 95 percent are left with little guidance about what it means to be a Christian at work, but also because they are surrounded every day by untold legions of non-Christians and nominal Christians to whom they could reveal God. He says, "Seemingly the church is missing one of its greatest opportunities for both discipleship and evangelism."

ONE PASTOR'S PARADIGM SHIFT

...having been built on the foundation of the apostles and prophets, Jesus Christ Himself being the chief cornerstone, in whom the whole building, being joined together, grows into a holy temple in the Lord, in whom you also are being built together for a dwelling place of God in the Spirit.

—EPHESIANS 2:20–22

The local church is designed to be a Holy Spirit–training outpost for equipping God's people to be kingdom warriors of love and servanthood on earth and to destroy the works of darkness. Paul said the church would be established on the apostles and prophets with Jesus as the cornerstone. The natures of these two offices are worth noting. The office of prophet sees the reality of situations; prophets see what is coming and how to discern the times we live in. They discern the deceptive ways of the world system and speak absolute truth at the risk of persecution for the sake of upholding truth. The office of the apostle is defined as one who is "sent out" to establish foundations and build upon it. Apostles are to lay spiritual foundations so that the other three offices of pastor, evangelist, and teacher fill in the missing bricks to the foundation.

However, one of the reasons we are experiencing a weak church is that the local church is no longer built upon these two offices because many churches do not even recognize that these offices exist today. Instead, the church is now built upon the office of pastor (and their preaching) and the evangelist. Lack of vision, fractured foundations, and compromised truth are often the consequences we suffer from building from this foundation. The evangelist's focus can lead to an overemphasis on the gospel of salvation versus the gospel of the kingdom that Jesus spoke more about during His lifetime. This has led to our weakened Christian worldview.

Let me share a personal story how these two offices operate to build the kingdom of God in one of the seven cultural mountains. A few years ago some leaders and I were invited to New York City by a very prominent executive inside a major media network. I have a friend who holds the office of prophet and has the gift of prophecy. I believe I have an apostolic teaching and convener calling in the faith at work arena. Our host invited my friend and me to share with a small group of media and arts and entertainment associates at a dinner party hosted in a high-rise condominium overlooking downtown Manhattan. I taught for about forty-five minutes, and then my friend spoke into the lives of each person in attendance. God spoke very personally to each of them in the room through my friend one by one, with each one breaking down in tears as they heard God speak so personally through my friend. Later our host was led to repent on behalf of the media, and he asked God to impact those who work inside the media.

It was a powerful meeting as evidenced by the fact all in the room were weeping and responding to the Holy Spirit. The prophetic gift breaks through religious barriers and preconceived ideas or prejudices and penetrates the heart to reveal the love of the Father. This would not happen in a meeting led by the office of pastor or evangelist. People would have felt cared for, and the unbeliever may have come to know Christ. However, a foundation would not have been established to build from, as was the case when the apostle and the prophet office ministered together.

I first met pastor Fred Hartley about five years ago when I was invited to be on a city transformation leadership team in Atlanta. Fred pastors a midsize congregation in a suburb of Atlanta and is also the founder of the College of Prayer, an international equipping ministry. Fred has written several books on prayer. Fred knew little about my work, but as we began getting to know one another, he took more of an interest in what I did. I shared a few of my books with him, but it was almost two years before Fred caught what I was doing and how it could impact his own local congregation. He wrote me this letter:

> Dear Os,
>
> I had the most amazing experience in church on Sunday. I wish you could have been here. Let me explain. During this last module of the College of Prayer, I was convicted as Vanessa Battle was teaching on marketplace ministry and my lack of prayer support for our marketplace leaders.
>
> During worship, I sat the people down and confessed that while I had recruited over 150 prayer partners for myself, I failed to pray for them in their marketplace, though their prayers are equally as valid as my own.
>
> I asked them to write their name on a piece of paper and underneath that to put down their employer and their position. Then I asked them to write down the name of their boss and the CEO of their company so I could pray for those in authority over them as well as praying

for their marketplace. You would have not have believed the response. It was overwhelming.

Our people flocked forward with their slips of paper. When I then led in prayer for everyone who responded, the place erupted in applause.

Our people are praying people, but they have never responded like that before. When I asked God to tear down the dividing wall between the sacred and the secular and led us in a prayer to declare our marketplace holy to God, the place just about erupted. I sensed the pleasure of God in the moment at a very profound level. The people felt validated! I told them we are going to take the nine-to-five window, as Os Hillman describes.

Thanks for being a good example to me, Os.

—Pastor Fred Hartley
Lilburn Alliance Church, Atlanta, Georgia

Many church members simply do not feel validated for the work they do five days a week. They often feel like second-class citizens. One schoolteacher commented, "I was called up to the front to the church to commission me as the teacher for the school-age children for the year. Later I wondered why I have never been recognized for teaching kids five days a week as a ministry."

A Church Growth Expert Recognizes a Movement

C. Peter Wagner has been watching movements in the church for more than fifty years. A former seminary professor and church growth expert, Wagner now leads the Wagner Leadership Institute and Global Harvest Ministries in Colorado Springs, Colorado. He also heads up the International Coalition of Apostles. He began watching the faith at work movement in the late nineties and saw that it was an important move of God that he felt was impacting the church at large and the local church. He began to draw a distinction between two types of churches—the nuclear church and the extended church.

He explains it this way: "Biblically, the word for *church*, *ekklesia*, means, 'the people of God.' God's people are the church, not only on Sunday when they gather together for worship and teaching (the nuclear church), but also on the other six days when they find themselves in the workplace (the extended church)." Wagner indicates that it has become increasingly clear that not only do these two forms of the church really exist, and that each is truly the biblical church, but also that they are quite different from each other, despite the fact that they contain largely the same people.

While simply acknowledging that there is a difference might seem rather innocuous, he states that the situation becomes more complex when we begin to explore the breadth of the gap between the nuclear church and the extended church. Wagner pointed to some respectable research that revealed the gap turns out to be much larger than most people might think. He says, "The nuclear church and the extended church each has a distinct culture, and each culture, as cultures do, operates according to its own rule book." Most extended church leaders understand both rule books, because they not only function in the workplace but are also active in a local church. However, Wagner pointed out that most nuclear church leaders understand only one rule book. He stated, "This can and does cause some of them to feel very uncomfortable with the notion that their own members customarily function, behind their backs, in a different *church* with different behavior patterns six days a week."

Wagner believes that it should go without saying that God's desire in this new season of the faith and work movement is that all His people move forward in harmony. It would be a severe setback to the kingdom of God if nuclear church leaders decided to condemn the rule book of the extended church for whatever reason and thereby widen the gap.[5]

Becoming an Equipping Center

One church in Atlanta, Georgia, is taking a step to equip the next generation around the seven-mountain mandate. Johnny and Elizabeth Enlow are pastors of Daystar Church in Atlanta. They launched the Daystar 7M School in September of 2011. They describe the purpose of this school this way:

> The Daystar 7M School, a ministry of Daystar Church in Atlanta, Georgia, is a one-year program open to students eighteen or older. The seven-mountain approach to the kingdom of God is valuable for anyone at any stage of life, but it is especially helpful for those who are still determining their career path. We welcome all adults and specifically encourage those who are in the process of deciding their life's direction to apply for this in-depth journey into God's heart and purposes. Though much of this yearlong adventure takes place in a classroom setting, it also involves a variety of hands-on ministry experiences, group work with other students, and field studies. Over the course of the year students will be able to develop a lasting bond with other students, staff, and members of Daystar Church. Our hope is that those who have gone through the school will never see their world or their God the same way again.

WHAT HAPPENS WHEN CHURCH MEMBERS
FEEL VALIDATED AND AFFIRMED?

Many times church leaders feel that if church members have a ministry outside the four walls of the local church, there will be a decrease in volunteerism, giving, and general support for the local congregation. That has proven to be false; it actually is the exact opposite. Giving increases and volunteerism increases, because the member, for the first time in his or her life, feels validated by the leadership for his or her specific calling. This validation draws members to a greater commitment to the local church, because it is serving them where they most need it—in their work life call. Churches need to consider that every member is a potential change agent in the making and recognize the privilege that church has to invest in their lives. One of the churches that Spada works with is Wooddale Church in Minneapolis. Pastor Geoff Bohleen stated, "I have had many calls, e-mails, and people stopping me in the hall to tell me their appreciation of various aspects of our workplace ministry."

Several years ago we introduced an equipping tool for churches, marketplace ministries, and businesses. We call it our *TGIF Co-branding Program*. We found that men and women love my *TGIF: Today God Is First* devotional. So what we decided to do was create a version of TGIF that organizations could use to build their own subscriber list using TGIF and brand it with their name on it. They totally control the subscribers. We added an article content website with articles on twenty-four different subjects men and women deal with daily in the workplace. We also branded that site with the organization's name. We added our affiliate bookstore, TGIFBookstore.com, to allow the organization to earn money from a branded store. TGIF Co-branding Program has been very effective as a support to what the local church or other organization might want to do to better equip men and women in the workplace. It frees the local church pastors from having to know everything about workplace topics, and gives their members a resource to get more in-depth teaching on various subjects related to their work life calling.

EQUIP CHANGE AGENTS

How do we reclaim the church mountain to fulfill its mandate to equip change agents? How can a congregation better affirm and mobilize its pew-sitters in ministry within their jobs? The following ideas and strategies can help you begin to mobilize men and women to see their work as a calling and ministry from God.

1. *Establish a team of intercessors to pray* for workplace
   believers and businesses, and to pray for God to establish a

ministry to workplace believers in your church. Present real-life examples of workplace transformation to inspire personal application in different types of workplace environments.

2. *Preach sermons related to workplace applications.* Form a team of workplace believers from different vocations to give input on the type of sermons that should be preached to address the needs of those in the workplace. Conduct a survey among those in the church that asks this question: How might our church help you apply your biblical faith in the context of your daily work life? Provide five specific things the church could do.

3. *Start an ongoing workplace ministry/outreach* that mobilizes your entire congregation into the workplace. WorkLife, one of the leading *life at work* voices in America, can launch a Work Life Support Center online for your church. You can access their website at www.hischurchatwork.org.

4. *Preach a series of messages on the priesthood of all believers in the context of work.* Preach on the fivefold ministry in Ephesians 4 and how these gifts and offices are found in the workplace. Remove formal titles of church staff that would tend to place them spiritually above members in the church. Reinforce the concept that each person's call is equal in the sight of God. (This does not mean church leaders are not the spiritual leaders and shepherds.) Avoid addressing or favoring only those *in business* or those with influence. Equip and train the whole workforce for ministry in the workplace, including mothers, students, executives, construction workers, and professionals.

5. *Affirm workplace believers that their call is equal* to vocational ministry call in its spiritual importance. Dedicate or commission members from various industries and seven mountain spheres on a given Sunday.

6. *Understand the problem* that often separates workplace believers from church leaders. This will help you see the heart of a workplace believer.

7. *Affirm workplace believers through church commissioning services* focused on the church recognizing and confirming their calling (vocation) in a formal way.

8. *Provide discipleship opportunities for your people.* Several workplace ministries offer online devotionals. My *TGIF: Today God Is First* is a free daily e-mail devotional that helps men and women apply biblical faith in their daily workplaces. We have a technology that allows TGIF to be uploaded free to your website.

9. *Consider Marketplace Leader's TGIF Co-branding Program* to use to equip men and women through three unique tools we offer that brands your church/organization name to these tools (www.MarketplaceLeaders.org).

10. *Begin a small-group ministry in the workplace.*

11. *Establish a SWAT team of intercessors* from your church willing to go into businesses and pray for the leaders. Their role is to go into different businesses to help discern issues that may be hindering God's blessing upon the business.

12. *Download PowerPoint presentations* by Os Hillman that can be used in teaching and training. See www.marketplace-leaders.org and www.Reclaim7Mountains.com.

13. *Teach a theology of work to your young people* so they do not have to relearn God's view of work.

14. *Allow one or two people each week to share a brief testimony* on how they experienced God's presence in their workplace that week.

15. *Equip the church library, bookstore or resource center* with helps on work and faith connections. (See www.tgifbookstore.com.)

16. *Sponsor special "work life experiences."* These might be a kid's day at work with their parents.

17. *Establish local church website news features* about members in their work. Other features could include profiles of biblical personalities who were in various industries. In the church member listing, add the industry (not the organization because these change frequently) of each working person.

18. *Sponsor employment helps* such as a job-seeking ministry, a care group for the unemployed or transitioning members, or internships for young people at members' places of work. See

www.CrossroadsCareer.org to get a chapter started in your church.

19. *Pastors should visit members in their workplace* in order to enlighten and enrich your work in the Scriptures, counseling, and preaching—while affirming your people. You will better identify with their challenges.

20. Encourage workplace believers to network online at www .marketplaceleaders.org; click on "Community."

For additional insights, read my book *Faith and Work Movement: What every pastor and Church Leader Should Know*, available at www.tgifbookstore.com. For information on TGIF Co-branding Program, go to www .MarketplaceLeaders.org and click on *TGIF Co-branding Program* under TGIF.

What would success look like on the church mountain?

- Local churches would better equip men and women for their calling in and through their working life instead of viewing them for what they can contribute within the four walls of the church.

- Community transformation efforts among intercessors, church leaders, and marketplace would become problem solvers in their community.

- Churches would desire to work together as one church in the community, and they would pool their resources and money to transform downtown slum areas and solve other community problems. Model cities would be created.

- Cities would be healthier and with less poverty because there would be less crime and more employment in the cities.

- There would be "As One" networks among churches, para-church groups, and marketplace ministries as they understand the John 17:20–23 principle of a unified effort and the multiplication value of networks.

- The local church would operate more as an equipping center to engage and release an army to influence culture. It will demonstrate an outward focus instead of an inward focus.

- The local church would prepare Christ's bride by helping them become mature in their faith, focusing on the gospel of the kingdom, not just salvation. The local church would have a commitment to occupy until the Lord returns instead of isolating ourselves from the world and its needs. The local church would seek to influence, not escape.

- The church will seek to bless the unbeliever, making the believer "salty" and thereby creating a fragrance that will create a desire and longing for relationship with God.

Chapter 21

CHANGE AGENTS CHANGING COMMUNITIES

And many of the Samaritans of that city believed in Him
because of the word of the woman who testified.

—John 4:39

C AN A TWENTY-FIVE-YEAR-OLD shake up a political action organization that results in a cut in federal funding and a cancelled contract with the US Census Bureau? You bet he can. James O'Keefe blew the lid off corruption within a national community, exposing a group called ACORN in September of 2009. He and his female assistant taped the corruption with a hidden camera, then went to the media with the very damaging footage. In the videos he posed as a pimp and his female assistant posed as a prostitute, and successfully showed ACORN employees in four of the agency's offices condoning a series of illicit actions as the couple sought advice on setting up a brothel with underage women from El Salvador. O'Keefe documented these on YouTube as well.

Fallout from the publicity prompted the US Senate to vote 83–7 to block Housing and Urban Development grants to ACORN.[1] O'Keefe is a conservative undercover reporter who simply wanted to make a difference by exposing corruption. Consider the irony of two young people with little funding who broke open a story that no network had been investigating. Age and money have nothing to do with being a change agent in culture, especially in this media age where anyone can post text or video images onto the Internet.

IMPACTING THE NEXT GENERATION

If we are going to impact future cultures, we will need young people who have a vision for what can happen when they enter into their destinies with a motive to solve problems and be used of God.

Many of today's next generation operate from no moral absolutes. George Barna defined those born between 1984 and 2002 as the *Mosaic Generation*, because they're "very mosaic in every aspect of their life.... There's [no attribute] that really dominates like you might have seen with prior generations."[2]

They are comprised of nonlinear thinkers who cut and paste their beliefs and values from a variety of sources. In a 2009 Barna Group survey, Barna describes the next generation like this: "Mosaics and Busters have come to expect experiences that appear unscripted and interactive, that allow them to be open and honest with their questions, that are technologically stimulating, that are done alongside peers and within trusted relationships, and that give them the chance to be creative and visual."[3] He believes that connecting with young people has always been a challenge, but today that struggle is at a much deeper level.

"It's a completely different set of values based upon a very varied interpretation of the meaning of life and how to achieve success or significance in one's life," said Barna in an interview. "They want spirituality; they want faith experiences; they want a taste of religion; but they don't want to have to go through all of the stuff that they see the adults doing at the typical church. But, because the Internet fits with their schedule—it's a 24/7 opportunity—they're using it to explore things they might not have access to otherwise."[4]

EMPLOYING THE NEXT GENERATION WORKER

For the last fifteen years I have devoted my life to helping Christians see that their working lives are not simply a place to collect a check, but a holy calling from God to reflect His glory and influence culture. I was delighted to come across Gabe Lyon's book *The Next Christians*. He describes a new type of follower of Jesus that engages the culture in ways my generation has avoided. They are not as evangelistic in their approach to cultural influence and are more open to building relationships within the secular channels of society, even the most liberal and un-Christian segments. And they see their work as a calling! Yeah, God!

> The next Christians view every corner of society as "in play." They may not overtly use their platforms to evangelize, but the redemptive elements of their work are unmistakable. They've checked their moralizing stick at the door but embrace the opportunity to naturally infuse faith into their businesses. If the conversations arise, they are thrilled to have them, but that isn't the only way they can be faithful. They understand that where they work is oftentimes the place God has called them to let his restoration flood the world.[5]

Debbie Farah is a first-generation Palestinian Christian founder and CEO of Bajalia Trading Company, an import business that uses trade, training, and other forms of community development to alleviate poverty and empower low-income people in third-world nations. Debbie's professional background reads like a who's who in corporate Fortune 500 marketing and retail. She has worked with high-profile clients like Neiman Marcus, Ritz Carlton, Coca-Cola, and even the US Army in her career as creative director in large ad agencies. Debbie saw the plight of the poor in these third-world nations and decided to do something about it. She is a change agent who is using her professional career knowledge and expertise to help the poor use their skills to earn a living by creating products for Debbie's import business. Debbie's nine-person company employs only under-thirty next gens. She has learned that there are unique characteristics of this next generation that must be recognized if we are to help them become change agents. She has also learned that the older generation must learn from this generation as well.

Some key differences that she sees in the work habits of this next generation are as follows:

- They are much more aware of the world as an international playing field and see the Web as the place to equalize big and small players.

- They are comfortable with diversity and generationally more cross-culturally sensitive.

- They place a high value on relationships and social networking and do not follow the nine-to-five structure of corporate America. They operate more like tribes. They desire flexibility in their working hours and are willing to work late hours if they can accommodate their social agendas at the same time they achieve their working goals.

- They prefer flexibility in order to maintain relationships while exercising creativity to accomplish measurable goals.

- They often need more mentoring and coaching with a hands-on approach. They ask lots of questions and do not accept the status quo just because that's the way something was done before. They will challenge long-held ideas and want their opinions and ideas valued.

- They tend to be risk-takers and see that as part of the adventure.

- They want meaning and purpose in the kind of work they do. They want to make a difference in society.

- They want to achieve things more quickly and often do not want to wait until they can afford to impact culture, unlike the baby-boomers. They want to have an impact now, not when they get to their "halftime" stage of life. They do not feel money is always the requirement to have impact.

- They are not comfortable working in segmented cubicles but prefer more open environments where they can better interact with associates.

- They often view the older generation as using words that are superficial.

- They want to see action, not just words.

- They look for genuine relationships and meaning in what and how they do it.

- They are creative and use the various technology media to accomplish their goals—such as web marketing, social networking, blogging, e-mail, and text messaging.

- They are often more drawn to start-up companies versus well-established companies because they feel they can use their creativity and entrepreneurial gifts to a greater degree. They believe they will be valued more in a start-up environment than a well-established corporate environment that may hinder their creativity.[6]

Martin Luther King Jr. was a young man who wanted to influence his culture. When he began to lead the civil rights movement, he was only twenty-six years old. There are change agents in the making in this generation, but it is going to require the older generation to relate differently to them in order to raise up a generation with a restored biblical worldview that will change the way they relate to and impact their world. It is also going to require the next generation to learn what it means to live as sons and daughters, which is a challenge since so many have not had physical and spiritual fathers.

RECLAIMING CULTURE ONE COMMUNITY AT A TIME

There is a grassroots movement taking place across the United States right now. It involves the formation of community-based Christian coalitions made up of local churches, workplace leaders, and intercessors who desire to see change in their communities. For the last ten years I have been traveling nationally and internationally and have watched this take place. These initiatives now have a common thread to them.

In March of 2005 I was speaking in a conference in Red Deer, Canada. There were about a thousand people in the audience when Cindy Jacobs made her way to the podium. Cindy is known for her prophetic ministry to nations and individuals. This was the second time Cindy has spoken over me, but never in a public setting like this. In that statement she said, "God is going to give you a model for city transformation that will be replicated around the world, but it will first begin in your own home town." Several years later I discovered what that model was. Today I see that model being used in no less than thirty cities across the United States and also in other nations. If we are going to reclaim culture, I believe local community transformation movements must be a part of that. It will mean that the seven cultural mountains will be affected on a localized level through these coalitions.

City transformation trinity

I believe there is a community transformation *trinity* of relationships that is the key to community transformation. Three groups of people are vital to bringing change to the spiritual climate in a city or community:

1. Intercessors who are called to intercede for the city

2. Pastors and nuclear church leaders who have a vision for their cities

3. Workplace leaders who want to use their marketplace influence for change within their communities.

These are men and women called to impact their cities through their spheres of influence in the seven specific cultural mountains. Landa Cope, who has taught in more than one hundred nations on the concept of focusing on the cultural mountains to influence culture, says that this has become the dominant strategy in community transformation efforts in other nations. America is actually ten to twenty years behind, compared to some nations.

I mentioned earlier that one of the great examples of cultural change took place in the early nineteenth century with William Wilberforce and the Clapham Circle. This small group of determined Christian leaders from various mountains of influence changed the world of their day by strategizing and accomplishing a long-term effort to eradicate slavery from the British Empire.

Earlier I told you about David Green and a group of change agent leaders in Oklahoma City. This group of leaders assembled regularly with the purpose of serving Christian leaders who desired to form their own community Clapham Circles. This resulted in the formation of Salt and Light Leadership Training (SALLT). SALLT brings together leaders of influence with a threefold purpose: first, to help the leaders understand the calling of God upon their lives, particularly as it pertains to the city to which they have been called; second, to help individuals understand how God provides solutions to our community problems and that these solutions are found in the Bible (also known as a biblical worldview). Finally, SALLT takes leaders through a process of being strategic in their calling. If the goal is to be a city of "salt and light" and thus pleasing to God, Christian leaders from the seven mountains of influence should gather and strategically plan long-term goals to that end. SALLT serves them in that process.

One of the goals Oklahoma City leaders identified as being a facet of a "salt and light city" is that it would be a city in which "the family" would thrive. To that end, one group of leaders has strategized and begun a long-term plan for workplaces in the city to become "family friendly" across the board. Thus their name for the organization they are developing: "Family Friendly Workplaces." The goal will be "to encourage family friendly workplaces in order to nurture God's plan for families."

In this plan leaders from the seven mountains identify how their respective influence can be wielded in unity to accomplish this goal. For example, SALLT leaders from the mountain of business will first have their own respective companies become a part of the organization-to-be. The group will help establish standards, provide resources, and determine methods of publicly praising workplaces that meet Christlike standards. Other mountains of influence will identify how they can bring their sphere of influence in support of such a goal (e.g., the mountain of government might identify regulations or laws that by their elimination or creation would encourage companies to become family friendly).

In the end, all the mountains will have helped strategize the plan and, over time, helped create an expectation in Oklahoma City that the "primo" places to work are those places that are considered "family friendly"—thus culture has been influenced to the glory of God in keeping with goals and methods of which He would approve.

WHAT IS REQUIRED FOR CITY AND COMMUNITY TRANSFORMATION?

There are four key ingredients required among Christian leaders to see a city transformed: prayer, humility, unity, and knowledge of God's ways.

Prayer

In every city in which transformation has taken place, believers have come together to pray for their city. Prayer changes the spiritual climate of a city.[7] The main areas of influence that must be the focus of our prayers include churches and businesses; the legal, political, educational, and medical fields; and the media/entertainment industry. Workplace leaders must be strategically aligned with intercessors to impact their city.

Humility

God uses men and women who recognize that they need each other and do not seek glory for their work. "He guides the humble in what is right and teaches them his way."[8] The workplace leaders God is using today care little about being in the limelight. The same is true of the shepherds of local churches in a community. When shepherds begin to pastor their community, the turf wars begin to evaporate. These leaders must have a kingdom perspective that avoids bringing attention to themselves or any one group in order to impact the city for Jesus Christ.

Unity

Jesus said, "May they be brought to complete unity to let the world know that you sent me and have loved them even as you have loved me."[9] God calls each of us individually and corporately to represent Christ to the world, but our independence, pride, and ego often prevent us from becoming unified in the purposes of Christ. Unity is built when we roll up our sleeves and determine to work together—pastors, priests, and people from every walk of life.

Knowledge of God's ways

Those of us in the workplace are often zealous for God, but we can move in presumption instead of faith that is rooted in knowledge of God's ways. Such was the case of David, who wanted to bring the ark of the covenant into the city of Jerusalem. He was zealous for God and celebrated as he brought the ark into the city. However, the ark was being carried into the city on a cart instead of by priests on poles, as God required. When a man named Uzzah reached out to catch the ark when the oxen stumbled, he was immediately struck dead by God.[10] David was devastated.

We must connect with our priests and pastors to jointly work on bringing the presence of God into our cities. Otherwise, we will fail like David and be guilty of presumption.

BLESSING THE CITY

The final piece of the puzzle that has been missing in city transformation efforts is the intentional efforts to bless the city. In their book *The Externally Focused Church,* Eric Swanson and Rick Rusaw cite a trend across the nation of churches becoming intentional about impacting social problems in the city. When Eric spoke at our 2008 Reclaim 7 Mountains International Conference, he gave an example from Pastor Robert Lewis of Fellowship Bible Church (FBC) in Little Rock, Arkansas. FBC had been content to be a successful, suburban megachurch. But Lewis grew increasingly dissatisfied with the impact

FBC was having on the community. He went to see the mayor and asked, "How can we help you?"

The mayor responded with a list of challenges facing the greater Little Rock area. FBC rose to the challenge by seeking to answer the question: "What can FBC do that would cause people to marvel and say, 'God is at work in a wonderful way, for no one could do these things unless God were with them?'" That one question led FBC to become what Lewis calls a *bridge-building church*.

For the past four years FBC has joined with more than one hundred churches and five thousand volunteers in the greater Little Rock area to serve their communities by building parks and playgrounds and refurbishing nearly fifty schools. They have set records for Red Cross blood donations and have enlisted thousands of new organ donors. They began reaching out to the community through *LifeSkill* classes (on finances, marriage, wellness, aging, etc.) in public forums like banks and hotel rooms, with more than five thousand people attending. In the past four years the churches of greater Little Rock have donated nearly a million dollars to community human service organizations that are effective in meeting the needs of at-risk youth. They have renovated homes and provided school uniforms, school supplies, winter coats, and Christmas toys for hundreds of children.

The churches of Little Rock let their light shine so that Jesus Christ was made real to the community. Once a church makes this mental shift regarding how it lives in its community, it is limited only by its creativity in how it can serve its community and be the salt and light it was meant to be.

When all of these efforts become focused, the net result is we begin to fulfill Deuteronomy 28:13–14 (NIV):

> The LORD will make you the head, not the tail. If you pay attention to the commands of the LORD your God that I give you this day and carefully follow them, you will always be at the top, never at the bottom. Do not turn aside from any of the commands I give you today, to the right or to the left, following other gods and serving them.

In almost every case where we see the church serving the city, it results in giving the church more influence in the city among its leaders. This is biblical Christianity. We win by serving and solving problems in the community as a unified body of Christ.

A FINAL WORD

In summary, if we want to begin to transform our cities, we must affirm workplace leaders who are the change agents in a city. They play a key role in establishing the church in the city. We must be intentional about bringing intercessors, workplace leaders, and pastors who have a vision for their city together with an intentional process that allocates money and resources to projects that will bless the city. Then we will begin to see the transformation of cities.

Joseph was a change agent whose life modeled the kingdom of God. His secular employer saw God in him:

> So Pharaoh asked them, "Can we find anyone like this man, one in whom is the spirit of God?" Then Pharaoh said to Joseph, "Since God has made all this known to you, there is no one so discerning and wise as you."
>
> —GENESIS 41:38–39, NIV

When we represent the kingdom of God in our lives and to others, we will naturally become change agents no matter where we reside. Are you ready to be a change agent for God's glory?

QUESTIONS FOR REFLECTION

1. One of the biggest needs of the next generation is to provide access to spiritual fathers and professional mentors. What might be some ways this could be done?

2. Name three ways you can encourage a next-generation individual to fulfill God's calling on his or her life.

3. What are the three core types of people needed to be effective in a community?

4. Name the four attributes needed among leaders in a community to be successful.

Epilogue

WE WILL REIGN TOGETHER AS ONE

> Now it shall come to pass in the latter days
> That the mountain of the LORD's house
> Shall be established on the top of the mountains,
> And shall be exalted above the hills;
> And all nations shall flow to it.
> Many people shall come and say,
> "Come, and let us go up to the mountain of the LORD,
> To the house of the God of Jacob;
> He will teach us His ways,
> And we shall walk in His paths."
>
> —ISAIAH 2:2–3

IN MICAH 4 we find these words:

> "In that day," says the LORD,
> "I will assemble the lame,
> I will gather the outcast
> And those whom I have afflicted;
> I will make the lame a remnant,
> And the outcast a strong nation;
> So the LORD will reign over them in Mount Zion
> From now on, even forever."
>
> —MICAH 4:6–7

I believe the Lord is preparing a people, a people who have had to walk with a limp. These are the Josephs of the last days prepared through hardship. It is a people who had to turn their plowshares into swords and their pruning hooks into spears to fight the battle at the top of the seven mountains[1] through their marketplace calling that required them to see their calling from a spiritual basis.

There will be a time when their marketplace tools will be reversed as Micah 4:3 describes. However, until then, God is preparing His remnant through hardship, often being outcasts because of our failures. He is removing all that we placed our confidence upon in order that He alone will be our confidence. It is only then that we truly become sons, living in right relationship with our heavenly Father rooted in love and reliance upon Him to complete all things. We will all join Him along with all the sheep nations to reign in Zion on that final day. Amen.

Appendix A

SUMMING IT UP

- The seven mountains of cultural influence are *business, government, media, arts and entertainment, education, the family,* and *religion.*

- Change agents go through six distinct phases of preparation— *(1) divine circumstances, (2) character development, (3) an isolation period, (4) personal cross bearing, (5) problem solving,* and *(6) joining networks.*

- Satan wants your past to become your future. He wants to convince you that you have no purpose or destiny.

- The more liberal and ungodly the change agents at the top, the more liberal and ungodly the culture.

- Our enemies didn't have to kill us; we simply disobeyed God, which entitled our enemies to take our mountains.

- Satan will always attack you in the place of your spiritual inheritance.

- Our level of adversity corresponds to the level of call and to the depth and width of the ministry and purpose He plans through your life.

- Influence in culture is only possible when those who want to exert influence have a message and a life that others see and desire.

- Constantine proclaimed Rome the Holy Roman Empire not for political reasons, but by merely stating the obvious, which was being demonstrated by the people. Christians transformed culture by the way they lived.

- Sometimes your talent takes you beyond where your integrity can keep you.

- Jesus reclaimed all that was lost in the garden so that man could once again rule with Him on the earth.[1]

- When the gospel of the kingdom comes into a life and a community, everything in its wake is impacted.

- We are to enforce and teach what Jesus has instructed us to do and what He has said. Our role is to enforce His will through intercessory prayer by claiming His promises and defeating the works of the enemy.

- The escape theology assumes the influence of the church will decrease on earth until Jesus returns.

- For most of us, we will have many jobs before we will fulfill God's ultimate work for our lives. This is often the place of convergence in our lives, when all of our gifts and talents align to perform our greatest work. God uses the early training, as He did David's, to prepare us for future battles and future experiences.

- Our role is to enforce His will through prayer by claiming His promises and defeating the works of the enemy. "God doesn't prune dead trees, only fruitful ones." Those God uses to significantly impact the kingdom are often required to experience the deepest level of adversity, which will light the torch to illuminate the often dark passageways for those yet to follow.

- We have preached the gospel of salvation, but we have not taught the people to apply the message of the gospel to their everyday life. This is the difference between the gospel of salvation and the gospel of the kingdom.

- Just as Moses laid his staff down, which symbolized his work, you and I must lay our vocations down and watch what God will do as we yield control to Him.

- The world is looking for a solution, not necessarily a Christian solution.

- Martin Luther said, "A gospel that does not deal with the issues of the day is not the gospel at all."

- God's training ground usually is made up of life experiences that will contribute to the ultimate assignment God has for us.

- The greater the calling, the greater the scrutiny from God.

- Change agents are most effective when they network with other change agents around a common cause.

- So often issues that are important to God get brought to our attention through our spouses.

- Preparation for a change agent always involves character development.

- The level of adversity corresponds to the level of call and to the depth and width of the ministry and purpose He plans through your life.

- It takes three nails for a complete crucifixion. It is often another person who pounds the third nail through betrayal to bury our flesh, which allows the work to be completed in us.

- Sometimes obedience does not yield less adversity; it actually increases it.

- God does not test us to find out what we will do; He tests us to let us know what we will do.

- The greater the calling, the greater warfare and suffering you will experience, but there will be greater revelation of God as well and often greater impact.

- As Joseph did with Pharaoh, we must appeal to the primary interest of those we are seeking to influence and take the religious component out even though that might be the root of our motivation.

- Since the beginning of time, culture has been defined by no more than three thousand change agents—a tiny fraction of the population. It is clearly a top-down scenario.

- The higher you go up any cultural mountain, the more demons there are assigned to you, and the more spiritual warfare you will encounter.

- Both God and Satan want you dead, but for different reasons. God wants to kill your flesh so His life can be fully lived through you. However, Satan wants to kill your destiny.

- God turns messes into messages and then messengers.

- God calls His change agents to operate from a place of weakness, not strength.

- God often invites us to live for a cause greater than ourselves through a battle we did not choose.

- The cross is a custom-designed assault to remove pride and self-assurance.

- The ways of God are fraught with unfairness, crisis, isolation, and doubts on the road to leadership.

- The apostle Paul understood that the higher you go up a mountain of influence, the greater the level of spiritual warfare. "For a great and effective door has opened to me, and there are many adversaries."[2]

- The core issue of any addiction or addiction tendency is rooted in a person's inability to believe they are loved by God.[3]

- Every marketplace believer has a calling to be both king and priest.

- Change agents solve societal problems.

- Many church members simply do not feel validated for the work they do five days a week.

- Many times church leaders feel that if church members have a ministry outside the four walls of the local church, there will be a decrease in volunteerism, giving, and general support for the local congregation. That has proven to be false; it actually is the exact opposite.

An important understanding must be restated as we close this book. Influence is a result of our love and obedience to God, not a goal to be achieved. Influence is the fruit of our obedience. Otherwise we begin to use fleshly strategies to exploit and subjugate others to our way of thinking. Jesus never sought to have dominion; rather, He encouraged others to love and obey God. Loren Cunningham once said, "Use your authority and you will lose your influence; use your influence and you will gain authority." When we do this, we will be attractive to the world. They will desire to follow. We become solution providers to the issues mankind will struggle with. Jesus solved people's problems, which resulted in greater influence in people's lives. Influence without humility and relationship (with Jesus and others) means we operate from our individual personal agendas. Let me encourage you to take to positive approach. Be a solution provider, which will earn you the right to influence.

Appendix B

CULTURE-SHAPING BOOKS, ORGANIZATIONS, AND WEBSITES

Books

- *To Change the World*, James Davisson Hunter
- *How Now Shall We Then Live?*, Chuck Colson
- *How Shall We Now Live*, Francis Schaeffer
- *Faith in the Halls of Power*, Michael Lindsay
- *The Seven Mountain Prophecy*, Johnny Enlow
- *Seven Mountain Mantle*, Johnny Enlow (Joseph Calling)
- *Idols for Destruction*, Herbert Schlossberg
- *The 9 to 5 Window*, Os Hillman
- *Upside of Adversity* (Joseph Calling)
- *If God Is in Control, Then Why...*, Craig Hill
- *The Book that Transforms Nations*, Loren Cunningham
- *The Next Christians*, Gabe Lyons
- *Transformation*, Ed Silvoso
- *An Introduction to the Old Testament Template*, Landa Cope
- *Roaring Lambs*, Bob Briner
- *Why Great Men Fall*, Wayde Goodall
- *Culturally Savvy Christians*, Dick Staub
- *The Marketing of Evil*, David Kupelian
- *Victorious Eschatology*, Harold Eberle
- *Rediscovering the Kingdom*, Myles Munroe
- *The Maxwell Leadership Bible*

- *Next Generation Leader*, Andy Stanley
- *UnChristian*, David Kinnaman and Gabe Lyons
- *Culture Shift: Engaging Current Issues With Timeless Truth*, R. Albert Mohler Jr.

Videos

Change Agent 12-part video series by Os Hillman
The Truth Project 12-part video series by Focus on the Family

CULTURE-CHANGE FOCUSED BUSINESS ORGANIZATIONS

- Marketplace Leaders, www.marketplaceleaders.org
- International Christian Chamber of Commerce, www.iccc.net
- Pinnacle Forum, www.pinnacleforum.com
- Fellowship of Companies for Christ, www.fcci.org
- Businessmen's Fellowship International, www.bmfusa.com
- Lance Wallnau, www.7MU.com
- Transformational Leadership, www.transformlead.com
- New Canaan Society, www.newcanaansociety.org
- Halftime, www.halftime.org
- Nehemiah Project, www.nehemiahproject.org
- The Next Christians/Q Ideas, www.qideas.org
- Salt and Light Leadership, www.saltandlightleadership.com
- Lead Like Jesus, www.leadlikejesus.com
- Christian Medical and Dental Associations, www.cmda.org
- Alpha in the Workplace, www.alpha.org/workplace
- PathNorth, http://www.pathnorth.com
- The Oak Initiative, www.theoakinitiative.org
- Harvest Evangelism, www.harvestevan.org

WORLDVIEW

- The Truth Project, www.thetruthproject.org
- Reclaim7Mountains.com, www.Reclaim7Mountains.com
- The Colson Center, www.colsoncenter.org
- Manhattan Declaration, www.manhattandeclaration.org
- Trinity Forum, www.ttf.org
- The Clapham Group, www.claphamgroup.com
- Centurions Program, www.colsoncenter.org/centurionstraining
- Marketplace Leaders, www.marketplaceleaders.org
- UnChristian, www.unchristian.com
- Worldview Matters, www.worldviewmatters.com
- Center for Christ & Culture, www.battlefortruth.org
- Center for Science & Culture, www.discovery.org
- L'Abri Fellowship, www.labri.org
- Q Ideas, www.qideas.org

GOVERNMENT

- Christian Legal Society, www.clsnet.org
- American Center for Law and Justice, www.aclj.org
- Alliance Defense Fund, www.alliancedefensefund.org
- Wallbuilders, www.wallbuilders.com
- Wilberforce Forum, www.colsoncenter.org/the-center/columns/wilberforce-forum
- The Fellowship (National Prayer Breakfast), www.thefellowshipfoundation.org

MEDIA

- *Relevant* magazine, www.relevantmagazine.com
- Christian Media Association, www.christianmedia.org

- National Religious Broadcasters, www.nrb.org
- World magazine, www.worldmag.com
- Christians in Media, www.writeanswer.org
- *Christianity Today* magazine, www.christianitytoday.com
- *Charisma* magazine, www.charismamag.com

Arts and Entertainment

- Hollywood Prayer Network, www.hollywoodprayernetwork.org
- Mastermedia, www.mastermedia.org
- Act ONE, www.actoneprogram.com
- Wedgwood Circle, www.wedgwoodcircle.com
- Sherwood Pictures, www.sherwoodpictures.com
- Walden Media, www.walden.com
- Paste magazine, www.pastemagazine.com
- White Owl Films, www.whiteowlfilms.com
- Genesis One Films, www.genesisonestudios.com
- GMT Studios, www.gmtstudios.com

Family

- Family Foundations International, www.familyfoundations.com
- Life Skills International, www.lifeskillsintl.org
- Be in Health, www.beinhealth.com
- Focus on the Family, www.FocusontheFamily.org
- National Coalition for the Protection of Children and Families, www.purehope.net
- EX3Watch.com
- Danny Wallace Ministries, www.dannywallace.org (homosexuality and abuse)

EDUCATION

- Christian Educators Association, www.ceai.org
- Christian Education Association, www.christianeducator.org
- Biblical Literacy Project, www.biblicalliteracyproject.org
- The Wilberforce Project, www.gordon.edu/Wilberforce
- The King's College, www.tkc.edu
- Regent University, www.regent.edu
- Regent School of Entrepreneurship, www.regent.edu/acad/global/

CHURCH

- Worklife Ministries, www.worklife.org
- International Coalition of Apostles, www.ica.org
- Daystar Church, www.daystar7mschool.org
- Marketplace Leaders, www.marketplaceleaders.org/church-based-ministry/

BLOGS/NEWSLETTERS/SOCIAL MEDIA/TOOLS

- Marketplace Leaders Community, www.mlcommunity.com
- The Call Self-assessment, www.marketplaceleaders.org
- www.todaygodisfirst.com
- Change Agent Network, www.becomeachangeagent.com

Notes

FOREWORD
1. Revelation 22:2.
2. Hebrews 12:27.
3. Psalm 105:22.
4. Psalm 22:6, NIV.
5. Isaiah 41:10, 15.

INTRODUCTION
CALLED TO A BIGGER STORY
1. See Judges 6:11–15.
2. 1 Peter 5:8.
3. See Psalm 4:2.
4. See Luke 19:10.

CHAPTER 1
CULTURE GONE AWRY
1. Henry Blackaby, *Experiencing God* (Nashville: Broadman and Holman, 1994), 66.

2. James Davison Hunter, "To Change the World," *The Trinity Forum Briefing*, vol. 3, no. 2, 2002, http://www.ttf.org/pdf/Bv3n2-Hunter-Text.pdf (accessed April 5, 2011).

3. Author interview with Loren Cunningham, November 2007.

4. James Davison Hunter, *To Change the World* (New York: Oxford University Press, 2010), 46.

5. Ephesians 5:27.

6. Matthew 22:37.

7. Gabe Lyons, *The Next Christians* (New York: Doubleday Religion, 2010), 165–166.

8. Barna.org, "Barna Survey Examines Changes in Worldview Among Christians Over the Past 13 Years," March 6, 2009, http://www.barna.org/barna-update/article/12-faithspirituality/252-barna-survey-examines-changes-in-worldview-among-christians-over-the-past-13-years (accessed April 6, 2011). This report draws information from four nationwide telephone interviews conducted by The Barna Group, each including between 1,002 to 1,005 adults randomly selected, during the years 1995, 2000, 2005, and 2008. The range of sampling error associated with a survey of 1,000 people is ±1.5 to ±3.5 percentage points at the 95% confidence level. Each of the surveys utilized minimal statistical weighting to calibrate the aggregate sample to known population percentages in relation to several key demographic variables. All interviews were conducted among a sampling of adults in the forty-eight continental states.

9. David Kinnaman and Gabe Lyons, *UnChristian* (Grand Rapids, MI: Baker Books, 2007), 75.

10. Henry Blackaby, *Holiness* (Nashville: Thomas Nelson, 2003), 20.

11. D. Michael Lindsay, *Faith in the Halls of Power* (New York: Oxford Press, 2007), 5–6.

12. David Barton, *America: To Pray or Not to Pray* (n.p.: Wallbuilder Press, 1991), as cited in Rob McCafferty, "What Happened When America Banned Prayer in Schools," April 29, 2003, http://www.pechurchnet.co.za/post/issues/education/ed20030429.htm (accessed April 6, 2011).

13. Kinnaman and Lyons, *UnChristian*, 47.

14. Loren Cunningham, *The Book That Transforms Nations* (n.p.: YWAM Publishing, 2007), 118.

15. CNN.com, "Obama Says U.S., Turkey Can Be Model for World," April 6, 2009, http://articles.cnn.com/2009-04-06/politics/obama.turkey_1_turkey -christian-nation-turkish-president-abdullah-gul?_s=PM:POLITICS (accessed April 6, 2011).

16. Rebecca Barnes and Lindy Lowry, "Special Report: The American Church in Crisis," *Outreach*, May/June 2006.

17. Bob Young, "Barna Report: Christianity No Longer the Default Religion in the U.S.?", January 15, 2009, http://www.bobyoungresources.com/articles/barna_default-religion.pdf (accessed April 6, 2011), citing Barna.org, "Christianity Is No Longer Americans' Default Faith," January 12, 2009, http://www.barna.org/barna-update/article/12-faithspirituality/15-christianity-is-no-longer-americans -default-faith (accessed April 6, 2011).

18. Barna.org, "Six Megathemes Emerge From Barna Group Research in 2010," December 13, 2010, http://www.barna.org/culture-articles/462-six -megathemes-emerge-from-2010 (accessed April 7, 2011).

19. Rogier Bos, "Next-Wave Interview With Stanley J. Grenz," Next-Wave.org, April 29, 1999, http://www.next-wave.org/may99/SG.htm (accessed April 7, 2011).

20. Patricia Aburdene, *Megatrends 2010* (Newburyport, MA: Hampton Roads Publishing, 2005).

21. Proverbs 14:12.

CHAPTER 2
KING KONG AND THE GARDEN OF EDEN

1. Psalm 115:16.

2. Genesis 1:28.

3. Psalm 24:1.

4. Landa Cope, *An Introduction to the Old Testament Template* (Burtigny, Switzerland: The Template Institute Press, 2006), 41.

5. Lyons, *The Next Christians*, 53.

6. Genesis 2:9.

7. Genesis 2:15–17.

8. Matthew 4:8.

9. John 12:31; 16:11.

10. 2 Corinthians 4:4.

11. 1 John 5:19.

12. See Luke 19:10.

13. Ezekiel 22:30; Matthew 28:18.

14. Proverbs 29:2.

15. 1 John 3:8.

16. See Matthew 6:10.

CHAPTER 3
DEVELOP A BIBLICAL WORLDVIEW

1. Oswald Chambers, *The Complete Works of Oswald Chambers* (Grand Rapids, MI: Discovery House Publishers, 2000), 937.

2. Charles Colson and Nancy Pearcey, *How Now Shall We Live?* (Carol Stream, IL: Tyndale, 1999), 14–15.

3. Cope, *An Introduction to the Old Testament Template*, 14–15.

4. Myles Munroe, *Kingdom Principles* (Shippensburg, PA: Destiny Image Publishers, 2006), 31.

5. Matthew 6:10.

6. Matthew 6:9–10.

7. Juan Callejas, "Almolonga: A Controversial Garden of Hope," The Institute, March 6, 2009, http://bradley.chattablogs.com/archives/2009/03/almolonga-a-con.html (accessed April 8, 2011).

8. G. Holden Pike, ed., *The Life and Works of Charles Haddon Spurgeon* (Edinburgh, UK: Banner of Truth, 1992), 4:210.

9. Jonathan Edwards, "Pressing Into the Kingdom of God," in *The Works of Jonathan Edwards*, vol. 1 (New York: Daniel Appleton and Co., 1835), 660.

10. John Wesley, *Sermons on Several Occasions* (New York: B. Waugh and T. Mason, 1836), 82.

11. Matthew 24:14.

12. Presentation to the International Coalition of Apostles, Dallas, Texas, 2007.

13. Revelation 19:7.

14. Susheela Singh, Jacqueline E. Darroch, and Akinrinola Bankole, "A, B and C in Uganda: The Roles of Abstinence, Monogamy, and Condom Use in HIV Decline," Guttamacher.org, December 2003, http://www.guttmacher.org/pubs/or_abc03.pdf (accessed April 8, 2011).

15. Ibid.

16. *The Journey to Transformation*, a twelve-month curriculum developed by George Otis Jr. Information about this curriculum is available at http://glowtorch.org/JourneytoTransformation/WhatistheJourneytoTransformation/tabid/2568/Default.aspx (accessed April 8, 2011).

17. "Transformation in Almolonga, Guatemala," Charisma News Service, March 24, 2000.

18. Romans 14:8.

19. Charles H. Spurgeon, "A Home Mission Sermon," June 26, 1859, The Spurgeon Archive, http://www.spurgeon.org/sermons/0259.htm (accessed April 8, 2011).

CHAPTER 4
ELIMINATE THE GREAT DIVIDE

1. 2 Corinthians 3:17–18, NIV.
2. 1 Corinthians 10:31, NIV.
3. Colossians 3:24, NIV.
4. See Revelation 1:6.
5. Os Guinness, *The Call* (Nashville: Thomas Nelson, 2003), 31–32.
6. Compare Romans 15:31, "service," and Ephesians 4:12, "ministry."
7. See Ruth 2:16.
8. See 1 Samuel 17:45–47.
9. Winston Churchill, *The Second World War*, vol. 1 (New York: Mariner Books, 1986), 601.

CHAPTER 5
GOD'S RECRUITMENT PROCESS

1. Exodus 33:15–16.
2. See Exodus 4:1–17.
3. Exodus 4:24–26.
4. 1 Corinthians 13:2–3, emphasis added.
5. Romans 11:29.
6. Matthew 17:20.

CHAPTER 6
SIX STAGES AND PROCESSES OF THE CALL OF A CHANGE AGENT

1. Frederick Buechner, *Wishful Thinking* (San Francisco: Harper San Francisco, 1993), 119.
2. 2 Samuel 7:8, NIV.
3. 1 Chronicles 29:17.
4. Acts 7:9.
5. See Psalm 66:10–12.
6. Psalm 144:1.
7. James 1:2–4.
8. Psalm 119:67.
9. Hebrews 5:8.
10. Matthew 6:15.
11. 2 Corinthians 12:9–10, NIV.

CHAPTER 7
EMBRACING THE CROSS THROUGH BROKENNESS

1. 1 Peter 1:6–8.
2. Philippians 2:5–8.
3. Jeanne Guyon, as quoted in Gene Edwards, *100 Days in the Secret Place* (Shippensburg, PA: Destiny Image Publishers, 2002), 45.
4. Matthew 6:15, NIV.
5. Matthew 5:44–45, NIV.
6. See Isaiah 45:3.

7. Oswald Chambers, *My Utmost for His Highest* (Grand Rapids, MI: Discovery House Publishers, 1963), December 9.

8. Romans 6:4, NIV.

9. A. W. Tozer, *The Root of the Righteous* (n.p.: Wingspread Publishers, 2007).

10. A. W. Tozer in *The Reaper*, February 1962, 459, as quoted in J. Oswald Sanders, *Spiritual Leadership* (Chicago: Moody Bible Institute, 1994), 29–30.

11. Matthew 16:24–25, NIV.

12. Romans 8:38–39.

13. Michael Molinos, as quoted in Edwards, *100 Days in the Secret Place*, 135.

CHAPTER 8
THE ROLE OF ISOLATION

1. Proverbs 13:12.

2. 1 Kings 19:9.

3. Charles Swindoll, *David* (Nashville: Thomas Nelson, 1997), 73.

4. Genesis 39:11–12.

5. 2 Samuel 22:20, NIV.

6. C. S. Lewis, *The Problem of Pain* (New York: HarperCollins, 2001), 91.

7. Daniel 2:22.

8. Proverbs 25:2.

9. Ezekiel 1:1–3.

10. Isaiah 45:3.

11. Hosea 2:14.

12. Jeremiah 33:1–3, NIV, emphasis added.

13. Psalm 31:20.

14. Psalm 142:7.

15. Robert Clinton, *The Making of a Leader* (Colorado Springs, CO: NavPress, 1988), 161.

16. 1 Samuel 22:5.

17. Isaiah 50:10, NIV.

CHAPTER 9
AVOID THE TRAPS OF PERFORMANCE, PASSION, POSITION, AND POSSESSIONS

1. 1 Corinthians 16:9.

2. Chambers, *My Utmost for His Highest*, March 25.

3. Swindoll, *David*, 139.

4. Matthew 4:1.

5. Matthew 4:3.

6. Matthew 4:9.

7. Brent Curtis and John Eldredge, *The Sacred Romance* (Nashville: Thomas Nelson, 1997), 130.

8. Ezekiel 36:26–27.

9. See 1 Kings 11:1–5.

10. Proverbs 6:32.

11. Philip Yancey, *Disappointment With God* (Grand Rapids, MI: Zondervan, 1988, 1992), 80.

12. John P. Splinter, "Having That Pesky 'Sex Talk' With Your Kid," National Coalition for the Protection of Children and Families, May 30, 2009, http://www.purehope.net/stlouisArticlesDetail.asp?id=199 (accessed April 12, 2011).

13. National Coalition for the Protection of Children and Families, "Pornography," http://www.purehope.net/statisticspornography.asp (accessed April 12, 2011).

14. MSNBC.com, "Porn Addiction Increases Across the Country," *Rita Crosby Live & Direct*, March 3, 2006, http://www.msnbc.msn.com/id/11640411/ns/msnbc_tv-rita_cosby_specials (accessed April 12, 2011).

15. Rebecca Hagelin, "Overdosing on Porn," *World and I Online*, March 2004, cited in John P. Splinter, "What It Means to Be a Man," National Coalition for the Protection of Children and Families, January 21, 2010, http://www.purehope.net/stlouisArticlesDetail.asp?id=235 (accessed April 12, 2011).

16. MSNBC.com, "Porn Addiction Increases Across the Country."

17. Splinter, "Having That Pesky 'Sex Talk' With Your Kid."

18. National Coalition for the Protection of Children and Families, "Child Advocacy: Kids' Connected World Brings Extra Duties for Parents," March 15, 2011, http://www.purehope.net/NewsDetail.asp?id=2000 (accessed April 12, 2011).

19. National Coalition for the Protection of Children and Families, "Child Pornography Prosecutors: Victims Are Getting Younger, Acts Are More Vile," January 31, 2011, http://www.purehope.net/NewsDetail.asp?id=1909 (accessed April 12, 2011).

20. Stephen Vaughn, *Freedom and Entertainment: Rating the Movies in an Age of New Media* (New York: Cambridge University Press, 2006), 166.

21. John P. Splinter, "Biblical Sexuality, Part 1: Pornography: A Cancer Killing Families and Churches," January 5, 2010, http://www.purehope.net/stlouisArticlesDetail.asp?id=187 (accessed April 12, 2011).

22. Jeremy Caplan, "Cheating 2.0: New Mobile Apps Make Adultery Easier," *Time*, June 29, 2009, http://www.time.com/time/business/article/0,8599,1907542,00.html?xid=newsletter-daily (accessed April 12, 2011).

23. Augustine, *Confessions*, translated by R. S. Pine-Coffin (New York: Penguin, 1961), 166.

24. Henry Wright, *Addictions* (Thomaston, GA: Be in Health Publications, 2003), 1.

25. Michael Novak, *Business as a Calling* (Washington DC: Free Press, 1996), 22.

26. Larry Crabb, *Shattered Dreams* (Colorado Springs, CO: Waterbrook Press), 126.

27. Dietrich Bonhoeffer, *Temptation* (New York: McMillan Publishing, 1953), 116–117.

28. Numbers 12:3.

29. 1 Timothy 6:10.

30. 2 Corinthians 9:7–8.

CHAPTER 10
UNDERSTAND YOUR SPIRITUAL AUTHORITY AND RESPONSIBILITY

1. Psalm 115:16.
2. Genesis 3:5.
3. Colossians 1:19–20.
4. 2 Chronicles 16:9.
5. Ezekiel 22:30.
6. Matthew 28:18–20.
7. 1 John 3:8.
8. Romans 8:26–27.
9. Isaiah 53:12.
10. Matthew 16:19.
11. Psalm 33:9.
12. Mark 11:23–24.
13. Proverbs 18:21; Hebrews 11:1–2.
14. Psalm 143:8.
15. Exodus 32:30–32.
16. Hebrews 7:23–28.
17. Isaiah 61:4–6.
18. Luke 23:34.
19. Hebrews 4:14–5:1.
20. Chambers, *My Utmost for His Highest*, December 13.
21. Romans 9:3–4, AMP.
22. Mark 15:38.
23. Luke 11:22.
24. Romans 8:26–27.

CHAPTER 11
GET READY TO EXPERIENCE SPIRITUAL WARFARE

1. C. S. Lewis, *The Screwtape Letters* (San Francisco: HarperCollins, 1942), 31.
2. Ibid., ix.
3. Barna.org, "Most American Christians Do Not Believe That Satan or the Holy Spirit Exist," April 10, 2009, http://www.barna.org/barna-update/article/12-faithspirituality/260-most-american-christians-do-not-believe-that-satan-or-the-holy-spirit-exis (accessed April 12, 2011).
4. Ibid.
5. 1 Peter 5:8.
6. Revelation 12:4.
7. Revelation 12:9.
8. Revelation 12:10.
9. Luke 10:17–20.
10. Nehemiah 4:7–10.
11. Nehemiah 4:17–18.
12. John Piper, "Be Devoted to Prayer," sermon preached December 29, 2002,

transcript viewed at DesiringGod.org, http://www.desiringgod.org/resource
-library/sermons/be-devoted-to-prayer (accessed April 12, 2011).

13. Isaiah 54:17.

14. 2 Corinthians 12:7.

CHAPTER 12
CHANGE AGENTS ARE PROBLEM SOLVERS

1. John 4:27.

2. John 4:40.

3. John 3:16.

4. Luke 19:10.

5. Matthew 6:10.

6. Matthew 28:18.

7. Mother Teresa, "One Strong Resolution: I Will Love," speech given to
United Nations, October 26, 1985, unedited transcript viewed at http://www
.piercedhearts.org/purity_heart_morality/mother_teresa_address_united_nations
.htm (accessed April 12, 2011).

8. Daniel 1:20.

9. Daniel 2:3–5.

10. Daniel 2:22.

11. Romans 9:17.

12. Johannes Gutenberg, cited in William Federer, *America's God and Country:
Encyclopedia of Quotations* (St. Louis, MO: Amerisearch, Inc., 2000), 270.

13. Focus on the Family, "Historical Figure: Johannes Gutenberg," The Truth
Project, http://www.mytruthproject.org/truthproject/downloads/bios/Gutenberg
.pdf (accessed April 14, 2011).

14. Lyons, *The Next Christians*, 8.

15. William Federer, *George Washington Carver: His Life and Faith in His
Own Words* (St. Louis, MO: Amerisearch, Inc., 2003), 67–68.

16. Mary Bellis, "George Washington Carver," About.com, http://inventors
.about.com/od/cstartinventors/a/GWC.htm (accessed April 14, 2011).

17. David Kuo, "Rick Warren's Second Reformation," interview on Belief.net,
http://www.beliefnet.com/Faiths/Christianity/2005/10/Rick-Warrens-Second
-Reformation.aspx (accessed April 14, 2011).

CHAPTER 13
CHANGE HAPPENS WHEN A SMALL NUMBER
OF CHANGE AGENTS BAND TOGETHER

1. Hunter, "To Change the World."

2. John 17:20–22.

3. Philippians 2:3–4.

4. For more information about the International Christian Chamber of Commerce, visit their website at www.iccc.net.

Chapter 14
Reclaiming the Family Mountain

1. Joshua 24:14–15.

2. Deuteronomy 11:26–28.

3. National Institute of Mental Health, "Any Disorder Among Adults," http://www.nimh.nih.gov/statistics/1ANYDIS_ADULT.shtml (accessed April 14, 2011).

4. Hebrews 13:5.

5. Craig Hill, *Marriage: Covenant or Contract?* (n.p.: Harvest Books, 1992).

6. National Right to Life, "Abortion in the United States—Statistics," http://www.nrlc.org/ABORTION/facts/abortionstats2.html (accessed April 14, 2011).

7. Paul Tournier, *Creative Suffering* (New York: Harper and Row Publishers, 1983), 1–2.

8. Tamara Audi, Justin Scheck, and Christopher Lawton, "California Votes for Prop 8," *The Wall Street Journal*, November 5, 2008, http://online.wsj.com/article/SB122586056759900673.html (accessed April 15, 2011).

9. Institute for American Values and University of Virginia's The National Marriage Project, "The State of Our Unions: Marriage in America 2009," December 2009, http://www.stateofourunions.org/2009/SOOU2009.pdf (accessed April 15, 2011).

10. Ibid.

11. Institute for American Values, "The Taxpayer Costs of Divorce and Unwed Childbearing: First-Ever Estimates for the Nation and all Fifty States," 2008, 7, http://www.americanvalues.org/pdfs/COFF.pdf (accessed April 15, 2011).

12. DivorceStatistics.org, "Divorce Statistics in America," http://www.divorcestatistics.org/ (accessed April 15, 2011).

13. DivorceRate.org, "Divorce Rate in Canada," http://www.divorcerate.org/divorce-rates-in-canada.html (accessed April 15, 2011).

14. DivorceRate.org, "Divorce Rate in Singapore," http://www.divorcerate.org/divorce-rates-in-singapore.html (accessed April 15, 2011).

15. DivorceRate.org, "Divorce Rate in UK," http://www.divorcerate.org/divorce-rates-in-uk.html (accessed April 15, 2011).

16. DivorceRate.org, "Divorce Rate in Japan," http://www.divorcerate.org/divorce-rate-japan.html (accessed April 15, 2011).

17. DivorceRate.org, "Divorce Rate in Australia," http://www.divorcerate.org/divorce-rates-in-australia.html (accessed April 15, 2011).

18. Institute for American Values, *Why Marriage Matters: Twenty-Six Conclusions From the Social Sciences*, second edition (New York: Institute for American Values, n.d.).

19. Cheryl Wetzstein, "Majority of Teens Live in 'Rejection' Families," *Washington Times*, December 15, 2010, http://www.washingtontimes.com/news/2010/dec/15/majority-of-teens-live-in-rejection-families/ (accessed April 15, 2011).

20. Marshall Kirk and Hunter Madsen, *After the Ball: How America Will Conquer Its Fear and Hatred of Gays in the '90s* (New York: Plume, 1990), xxvii.

21. Ibid.

22. David Kupelian, *The Marketing of Evil* (Nashville: Cumberland House Publishing, 2005), 33–34.

23. Joel Connelly, "ABC/WashPost: Majority for Same-Sex Marriage," *Seattle PI* (blog), March 18, 2011, http://blog.seattlepi.com/seattlepolitics/2011/03/18/abcwashpost-majority-for-same-sex-marriage/ (accessed April 15, 2011).

24. Kirk and Madsen, *After the Ball*, 184.

25. Kupelian, *The Marketing of Evil*, 35.

26. Romans 1:24–27.

27. Kinnaman and Lyons, *UnChristian*, 27.

28. Personal conversation with author.

29. See John 8:3–11.

30. Galatians 3:19–21.

31. Message given at a family foundations conference in 2010.

32. Noel and Phyl Gibson, *Evicting Demonic Squatters and Breaking Bondages* (n.p.: Freedom in Christ Ministries Trust, 1987).

33. Exodus 20:5–6.

CHAPTER 15
RECLAIMING THE MOUNTAIN OF GOVERNMENT

1. Anonymous.

2. Adapted from Johnny Enlow, *The Seven Mountain Prophecy* (Lake Mary, FL: Creation House, 2008), 61.

3. The Avalon Project, "Washington's Farewell Address, 1796," Yale Law School, http://avalon.law.yale.edu/18th_century/washing.asp (accessed April 15, 2011).

4. Newt Gingrich, *Rediscovering God in America: Reflections on the Role of Faith in Our Nation's History and Future* (Nashville: Integrity Publishers, 2006), 39.

5. Adapted from the text of the video *America's Godly Heritage* by David Barton.

6. Ibid.

7. Patrick Henry, speech given March 23, 1775, Christian Heritage of America, http://www.alfredny.biz/Christian-Heritage-of-America/patrick-henry.htm (accessed April 15, 2011).

8. Patrick Henry, 1776, Christian Heritage of America, http://www.alfredny.biz/Christian-Heritage-of-America/index.htm (accessed April 15, 2011). While some question the attribution of this statement to Henry, conservative Christian historians say it is in line with other statements Henry made.

9. Alexis de Tocqueville, *Democracy in America*, vol 1, trans. by Henry Reeve (New York: The Colonial Press, 1899), 313, 310, 305.

10. James Madison, *Notes of Debates in the Federal Convention of 1787* (New York: W. W. Norton and Co., 1987), 209–210.

11. Adapted from the text of the video *America's Godly Heritage* by David Barton.

12. Thomas Jefferson, "Jefferson's Letter to the Danbury Baptists," Library of Congress, http://www.loc.gov/loc/lcib/9806/danpre.html (accessed April 18, 2011).

13. "America the Beautiful" by Katharine Bates and Samuel Ward. Public domain.

14. Kerby Anderson, "Ten Commandments in America," Probe Ministries, http://www.probe.org/site/c.fdKEIMNsEoG/b.4218093/k.824A/Ten_Commandments_in_America.htm (accessed April 18, 2011).

15. US Department of the Treasury, "History of 'In God We Trust,'" http://www.treasury.gov/about/education/Pages/in-god-we-trust.aspx (accessed April 18, 2011).

16. Deuteronomy 8:11–17.

17. Deuteronomy 8:18–20.

18. Cited in Laura Abington, "Dr. Abrahm Kuyper," paper presented May 13, 2008, http://trinitynorman.org/uploads/media/Abraham_Kuyper.pdf (accessed April 18, 2011).

19. Jeremiah 17:9–10.

20. Revelation 2:5.

21. Genesis 12:3.

CHAPTER 16
RECLAIMING ARTS AND ENTERTAINMENT

1. Lawrence Khong, *Give Me the Multitudes* (Singapore: Touch Ministries International, 2008), 5.

2. Information in this section is taken from Peter Schweizer, *Reagan's War* (New York: Anchor Books, 2002), 6–16.

3. "Visual Faith: A Christian Recovery of the Arts, A Conversation with Dr. William Dyrness," *Cutting Edge* 6, no. 1 (Winder 2002), 9–11, referenced in Cunningham, *The Book That Transforms Nations*, 62.

4. WhiteOwlFilms.com, "The Hollywood Minefield," http://whiteowlfilms.com/minefield.html (accessed May 16, 2011).

5. Brian Godawa, *Hollywood Worldviews*, cited in Dick Staub, *The Culturally Savvy Christian* (San Francisco: Jossey Press, 2007), 45.

6. CBSNews.com, "Tyler Perry's Amazing Journey to the Top," October 25, 2009, http://www.cbsnews.com/stories/2009/10/22/60minutes/main5410095.shtml (accessed April 18, 2011).

7. 1 Corinthians 16:9.

8. Candice Watters, "Fireproof," *Boundless Webzine*, September 26, 2008, http://www.boundless.org/2005/articles/a0001854.cfm (accessed April 18, 2011).

9. Phil Cooke, "Hollywood Report: Is God Making a Difference in Tinsel Town?" ChristianAnswers.net, December 5, 2004, http://www.christiananswers.net/spotlight/movies/discernment/findinggodinhollywood.html (accessed April 18, 2011).

10. As cited at AboutUs.org, "FoxFaithMovies.com Sells Family and Faith Oriented Movies," http://www.aboutus.org/FoxFaithMovies.com#- (accessed April 18, 2011).

11. Megan Bashan, "WALL-E World," *World*, June 28, 2008, http://www.worldmag.com/articles/14127 (accessed April 19, 2011).

12. Mark Moring, "Just What the Docter Ordered," *CT Entertainment* (blog), March 18, 2009, http://blog.christianitytoday.com/ctentertainment/2009/03/just-what-the-docter-ordered.html (accessed April 19, 2011).

13. Bill Berkowitz, "The Movie, the Media, and the Conservative Politics of Philip Anschutz," MediaTransparency.org, December 2, 2005, http://old.mediatransparency.org/story.php?storyID=97 (accessed April 19, 2011).

14. AMTCWorld.com, "For Christ," http://www.amtcworld.com/reading-room (accessed April 19, 2011).

15. Galatians 2:2, emphasis added.

CHAPTER 17
RECLAIMING THE MEDIA MOUNTAIN

1. Adapted from Enlow, *The Seven Mountain Prophecy*.

2. Francis Schaeffer, *How Should We Then Live?* (Wheaton, IL: Crossway, 1983).

3. Kupelian, *The Marketing of Evil*, 171.

4. Culture and Media Institute, "National Cultural Values Survey, http://www.docstoc.com/docs/30793947/The-National-Cultural-Values-Survey (accessed April 19, 2011).

5. Enlow, *The Seven Mountain Prophecy*, 49.

6. As cited in BiographyOnline.net, "Short Biography of Oprah Winfrey," http://www.biographyonline.net/humanitarian/oprah-winfrey.html (accessed April 19, 2011).

7. LaTonya Taylor, "The Church of O," *Christianity Today*, April 1, 2002, http://www.christianitytoday.com/ct/2002/april1/1.38.html (accessed April 19, 2011).

8. Kupelian, *The Marketing of Evil*, 171.

9. Cited in David P. Baron, "Research Paper No. 1845: Persistent Media Bias," August 2004, http://www.wallis.rochester.edu/conference11/mediabias.pdf (accessed April 19, 2011).

10. Ibid.

11. Ibid.

12. Kupelian, *The Marketing of Evil*, 174.

13. Staub, *The Culturally Savvy Christian*, 43.

14. Cited in Bernard Goldberg, *A Slobbering Love Affair* (Washington DC: Regnery Publications, 2009), 19.

15. Ibid., 21.

16. Ibid., 15–16.

17. Cited in Baron, "Research Paper No. 1845: Persistent Media Bias."

18. Matthew 10:16.

19. Daniel 3:16–18.

CHAPTER 18
RECLAIMING THE MOUNTAIN OF BUSINESS

1. Michael O. Sajbel, "Plot Summary for *The Ultimate Gift*," IMDB.com, http://www.imdb.com/title/tt0482629/plotsummary (accessed April 19, 2011).

2. Blake Mycoskie, "Fulfilling My Life's Mission Through the TOMS Shoes Movement," HuffingtonPost.com, http://www.huffingtonpost.com/blake -mycoskie/fulfilling-my-lifes-missi_b_362589.html (accessed April 19, 2011).

3. Mary Bellis, "Bill Gates—Biography and History," About.com, http:// inventors.about.com/od/gstartinventors/a/Bill_Gates.htm (accessed April 19, 2011).

4. Solarnavigator.net, "The World's Richest Men in £32 Billion Giveaway—27 June 2006," http://www.solarnavigator.net/sponsorship/bill_melinda_gates_ warren_buffett.htm (accessed April 19, 2011).

5. Preston Gralla, "Microsoft Turns 35: Best, Worst, and Most Notable Moments," ComputerWorld.com, March 24, 2010, http://www.computerworld .com/s/article/print/9173238/Microsoft_turns_35_Best_worst_and_most_notable_ moments (accessed April 19, 2011).

6. Alex Crippen, "Warren Buffett and Bill Gates Share Their 'Optimism' With Eager Columbia Business School Students," CNBC.com, November 12, 2009, http://www.cnbc.com/id/33888348 (accessed April 19, 2011).

7. Carol J. Loomis, "The $600 Billion Challenge," *Fortune* (blog), CNN.com, June 16, 2010, http://features.blogs.fortune.cnn.com/2010/06/16/gates-buffett-600 -billion-dollar-philanthropy-challenge/ (accessed April 19, 2011).

8. Ibid.

9. Paul Thurrott, "Facebook Co-Founders to Give Away Half of Fortunes to Charity," Windows IT Pro, December 9, 2010, http://www.windowsitpro.com/ article/paul-thurrotts-wininfo/Facebook-Co-Founders-to-Give-Away-Half-of -Fortunes-to-Charity (accessed April 19, 2011).

Chapter 19
Reclaiming the Education Mountain

1. Bible Literacy Project, "Breakthrough Public School Bible Textbook Receives Wide Acclaim from Scholars, the Media, and National Faith Leaders," press release, http://www.bibleliteracy.net/Site/PressRoom/PressRelease070320 .htm (accessed April 20, 2011).

2. David Van Biema, "Why We Should Teach the Bible in Public School," *Time* cover, April 2, 2007, http://www.time.com/time/covers/0,16641,20070402,00 .html (accessed April 20, 2011).

3. Bible Literacy Project, "Breakthrough Public School Bible Textbook Receives Wide Acclaim from Scholars, the Media, and National Faith Leaders."

4. Bible Literacy Project, "Bible Literacy Report: What Do American Teens Need to Know and What Do They Know?", Executive Summary, 2005, http:// www.bibleliteracy.org/bibcdocs/BLRExecutiveSummary071008.pdf (accessed April 20, 2011).

5. Bible Literacy Project, "Bible Literacy Report: What Do American Teens Need to Know and What Do They Know?", http://www.bibleliteracy.org/Secure/ Documents/BibleLiteracyReport2005.pdf (accessed April 20, 2011).

6. Adapted from Enlow, *The Seven Mountain Prophecy*, 79.

7. Wikipedia.org, "The New England Primer," http://en.wikipedia.org/wiki/ The_New_England_Primer (accessed April 20, 2011).

8. *Vidal v. Girard* (1844), cited in *Hackett v. Brooksville Graded School District et al.* (1905), *The Southwestern Reporter* 87, June 7–July 12, 1905 (St. Paul, MN: West Publishing Company, 1905), 795.

9. Noah Webster, *History of the United States* (New Haven, CT: Durrie and Peck, 1832), 339.

10. Cited in *The New Encyclopedia of Social Reform*, ed. William D. P. Bliss and Rudoph M. Binder (New York: Funk and Wagnalls, 1908), 1057.

11. Sabrina Holcomb, "Answering the Call," part 1, *NEAToday*, January 2006, http://www.nea.org/home/11608.htm (accessed April 20, 2011); Sabrina Holcomb, "Answering the Call," part 2, *NEAToday*, February 2006, http://www.nea.org/home/12172.htm (accessed April 20, 2011).

12. DiscovertheNetworks.org, "National Education Association (NEA)," http://www.discoverthenetworks.org/groupProfile.asp?grpid=7428 (accessed April 20, 2011).

13. NEA.org, "NEA President to Administration: 'Takes Working Together to Improve Schools,'" March 20, 2010 press release, http://www.nea.org/home/38531.htm (accessed April 20, 2011).

14. *Congressional Quarterly*, quoted in William Bennett, *Index of Leading Cultural Indicators*, (New York: Simon & Schuster, 1994), 83.

15. David Barton, *America: To Pray or Not to Pray* (Aledo, TX: Wallbuilders Press, 1991).

16. Ibid.

17. Harvard GSAS Christian Community, "About Our Shield and Logo," http://www.hcs.harvard.edu/~gsascf/shield.html (accessed April 20, 2011).

18. Ibid.

19. America's Youth for Truth, "America's True Beginnings," http://www.americasyouthfortruth.org/americ_beg.htm (accessed April 20, 2011).

20. The Social Transformation Conference, "Overview," http://socialtransformation2011.org/?page_id=253 (accessed April 20, 2011).

21. Columbia University, "A Brief History of Columbia," http://www.columbia.edu/content/history.html (accessed April 20, 2011).

22. Richard Brookhiser, *Gentleman Revolutionary: Gouverneur Morris, the Rake Who Wrote the Constitution* (New York: Free Press, 2004).

23. Ronald Nash, *The Closing of the American Heart* (Los Angeles, CA: Probe Books, 1990).

24. The King's College, "About King's: Mission Statement," http://www.tkc.edu/abouttkc/mission.html (accessed April 20, 2011).

Chapter 20
Reclaiming the Church Mountain

1. Sunday Adelaja, *ChurchShift* (Lake Mary, FL: Charisma House, 2008), 7.

2. Ibid.

3. Ibid., 9.

4. Mark Greene, "Imagine How We Can Reach the UK," The London Institute for Contemporary Christianity, http://www.licc.org.uk/uploaded_media/1233749611-Imagine.pdf (accessed April 20, 2011).

5. C. Peter Wagner, in his foreword to *Faith and Work Movement* (Atlanta, GA: Aslan Publishing, 2004), viii.

Chapter 21
Change Agents Changing Communities

1. Associated Press, "Senate Blocks HUD Grants to ACORN," *Los Angeles Times*, September 15, 2009, http://articles.latimes.com/2009/sep/15/nation/na-acorn15 (accessed April 20, 2011).

2. Jon Walker, "Youngest Generation Comfortable With Contradictions, Barna Says," BaptistPress.org, February 4, 2002, http://baptistpress.org/bpnews.asp?ID=12664 (accessed April 20, 2011).

3. Barna.org, "New Research Explores How Different Generations View and Use the Bible," October 19, 2009, http://www.barna.org/barna-update/article/12-faithspirituality/317-new-research-explores-how-different-generations-view-and-use-the-bible (accessed April 20, 2011).

4. Walker, "Youngest Generation Comfortable With Contradictions, Barna Says."

5. Lyons, *The Next Christians*, 112.

6. This material from Debbie Farah is adapted from her presentation and the 2009 Reclaim 7 Mountains Conference held in Atlanta, Georgia, in February 2009.

7. 2 Chronicles 7:14.

8. Psalm 25:9, NIV.

9. John 17:23, NIV.

10. 2 Samuel 6:6–7.

Epilogue
We Will Reign Together as One

1. See Joel 3:10.

Appendix A
Summing It Up

1. Luke 19:10.

2. 1 Corinthians 16:9.

3. Henry Wright, *Addictions* (Thomaston, GA: Be in Health Publications, 2003), 1.

ADDITIONAL RESOURCES
BY OS HILLMAN

Become a Change Agent! Join the Change Agent Network

Each month receive in-depth biblical teaching on various topics related to your workplace calling, marketplace tips, proven business principles, teleseminars, webinars, and networking with other change agents, and free and discounted resources via this e-zine and online private membership-based website. Visit www.becomeachangeagent.com to learn more.

The Change Agent Intensive Weekend Workshop

This is Os Hillman's core workshop based on the *Become a Change Agent* book. The weekend training consists of two and a half days and is limited to fifty participants. This workshop helps men and women discover their purpose in work and life, the six stages of a call for a change agent, seven-mountain strategies and much more. It is loaded with practical principles to understand God's method of calling, biblical decision making, and the role adversity plays in every believer's life toward becoming a change agent. Visit www.marketplaceleaders.org to learn more.

FREE TGIF: Today God Is First E-mail Devotional

Start your day by reading an e-mail that encourages you to experience the Lord's presence at work through this popular e-mail devotional that is subscribed to by hundreds of thousands daily. Subscribe by going to www.TodayGodIsFirst.com.

Experiencing the Father's Love: Learning to Live as Sons and Daughters of Our Heavenly Father

When God thinks of you, love swells in His heart. Do you believe it? Os helps readers understand what it means to live as sons and daughters of our heavenly Father.

The 9 To 5 Window: How Faith Can Transform The Workplace

Provides an in-depth look at this new move of God and how Christians can practically implement their faith with their work life.

The Upside of Adversity: From the Pit to Greatness

Through a challenging seven-year process, Os learned that God was at work using these painful circumstances to prepare him for the calling God had on his life. So will you.

TGIF: Today God Is First, Volumes 1 & 2
365 Meditations on the Principles of Christ in the Workplace
The daily e-mail devotional in book form! *Today God Is First* provides daily meditations that will help you focus your priority on knowing Jesus more intimately every day. See www.TodayGodIsFirst.com for free e-mail subscription. Also available as an iPhone app—TGIF Devotional.

Making Godly Decisions
How can you know if you are making a decision that will be blessed by God? In *Making Godly Decisions,* you will learn the principles for making good decisions that are also godly decisions.

The Purposes of Money
Why does God prosper some, while others still live in need? Can we trust God to provide when we don't have enough? In this book you will discover five fallacies of belief that most people live by regarding money and the five reasons God provides us money.

Are You a Biblical Worker?
Here's a self-assessment tool to help you discover where you are in your biblical knowledge of applying faith in your workplace. The inventory test features fifty True/False/Sometimes questions and answers.

Faith@Work Movement: What Every Pastor and Church Leader Should Know
Is there a real move of God in the workplace? If so, what do pastors and church leaders need to know? How can the church mobilize workplace believers to impact their city and nation? Os answers these and many more questions about the modern-day faith at work movement.

TGIF Small Group Bible Study
The popular *TGIF: Today God Is First* book is now a twelve-week, small group Bible study that is ideal for workplace groups. This study includes discussion questions and a workplace application with added scriptures that will allow the leader to extend or reduce the study time.

Faith & Work: Do They Mix?
When you have an intimate relationship with Jesus, you will understand that your faith and work are not separate in God's eyes. This book will help you understand why your work IS your ministry. Os provides a theology of work basis for bringing faith into your work life.

Visit Our Websites

www.MarketplaceLeaders.org
www.Reclaim7Mountains.com
www.tgifbookstore.com
www.UpsideofAdversity.com
www.mlcommunity.com
www.becomeachangeagent.com

Marketplace Leaders
3520 Habersham Club Drive
Cumming, GA 30041
Phone: 678-455-6262
E-mail: info@marketplaceleaders.org
Website: www.marketplaceleaders.org